SOARING ON
WINGED VERSE

SOARING ON WINGED VERSE

The Life of Ethiopian Poet-Playwright
TSEGAYE GABRE-MEDHIN

Fasil Yitbarek

Edited and with an Introduction by
Heran Sereke-Brhan

TSEHAI
Publishers & Distributors

Tsehai books may be purchased for educational, business, or sales promotional use. For more information, please contact our special sales department.

Tsehai Publishers
Loyola Marymount University
1 LMU Drive, UH 3012, Los Angeles, CA 90045

www.tsehaipublishers.com
info@tsehaipublishers.com

ISBN: 978-1-59907-056-8 (Paper back)
ISBN: 978-1-59907-057-5 (Hardcover)

First Edition: 2013

Publisher: Elias Wondimu
Staff Editor: Ellen Hoffs
Cover Illustration: Ezra Wube
Layout Designer: Tessa Smith
Cover Designer: Kerri Blackstone
Layout and cover design assistant: Sara Martinez

A catalog record for this book is available from:
Institute of Ethiopian Studies Library at Addis Ababa University
U.S. Library of Congress Catalog Card Number, Washington, D.C.
British Library Cataloguing in Publication Data

10 9 8 7 6 5 4 3 2 1

Printed in the United States of America

For those whose creative inspiration springs
from their love of Ethiopia

Contents

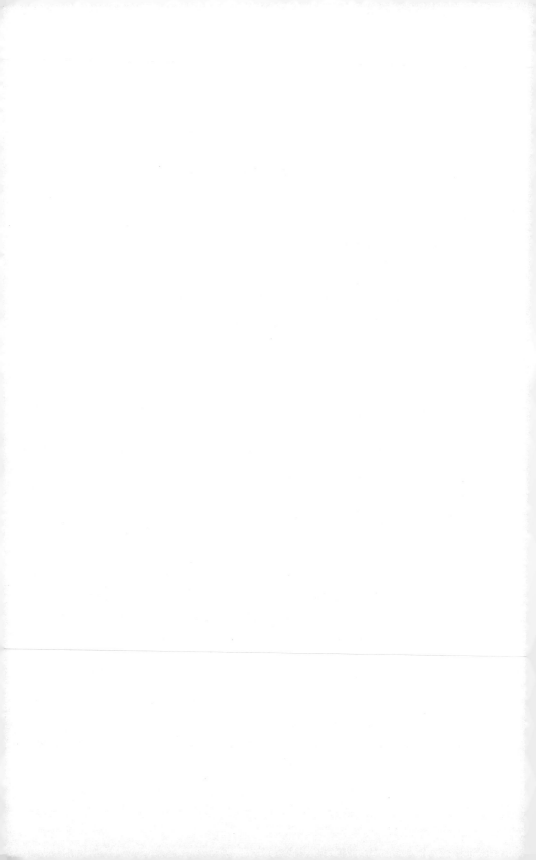

Acknowledgments

My thanks to Heran Sereke-Brhan, whose constant support I have counted on throughout the writing of this biography. Her tireless reviews of the manuscript and her incisive remarks have greatly contributed to the book.

I am indebted to those who provided me with the materials I needed to complete the second half of the biography: performance artists Alemtsehai Wodajo and Getachew Debalke, poet-playwright Ayalneh Mulatu, and director Abate Mekuria.

Credit is also due to the family of Tsegaye Gabre-Medhin, his wife Woizero Lakech Bitew, and his daughters Yodit, Mahlet and Adey for their support and steadfast willingness to answer my endless questions.

❖ ❖ ❖

The publisher would like to thank the author for writing a captivating biography and Heran Sereke-Brhan for working with us closely in producing this book. We would also like to extend our gratitude to Tsegaye Gabre-Medhin's daughters Yodit, Mahlet and Adey for supplying the necessary images.

We thank Ellen Hoffs, our Editor, for her excellent editorial work and Professor Theresia de Vroom for reading the manuscript and providing us with useful suggestions.

We are also grateful to our design team: Tessa Smith, layout designer; Kerri Blackstone, cover designer; Sara Martinez, layout and cover design assistant; and Ezra Wube, who provided the cover illustration.

Preface

When Tsegaye Gabre-Medhin asked me to write his biography, I felt equally honored and daunted. I knew it would not be easy to do a fair job of telling the life story of such a great person between the covers of a book. After mulling things over for a while, I accepted the challenge. We agreed that he would be my sole source for materials needed for the biography, which would be gathered through tape-recorded interviews in Amharic. Tsegaye wanted the book to be written in English so that it would be accessible to a diverse audience.

We met once a week, whenever we could, for a couple of hours at his home. I asked him questions to which he responded at length. There were days when he was too tired to talk or when I wasn't able to meet. Despite these occasional disruptions, we carried on and managed to cover the years up until 1974 when Tsegaye passed away unexpectedly on February 25, 2006. The remaining content, including materials used to fill the gaps in some early chapters, are scoured from various published secondary and Internet sources, and from speaking to people who knew Tsegaye closely. In some instances, I have taken the liberty to dramatize stories with dialogue without interfering with the facts in any way.

This biography is by no means a complete portrayal of Tsegaye's life. I have tried to include an account of his childhood, his early education, his adulthood, and the defining moments of his life. I've attempted to convey important events and stories of his artistic ventures, his triumphs and his disappointments, and above all, his accomplishments. Yet there are bound to be inadvertent gaps and omissions. Even among the stories in this book, there might be factual inaccuracies and imprecise details, for it is possible that those who shared their recollections, including Tsegaye himself, might have misremembered things.

Tsegaye's artistic achievements are monumental. His tireless commitment of devoting his creative pursuits for the good of his beloved Ethiopia is truly remarkable. His poems are eulogies to the country he loved, its history, and its culture. They are paeans to the hills and meadows, to the valleys and rivers of the land he cherished. His plays are portraits of Ethiopian realities. They extol the beauty of diversity and the fascinating profusion of languages, beliefs, and customs. They marvel at the wisdom of common folk and their ability to peacefully coexist. His historical plays pay tribute to towering figures of the past who gave their lives in defense of their country against invaders. His works of social criticism bravely denounce injustice and give voice to the misery of the powerless. Tsegaye is a prolific poet and playwright whose enthralling poems and stirring plays, imbued with his profound love for his people, his pride in his identity and heritage, continue to inspire and move audiences. His art is the art of love.

I chose the title *Soaring on Winged Verse* in an attempt to capture the frequent image I have of Tsegaye in the last years of his life. During my visits to his home in New York City, there were occasions when I would find him sitting in an armchair with pen in hand and a notebook on his lap. His eyes would glance at me, but it would be a few moments before my presence brought him back from the poetic flight he'd taken in search of verses he had scribbled on his notepad.

Tsegaye was a born poet, a perennial verse weaver—one who seemed to live for the very joy of conceiving and creating poetry.

–Fasil Yitbarek

Introduction

It was with excitement and some trepidation that Tsegaye Gabre-Medhin's family, the author Fasil Yitbarek and I put the final touches on this account of Tsegaye's life. Although it was a project that began with Tsegaye's passionate participation, we were to arrive at the finish line without his immediate guidance. We pressed on, grappling with the right and wrong of facts, the significance of events, and the relative importance afforded them in his story. Writing and editing alone took about three years. We struggled at length with the ethical dilemmas of using terms, naming names, and detailing happenings that might affect those that are still living.

As the flurry of e-mails and phone calls of our discussions settled, a simple truth emerged. Perhaps what was important was not so much the 'accuracy' of details in absolute terms, but the primacy of perception in reflecting on one's past. In these pages, we will learn something about how Tsegaye, the child, the young student, the man, and later the accomplished poet and playwright, was shaped by his surroundings. But we will learn more about his perceptions of his own transformation, his growing sense of place and purpose, and his increasingly urgent self-appointed task of interpreting the dreams and disappointments of his people on stage. In the years leading up to 1974, Tsegaye's telling of his life story is first-hand. In the characters he introduces, the images he paints, and the encounters he enlivens, we find a keen and observant mind at work—one that weaves the sometimes disparate settings of his life, the changing values of his times, and his own ever-evolving identity—into a cohesive whole.

From the outset, Tsegaye's imperiled life summons and unwittingly embraces multiple cultural sensibilities. Religious practices dubbed 'indigenous' or 'traditional' on the one hand, and those assumed to be 'conventional' or more 'institutionalized' on the other, seem to hold equal sway on Tsegaye's world. Thus it was that his anxious mother prayed fervently to Saint Abune Gabre-Menfes Kidus for the birth of a son, and when born and taken ill, consulted with the local priest, and finally the resourceful traditional healer, to cure him. Like most in her surroundings, Feleqech saw no contradiction in turning to symbolically endorsed church representatives or consulting with influential indigenous alternatives, as the occasion saw fit. Other family members similarly worshipped the Christian God along with the Oromo Waqa, or sometimes Waqa alone, depending on their varying levels of skepticism—thus broadening the young Tsegaye's realm of spiritual references.

We are invited to consider and contrast other memories. There's one in which Tsegaye recalls standing among his age-mates anticipating Jeti's arrival. With great majesty and pomp befitting a grand performance, the blind septuagenarian would ride her white horse Gute Daňa to the hilltop to bless the young initiates of Gada. Then a young shepherd who ran about with friends, drank milk straight from the cow's udder, and surreptitiously nibbled on the forbidden rarity of sheep testicles, Tsegaye recounts a boyhood filled with freedom and attendant mischief, marked intermittently by important rites of passage. Next we find him haplessly caught in the regimented discipline of Ethiopian Orthodox priests, (members of his own family seeking refuge from the Italian invasion), sternly admonishing him to memorize and recite Old Testament verses in the liturgical Ge'ez, to which the young Tsegaye felt little kinship.

It is no surprise then that these dual cultural and religious leanings serve as an inspiration to some of his later writings. One can safely suggest that even before Tsegaye could foresee his intellectual path or determine his creative pursuits, he had laid equal claim on these cultural worlds—and they on him. Over his lifetime, a detectable tension in duality is also transposed onto his writings, taking on various broadly contrasting forms: pre-Christian/Christian, 'traditional'/'modern,' nobility/commoner, martyr/collaborator, foreign-educated intellectual/keeper of home bred folk wisdom, among them. Each seems to have provided a treasure trove of ideas through which Tsegaye could explore differences and sameness, and probe deeper into universal themes of truth, justice, courage, and human vulnerability.

Like many Ethiopians who draw their ancestry from various ethnic groups, Tsegaye's story is rich with instances of honoring, navigating, confronting, asserting, and assuming a complex array of identities, all of which are important parts of a whole. His father Robale decided early on to change his name "overnight" to Gabre-Medhin, yet took great pride in reciting the name of Oromo forefathers nine generations back at important ceremonies—a tradition that Tsegaye duly passed on to his own children. Tsegaye's mother was from the Ankober area, one-time capital of the Shewan dynasty founded by King Sahle Sellassie. Yet we are not privy to barriers of language or culture between them—Tsegaye's uncle

Soboqa, a gifted orator, may well have wished for a similar marital outcome when he set about wooing the Amhara woman with whom he was briefly enamored.

Instead, Tsegaye's young ears were tickled by the languages spoken around him. His first language was Oromiffa, a factor that may have later contributed to Tsegaye's love of rhythmic musicality and alliteration in language. As one of Aleqa Me'amir's young students, he openly reveled in his ability to coin verses and play with imagery in Amharic, to the delight of his exacting teacher. So moved was he by Aleqa Me'amir's unequivocal encouragement that, upon receiving the coveted Haile Sellassie Prize for Literature in 1966, Tsegaye would single him out as his most influential teacher.

Notably, whereas Tsegaye accepted his teacher's pronouncement of him as a "gifted Oromo[1] boy", he is instantly reviled and angered by the same term imposed on him at the Ministry of Education Registrar's Office. He experiences the very act of choosing one identity over another as an assault on his person, and worse yet, on his creative imagination. In his later research work and his presentations, Tsegaye would become increasingly vocal about his beloved country's unity and the significance of her ancient integrity. Tsegaye broadened his discourse to include the continent, embracing discussions of African antiquity and vibrant cultural claims put forth by such intellectuals as Cheikh Anta Diop and Léopold Senghor.

As most young men of his generation, Tsegaye's accelerated journey through traditional, formal, and then foreign institutions of education was guided by Emperor Haile Sellassie's urgent agenda of modernizing Ethiopia. The emperor's vision was to create a civilian workforce or 'meritocracy' that would ultimately displace the nobility's claims to power and propel the country forward on the 'path of progress'. We sympathize with a young Tsegaye whose move from Goromti to Ambo seems to have irrevocably disrupted an idyllic childhood. We experience the newness of a town through his bewildering moments at the raucous Ambo market where he arrived on the back of a mule holding on to his favorite aunt Adde Argaatu. His mother lay ill in a hospital there. Yet this very setting where she had gone to seek 'modern medicine' appeared utterly surreal to her young son, and did little to soothe Tsegaye's jangled nerves, much less to solicit his suitable response.

Though he conducted a clandestine arms trade against the invaders during the Occupation, Gabre-Medhin recognized the future value of the '*ascola*' grammar school and decided to send his son there. The strange habits and looks

---

1   Throughout the text of this book, we have substituted the word 'Oromo' for the earlier term 'Galla,' as the latter is deemed derogatory. Tsegaye himself used 'Galla' in describing these two incidents.

of his Italian teachers did little to deter Tsegaye's curiosity. Instead he entreats us to a magnified examination of the headmaster's features, replete with a whiff of his cologne, even as the latter hoists the stranded Tsegaye onto his shoulders and sets off on his rescue mission across the flooded Huluqa River. Soon after, Tsegaye graduates from Haile Selassie I Primary School in Ambo and is accepted to the prestigious General Wingate Secondary School. His parents and the community rejoice, lauding his achievement as 'a future student of Wongel,' mistakenly appropriating the Amharic word for Gospel for that of the British General's name, and marveling at Tsegaye's speedy journey to the epitome of learning as they knew it.

Once in Addis Ababa, the hastening pace of change, along with Tsegaye's curiosity and quick-witted resourcefulness, shared by many of his generation, become more apparent. Come time to leave his station at Wingate and pursue schooling at the Addis Ababa Commercial Secondary School, Tsegaye successfully beseeches Wingate's reluctant and unsuspecting headmaster Mr. Hairring with solemn words from the *King Dionysius* play he had memorized and acted in years before. Next, he impresses his examiners at the secondary school with confident delivery of the only word he knew to write in shorthand (his name), and gets accepted. And while awaiting word of his admission, Tsegaye is lured by his own curiosity to play with a live electric wire—a symbolic feature of a modernizing Addis Ababa—narrowly escaping electrocution.

Soon after, Tsegaye moves to Piazza, an upcoming trendy neighborhood of Addis Ababa, and we are afforded brief glimpses of a rapidly modernizing city. There the young educated elite and the aspiring middle class are beginning to create a new lifestyle for themselves. Most had been educated abroad and had returned to Addis Ababa in the 1960s, eager to contribute to change, and optimistic about their bright future. 'Addis Spring' was in early bloom as poets, writers, musicians, and painters explored new creative directions and established formal and informal peer groups to discuss their works.

Shared world-views of the generation of artists who came of age in the 1960s were earlier shaped by well-rounded Ethiopian school curricula that included the arts. Upon return from their studies abroad, these views were further expanded and enriched. The unspoken aesthetic of 'Ethiopianizing' forms of visual and performance arts prevailed. Poets, painters, writers, and musicians engaged in bringing Ethiopia to the world and the world to Ethiopia did so through thoughtful reflections and ruminations on identity and modernization. Notable artistic collaborations between Tsegaye and painter-poet Gebre-Kristos Desta, as well as composers Nerses Nalbandian and Mulatu Astatke, resulted in unforgettable stage sets and musical scores. The dynamic partnership between director

Abate Mekuria and Tsegaye would create classics that drew long queues and extended performances at the theatre.

Theatre was a choice destination for young urbanites, a place to meet like-minded friends, or better yet, future mates. The few educated women were sought after for company, but cultural decorum dictated their stately public behavior, making them an even rarer presence in stage performances. In fact, the first theatre actors a generation earlier were all men who had perfected the art of imitating women, and did so to comical effect. If finding and training actresses was a challenge in his early years as playwright, literary researchers have commented on Tsegaye's uncanny ability to write poems in a woman's 'voice,' laying bare critical views on power, gender, and representations of womanhood. Tsegaye's telling of his story belies related observations. His father's position of authority is tempered by his aunt Adde Argaatu's influence and his mother Feleqech's resourceful interventions. In Tsegaye's memories and creative musings, women characters consistently seem to represent solace, justice, and a palatable resonance for truth.

The newness of theatre as an art form, and its unmistakable grip on public imagination is aptly demonstrated by Gabre-Medhin's first experience as audience member of his son's play. His active participation in Othello's unfolding story and increasingly indignant response to Iago's deceit finally erupts in Gabre-Medhin's loud protests and near-rage, despite Tsegaye's whispered assurances. Colonel Mengistu Haile-Mariam's terse body guards would react similarly years later, as the opening scene of *Enat Alem Tenu* (the adaptation of Brecht's *Mother Courage*) revealed a dark stage and scuffle that they mistook as a ruse and potential attempt on the leader's life.

Tsegaye's own encounter with theatre was no less profound. From the time he took turns standing on his friend's shoulder to peep in on a performance at eight to when he penned his first play at 13, Tsegaye imagination seemed alight with possibilities of the stage. His production of *The Story of King Dionysius and his Two Brothers* required enough of his persuasive skills to convince a cast of friends to join. He dangled the irresistible promise of delicious yogurt following a near all-night rehearsal to prepare a performance for no less an august audience than Emperor Haile Sellassie. At Tsegaye's memorial service in Ethiopia in February 2006, a grieving but bemused friend so recruited would comment on the intense urgency of it all for Tsegaye and how his infectious enthusiasm had the cast dutifully memorizing parts in barely discernible English in support of their determined friend.

This performance marked the first encounter between Tsegaye and Emperor Haile Sellassie. Touched and duly charmed by his efforts, the emperor would offer his own gifts of appreciation, taking note all the while of the young boy's talent and aspirations. The emperor perceived the arts to be an integral part of modern education and enjoyed his public role as its patron. Remarkably, he would remember Tsegaye from this encounter and continue to follow his progress over decades. Yet this was more the norm than the exception. Emperor Haile Sellassie was actively involved in guiding promising talent, availing scholarships abroad to young artists, and overseeing their placement in the government's cultural establishments upon return. Even when Tsegaye's tone grew more critical, the delicate balance of sustained engagement and imposed restraint that characterized their relationship lends insight into the emperor's overall demeanor—both paternal and visionary in parts.

By most accounts, Tsegaye's plays transformed Ethiopian theatre, aptly capturing the schisms of modernization. Whereas most earlier works dramatized religious teachings and were heavily moralizing in content, Tsegaye's writings exposed darker social ills and struggles. His childhood observations and early adult experiences of class differences and perceptions of 'otherness' would manifest in unforgettable characters driven by the consuming search for justice or the unquenchable thirst for power. Under the guise of madness or from otherwise marginalized spaces, characters would put into words the prevailing restlessness and yearning for change.

The very titles Tsegaye chose would prove insolent to gentrified sensibilities, as *Joro Degif* (Mumps), *Askeyami Lijagered* (The Ugly Girl) and *Listro* (Shoeshine Boy) took to the stage and introduced their own linguistic and visual aesthetics. Both in his original works and in his seamless adaptations of Shakespeare, Molière or Brecht, Tsegaye transposed Ethiopian content and cultural nuances that captivated audiences and, not surprisingly, raised alarm among censorship units. Tsegaye's own struggles are illustrative, but the history of censorship and the arts deserves a more thorough study than can be attempted here. Suffice it to say that the cache of rejected play scripts and book manuscripts, if archived, will serve as invaluable source material for cultural historians wishing to explore the confluence of politics, representation, and creative freedom.

In our effort to re-introduce Tsegaye's life and works through performances and publications, it is our greatest wish to see him take his place among African literary luminaries. We hope that his recollection of childhood memories and reflective recounting will find resonance in Wole Soyinka's *Aké* and Ngũgĩ Wa Thiong'o's *Dreams in a Time of War*. From Tsegaye's fearless imagination, we will learn to resurrect our heroes and bestow them with timeless presence. From his fierce love of country and continent, we will find courage to encounter others without judgment then embrace our own reflections without reserve. From his unwavering commitment to craft, we will be emboldened to explore and expand the very limits of language and revel in its fullness and beauty.

In these pages we will meet Tsegaye—poet, playwright, man of his times— and journey with him to his past, even as he bids us to dream forward.

–Heran Sereke-Brhan
October, 2011

Chapter 1

GABRE-MEDHIN COULDN'T BELIEVE what he saw on his way to the open-air market, the Merkato, in Addis Ababa. There was a man, respectable looking to all appearances, committing an illegal act in broad daylight. The law had forbidden exchanging the legal currency, Menilek's allad, for East African shillings and Yemeni Piasters, and here before him the black marketeer was doing just that. Gabre-Medhin had no choice but to do what any upright citizen would do upon witnessing a crime. He cried foul screaming "Oooo! Oooo! Oooo!" People knew what that meant. The high-pitched, drawn out call, like a blaring bugle, signaled trouble. It meant someone was in distress.

"Bind me to him in the name of the God of Menilek! Bind us together and send us to the house of justice!" pleaded Gabre-Medhin with the people thronging around him, pointing at the man he had caught dealing in forbidden currency.

Little did Gabre-Medhin know that the man he had just accused of committing a crime was a crony of the Crown Prince, *Ras* Teferi, who would one day become Haile-Selassie. The prince and his friends could thumb their noses at Menilek's decree with impunity knowing that the emperor *Atse* Menilek was powerless to do anything about it. The emperor had been in a coma for a long time, while a power struggle was brewing under the watchful eye of Empress Tayitu. Supporters of Ras Teferi had begun asserting their strength by undermining the power of the official heir, *Lij* Iyasu, even engaging in illegal acts to flaunt young Ras Teferi's rise to the throne.

Meanwhile, the rituals of justice carried on. The citizens who had witnessed this breach of Menilek's law had to do what custom dictated, bind the accuser with the accused and send them to the nearest *chilot*, or seat of justice. A random passerby proceeded to tie the ends of the cotton cloth the two men had donned over their shirts—no self respecting man or woman, rich or poor, ventured out without wearing a length of white cloth woven of cotton, called *netela*—and told them to go to *Basha* Wolde's Chilot in Arat Kilo. The strength of the knot that linked the two men was merely symbolic; the true force of their commitment to reach the court came from the authority that their binders had invoked.

"Go to the house of justice in the name of the God of Menilek!" they warned, and there was no turning away. The two men would have to arrive together to where an interpreter of the law would give them a fair hearing. They might, of course, glare at each other on their way to court. They might sling a few angry words and even tug and scuffle. But get to their destination they would, goaded further by folks along the way. "Go stand before the law without fail!" passersby would urge them. "Even a river obeys when one calls the name of Menilek!"

Gabre-Medhin was a tradesman. He had been one since giving up his job at Emperor Menilek's palace where he served as an attendant in the dining hall. As owner of a small business with hired tailors and two sewing machines, he made a living by selling ready-made clothes in Merkato. He had abandoned his respectable career at the palace in the capital and started a retail business at a time when trade was not held in high regard, because he no longer had the patronage of *Fitawrari* Ibsa. As a result, his job at the palace had become precarious.

Ibsa, Gabre-Medhin's relative from Mecha region, was a late minister of Menilek's regime and, in his final years, governor of Wollega. But he was dead, betrayed by an unfaithful wife who was caught in bed with *Dejazmach* Wolle of Warrababo. Eager to salvage their master's honor, the minister's loyal servants had killed the seducer. And yet, it was not the servants who were held to account for the guilt of murdering a person of rank, but Ibsa himself. He was placed under house arrest. Of course, Emperor Menilek would have pardoned him, but he was at death's door. If Ibsa stood trial, his judge would be either Prince Teferi or one of his men. And that, he was certain, would be a shameful end to his glory days. He would rather escape the humiliation. And he did. By poisoning himself.

At the hearing of the illegal currency case, a strange turn of events had landed Gabre-Medhin, the plaintiff, in the defendant's corner. He was now the one that the stern hand of the law threatened to punish. His guilt: slandering an honorable citizen! The young man seated at the judge's bench was Prince Teferi himself. And there was Gabre-Medhin, a self-professed loyalist of a dying regime, accused of slinging mud at the wrong man. He was held in the manner in which offenders were kept in court then—his wrists tied to his ankles—and was brought before the judge who sat under the shade of a tree. As for the man he had caught breaking the law, he was freed. He stood brazenly chatting with the Prince's courtiers.

There was no way out of the predicament Gabre-Medhin had put himself in, it seemed. No self-appointed defender of the fading rule of Menilek would get off lightly in the court of Prince Teferi, and Gabre-Medhin wouldn't have been the exception, had it not been for the well-timed intervention by his own wife, Fele-qech. At the exact moment when Teferi excused himself and was about to step away from the bench to attend to some matter whispered to him by an aide, she ran to him shouting "*Abet! Abet! Leul* Teferi! May the Lord show you the way of mercy!" She swiftly took off her *netela* and threw it on the ground before him. The import of Feleqech's action was not lost on Teferi. The netela was her dignity, and for him to walk on it would have been tantamount to trampling on the body of a distraught woman seeking justice for the father of her children. That would be an act unworthy of one who promised to be a fair successor of Menilek; Gabre-Medhin knew that. By daring the Prince to step on her netela, Feleqech had posed a delicate challenge.

Her courage gave Gabre-Medhin hope and emboldened him to protest against the unfairness of his treatment. Doubled up like a contortionist, he began shouting: "No one holds the rein but the rider; no man upholds the law but the leader." Prince Teferi was in a quandary. Faced with Feleqech's potent ploy of a netela thrown in his path and her husband's loud censure of his failure to enforce the living law, the prince chose the wiser course and spared himself embarrassment by acquitting the man.

Gabre-Medhin was free in the end, but the brush with the nascent rule of Prince Teferi had imperiled his life. Pointing an accusing finger at a crony of the Crown Prince had singled him out as hostile to the new order. He had proven to be a loyalist of the waning regime of his beloved Emperor Menilek. His days of prosperity in the capital had come to an end. It was time he moved out of Addis Ababa. He would be better off taking his wife and their three children, and going to Bodda. He had a sister there, Adde Argaatu. He would be able to provide for his family there.

Chapter 2

Wuen Gabre-Medhin first laid eyes on Feleqech, he was called by his pre-baptismal name, Robale. He was a soldier then, and she, a mere nine-year-old fleeing town with her mother, *Woizero* Wolete Selassie. A power struggle between Lij Iyasu of Wollo and Teferi Mekonnen of Shewa over the succession of the ailing monarch had evolved into a bloody war that erupted on October 17, 1916. Being Emperor Menilek's grandson, Iyasu had a rightful claim to the throne, but Shewan nobility were unwilling to crown him. How could they appoint Lij Iyasu, the dissolute son of *Nigus* Mikael of Wollo, whose father was a recent convert to Christianity and who had himself openly flirted with the idea of embracing Islam, as their ruler?

Ankober, the historical capital of the Shewan Dynasty, was burned to the ground, as were surrounding villages. Many fled to save their lives; families abandoned the town and traveled to the safer interiors of Shewa in the company of soldiers.

The fourteen-year-old Robale, a sergeant in the army of Fitawrari Habte-Giorgis, was assigned to be an armed escort in charge of guarding refugees. Among the group of Ankober folk in his custody was a woman called Wolete-Selassie, Basha Dañe Haile's wife, traveling with her young daughter to their home in the capital, Addis Ababa.

Wolete-Selassie set out on foot to Addis Ababa with about a dozen sheep she had raised and the dearest possessions she had salvaged from her burning house. There was nothing to be afraid of on the long trek to her husband's home. The marauding soldiers and their flying bullets were far behind. With these young riflemen by their side to protect them till they reached a safe haven, Feleqech and her fellow travelers had no fear of being waylaid by roaming bandits. True, there had been rumors of the defenders themselves becoming thugs. Wolette-Selassie had heard of such guardian angels taking advantage and abusing the very people they were supposed to protect. They robbed defenseless folks of their possessions, killed and feasted on their livestock. But there was this serious-looking sergeant, a lanky boy named Robale, who put her mind at ease. Polite, reserved and reliable, he had earned her trust from the start by making it clear to his fellow soldiers that he meant to protect the people in his care. If some of the riflemen had harbored mischievous ideas, Robale's conduct banished such thoughts from their heads.

"I was sleepless with worry wondering what might have happened to you," said Basha Dañe sighing in relief as his family arrived home unharmed in the Qebenna neighborhood of Addis Ababa.

"Yes. We are alright, thank God. St. Mary herself put us in the hand of a true guardian. I knew he was trustworthy the moment I saw him. I was sure we would be well taken care of."

"What is this young soldier's name?" asked her husband.

"Robale. A good-mannered lad who kept those other soldiers in their place. May the Lord bless his life."

Basha Dañe thought awhile stroking his beard and said: "I'd like to thank him myself. One should be grateful for kindness. I'll slaughter a sheep and invite Robale and the other boys for dinner."

Chatting with the young sergeant after dinner the following day, Basha Dañe was glad to learn that Robale was related to Fitawrari Ibsa's family.

"What a happy coincidence!" he exclaimed. "You are of the same clan as Fitawrari Ibsa."

Ibsa, Basha Dañe's boss, was in charge of allocating funds for the numerous churches that Atse Menilek wanted to build in Addis Ababa. Basha Dañe, an expert in building materials, played a vital role in the project by selecting the finest wood pillars and foundation stones for some of the grand churches that would later adorn the capital. "I will tell Fitawrari Ibsa what a fine young man you are," said Basha Dañe. True to his word, he sang Robale's praise to his superior. Ibsa was impressed. He had Robale summoned to the palace following the defeat of Nigus Mikael's army in Ankober, and helped the young man secure work as an attendant in the palace's dining hall.

The job was a good start to a promising future; a cushy perch far better than any foot soldier could dream of. His duties were neither frivolous nor demanding. Assisting the dining hall staff in tending to the needs of eminent guests at the frequent royal feasts, Robale couldn't have been happier. He liked it there; it was all first-rate, he thought. Only one thing troubled him: a few of his colleagues mocked him. They made fun of his Oromo name just because it sounded like an Amharic word that meant hoodlum. "Worobelle," they jokingly called him, but he resented it. He brooded about it for days then made up his mind to renounce the bothersome name and adopt his baptismal name instead. He became Gabre-Medhin overnight.

❖ ❖ ❖

Basha Dañe lived in Qebenna, close to Fitawrari Ibsa's home in Amist Kilo. He was a busy man, working hard to fulfill Menilek's dream of erecting many fine churches. His future seemed secure, what with his own reputation as the best in his trade and his wife's occasional visits to Ibsa carrying her fine cooking in a basket. Such thoughtful gestures, Wolete-Selassie believed, would help her husband's career prospects. Paying homage to his superior would only make things brighter for Basha Dañe, she thought, and periodically brought offerings of chicken and lamb stew to Fitawrari Ibsa. Then one day, he asked her to stay and sprang a question that took her by pleasant surprise.

"Why don't you give your daughter in marriage to my protégé, Gabre-Medhin?" he asked. She knew Gabre-Medhin. How could she forget that shy youthful sergeant who had protected them on their panicked flight to Addis Ababa? He was doing well for himself; she had been told. Situated in the capital, he was on a path to a good life. A decent young man with a respectable occupation was a double blessing; she could wish for no better husband than him for her daughter. But how could she give her consent without consulting her husband? Shouldn't she let him know first before giving her word to Fitawrari? Shouldn't he have equal say on the matter, if not more?

"So what do you say, Wolete-Selassie?" Ibsa prodded.

She was in a fix. What would Basha Dañe say when he found out that that his wife had agreed, on her own, to give their daughter away in marriage? He would resent it, for sure. But she would try to talk sense into him. He would understand. For if she missed the chance and Ibsa changed his mind, she would never forgive herself.

She rose from her seat and expressed her consent.

"It's settled! You will marry Feleqech," Fitawrari told Gabre-Medhin. "Her mother has agreed, as will her father, I'm certain." The news made the young man beam with joy. In profound gratitude, he bent down and kissed his patron's knee.

Feleqech was thirteen then. She was only nine when Gabre-Medhin first saw her among the displaced families he was escorting to Addis Ababa. He had seen her here in the capital a few more times since then. He had run into mother and daughter on their way to or from the market or church. The mother kissed him whenever they met and asked him how he was doing, while Feleqech stood watching, glancing guardedly and smiling shyly. Her reserve pleased him, and her reverence for her mother won his approval. He liked her finely combed hair and her ladylike airs. But it was her smile, more than anything else, that he had been unable to resist. Feleqech's winsome smile unleashed a storm inside him, which spurred him on to trouble Fitawrari Ibsa to intercede on his behalf before he lost her to someone else. Coming from a person as eminent as Ibsa, the request had a sure prospect of being granted, he figured.

He was right.

Chapter 3

AFTER LEAVING ADDIS Ababa in the wake of Ibsa's death, Gabre-Medhin went to Bodda, a village 20 kilometers west of Ambo, the place where his elder sister Adde Argaatu lived. For one like him who had tasted the city life in the bustling capital, this exile to the quiet humdrum life in the country would have been hard to accept. But to his surprise, Bodda was no longer the sleepy hamlet of former days. This birthplace of Menilek's Minister of War, Fitawrari Habte-Giorgis, had blossomed into a vibrant little town holding forth the promise of peace and prosperity. Gabre-Medhin had bought sewing machines with money he had saved in Addis. He knew he would make a good living in Bodda. His family would lack for naught; nor would his aging sister, Adde Argaatu. She had taken him in and raised him after their mother's death, but she was poor and lonely now. She needed someone to look after her, and here was Gabre-Medhin's chance to repay her kindness.

He built a fine home for his family and another one nearby for his sister. He hired tailors to work on his sewing machines and embarked in earnest on this serene chapter of his life. No more dreams of a prestigious career in government service; no more fear and insecurity in the ruthless world of politics where thirst for power turned men into beasts. Even his dismay at the speedy demise of Emperor Menilek's rule had faded away, and life in the rural town was shaping up to be joyful. He would be faring well in Bodda, God willing. He was a lucky man. Lucky in many ways except in one: he didn't have a son. He had fathered four girls but no male child to carry on his legacy.

This absence of a son rankled his relatives who thought it was foolish of Gabre-Medhin to waste his prime years with a woman who would only give him daughters, and they made no secret of their outrage.

"You gave her four chances, man. And four times, she gave you a girl. What are you waiting for? A fifth girl?"

"Let this Amhara woman go before it is too late. Don't let your name die with you for God's sake!"

His first child, a strapping baby boy, had died in infancy. There was another boy too; a son Gabre-Medhin had named Zewde—my crown. Zewde was alive but not well. A childhood accident had left him brain damaged.

"Get yourself an Oromo woman and put an end to this curse. You wouldn't want to die like a nobody without a son to look after you in your old age, would you?"

Their ceaseless harping wore down Gabre-Medhin's resolve. There was wisdom in their counsel; he couldn't deny it. The very thought of getting old and dying without a descendant to bear his lineage was frightening. So, little by little, he yielded to their plea and grew cold and aloof towards his wife. Then the most callous of his kin, taking their cue from him, became downright hostile towards her. With whispered slights and biting innuendos, they let her know that her place as matriarch of the family was no longer secure. A divorce was looming, Feleqech realized. For failing to bear a healthy son, she was going to lose the man she loved, and there was no one to help her, for no mortal had the authority to reverse her fate. Nothing short of a miracle could bless her womb with a son and save her from the shame and pain of a broken marriage. She needed a rescue; a divine favor only her patron saint, Abune Gebre-Menfes Kiddus of Bodda, could grant. She needed to ask him to intercede for her.

In the tradition of Ethiopian Orthodox Christianity, when a believer is confronted with a grave problem that she is powerless to resolve on her own, she turns to a last resort known as *silet*, an earnest pledge to make an offering to a saint or angel in return for the fulfillment of her request. The repayment of such divine favor could be in the form of goods or services whose worth varies in proportion to the favor granted. Silet is a serious vow to show gratitude by giving back what one can after receiving a celestial boon. It is a solemn covenant made in tears and prayer. But there are some desperate souls who find themselves in distress so dire that they present their silet covered in ashes and clad in chaffing sackcloth, helpless suppli- cants who hope to earn heavenly compassion by subjecting themselves to brutal pain and self-abasement. Feleqech was of this latter group. It was her marriage that was at stake after all; her future was in jeopardy through no fault of her own.

"I'm going to offer a silet to Abuye," she confided in Adde Argaatu, her sister- in-law, and the one true friend she had left. "I'll weep at his feet and implore him to save me from being thrown out of my home. I'd rather die than be separated from my husband and my daughters," she said, and her voice broke as tears stung her eyes.

Adde Argaatu knew the woes of losing a child. She had lost her only son, Fufa Irana, who had been killed in the Battle of Sagale.

"Who said you'll be separated from your family?" she said holding Feleqech's hands in hers. "That'll never happen; you hear me? You'll have a boy any day now and put all these busybodies to shame. Mark my words."

But Feleqech was not sure, and in the closeness of her comrade, she found it difficult to contain her grief and dissolved in tears. Adde Argaatu couldn't bear to see her suffering. Her lips trembling in a losing battle to stem her own tears, she told Feleqech: "You don't believe me when I tell you that you'll have a son? Call me a liar if your next child isn't a boy. Why are you crying? To make those meddlers happy? Don't break your heart grieving, my darling. Hushhh. You'll give Gabre-Medhin a son and that'll be the end of your torment."

Feleqech wiped her face with the edge of her netela and sighed.

"When are you going to Dereba Abbo?" asked Adde Argaatu.

"Tomorrow morning."

"I'll come with you. You won't be alone."

The following morning, the two quietly headed to the church in search of a miracle. Adde Argaatu worshipped Waqa, the Oromo God of sun and sky. She had no place in her heart for the Christian deity. The only reason she set foot on the grounds of Dereba Abbo was to show her solidarity to her friend. This was Feleqech's only hope of saving her marriage; the silet was her last chance at redemption. Adde Argaatu wouldn't desert her in her time of need.

The church was closed, as it always was on ordinary weekdays. There was no one to spy on Feleqech at her moment of despair. No one to witness her pain in a deserted churchyard. Away from venomous tongues and prying eyes, she stripped off her white cotton dress and wrapped herself up with sackcloth. She then fell to her knees and began to weep as her friend watched and wept with her. She crawled on her bare knees sobbing and pleading with the saint for a miracle. She mumbled her plea while tears streamed down her face. She called upon Abuye, the Saint Abune Gebre-Menfes Kiddus, and asked him to give her a son. She begged him to shield her from the fate of an unwanted wife. The rocky ground had no mercy; it lacerated her knees and turned them bruised and bloody. She winced, but didn't get up until she crawled around the church three times and concluded her silet by fervently reciting her pledge.

What was her silet to the Saint? What did she promise to give Abuye in return for brightening the remainder of her years with hope? Was it a sheep or an ox that she was to slaughter in his name and feed to the needy? Did she hope to appease the saint with gifts of beautiful curtains for the sacristy of his church? Vestments embroidered with gold threads for his servants? Bejeweled umbrellas to glitter over the Ark of the Covenant on high holidays? No. Feleqech made no such promises.

What she committed to, if she was blessed with a son, was to repay the favor in-kind by giving back the life that would be conceived in her womb. Yes, she vowed to commit her son to a life of service in the church of Dereba Abbo. Imagining her own boy becoming a deacon and gladdening the saint with absolute devotion, "Give me a son and I will give him back to you," she said.

Lo and behold! The saint heard her prayer and fulfilled her heart's desire. She gave birth to a healthy baby boy on August 17, 1936, and named him Tsegaye, "my grace." The birth of a son shamed her detractors to silence and resurrected the loving husband of former years in Gabre-Medhin. The threat of being cast out of her home melted away like frost in the sun and, she was restored to her rightful place as the true materfamilias.

But once Tsegaye was born, Gabre-Medhin would have none of Feleqech's talk of putting his beloved son on the path to priesthood. His faith in the Christian God was enduring, but he despised the clergy. Having seen scores of malicious priests and their devious ways in Menelik's palace, he had no faith in the sanctity of the so-called "House of God", filled with ungodly serpents as it was. To his wife's tearful insistence that failing to honor a solemn vow was an ill-fated sacrilege, he answered: "Our son will receive modern education, get a well-paying job, and make a generous donation to the church. I won't let him waste away his life in priesthood." Feleqech had no choice but to hold her tongue and see what the future would bring.

Then ominously enough, in the third month of his birth, Tsegaye became ill. A lump as hard as a pebble appeared on the tender flesh of his groin and quickly grew into a wide swelling that spread to his thigh. He became irritable and refused to be fed. Fever racked his body. He grew weak within days and the family began to wonder if Gabre-Medhin's long-awaited son and heir, fine and healthy till then, was going to be taken away before his life had barely begun. To Feleqech though, the infant's illness could mean only one thing: the saint was angry at her for denying him his prize. She was scared. A broken silet was a serious matter, and even Saint Abbo, compassionate as he was said to be, wouldn't take that lightly. She had meant it when she made the pledge; she would have kept her word had it been up to her. But Gabre-Medhin was the father. He had the last word, and his word was that Tsegaye would not go down the path of a clerical life. Not even this imminent threat to the child's life, which Feleqech knew was sent by an offended saint, would dissuade the patriarch from his stubborn conviction that Tsegaye should be the family's trail blazer to the world of modern education.

Feleqech was in despair. Her husband wouldn't let Abuye collect his due even when it seemed nothing short of that would induce the saint's pity. In the meantime, her son's condition was getting worse. He hadn't eaten for two days, and the fever had persisted. The swelling had grown bigger and looked angrier. Something had to be done. Feleqech had to find someone worthy enough to intervene and ask the displeased saint to have mercy. There was only one such man she could think of: the archpriest of Dereba Abbo, Bodda's only church. If there was ever any hope for a divine favor, it would be found through the priest's mediation.

His name was *Abba* Tekle-Tsadiq, a haggard, gray-bearded man who had made a vow of celibacy and a commitment to serving the church to the end of his days. He was in charge of upholding the faith among Bodda's few halfhearted Christians and their heathenish neighbors. Together with two other priests and a couple of shepherds, who doubled as deacons whenever they could, he carried out his priestly duties and conducted Sunday services. He officiated at Christian weddings and baptismal rites. On high holidays, he brought out the Ark of the Covenant for people to pay homage to and to follow singing and ululating. He read pages of the Scriptures and those of the Miracles of the Saint to the flock. With tales of the fantastic deeds the saint was said to have performed, he struck awe in the hearts of his listeners, and he did it all while reading in one language and speaking in another, for no one beside full-fledged priests spoke Ge'ez; the ancient language that had found sanctuary from extinction in the bosom of the church. Abba Tekle-Tsadiq, God's supreme agent, was a tireless preacher of righteousness to the sinful folks in the village, a dour prophet of doom who enjoyed giving the laity hair-raising accounts of hell by way of warning them to stay away from sin. He was the Father Confessor to all Christian families in Bodda, given divine authority to hear honest accounts of their sins and to bestow blessings. Now that Feleqech was faced with a heaven-sent threat that she was powerless to ward off, the Soul Father, she thought, was her best hope.

"Go tell him my child is dying. Tell him that I beg him to come and pray for my son," she told Askale, her eldest daughter.

The priest came promptly, barefoot and out of breath, with his head thickly wound with a long strip of white cloth, a symbol of his priestly calling. Holding a small wooden cross in his hand and a couple of prayer books in cases of cowhide slung over his shoulder, he hurried to Feleqetch's home. Once there, he quickly glanced at Tsegaye and told the mother what he intended to do.

"He needs a seven-day course of prayer and holy water," he said. "Get me a pail of clean water. There is no time to waste."

Tears of hope filled Feleqech's eyes as Askale went to fetch water.

"How long has he been like this?" the priest asked, slowly pulling out one of his books and sitting in a wooden chair.

"Four days now, Father. He is getting worse by the day."

He blew thrice on the bowl of water placed before him and began praying. "In the name of the Father, the Son, and of the Holy Ghost," he intoned the first words of his prayer. For over an hour he prayed, reading from his books and reciting from memory. In a voice like the drone of a giant beetle, his shaggy beard wagging as a torrent of Ge'ez words tumbled from his mouth, he launched an attack on whatever might have cast its evil shadow on Tsegaye. Every once in a while, he scooped a handful of holy water with his hand and sprinkled it on the child's face. Tsegaye whimpered but didn't scream. He had lost the strength to protest aloud.

"We shall see a sign by tomorrow," he announced at the end of the first session. "The holy water has begun its work. Your son will be better." There was confidence in his voice; cocksure self-assurance enough to kindle hope in Feleqech's heart. "No adversary can withstand the cross for seven days," he added, brandishing his wooden cross as he leaned forward to reap the reward for his exertions: a bowl of beef stew with *injera,* the thin flimsy bread pockmarked with a thousand tiny craters, to which he did ample justice.

To the priest's chagrin, Tsegaye's health didn't improve the following day. In fact, on the third day of the seven-day prayer vigil, his condition grew worse; it appeared as though he wouldn't last another day. And when he stopped stirring even when ice-cold holy water fell on his forehead, Feleqech heard herself whispering the words of yet another silet to the Saint. "Thirty sticks of taper for your church; if you show my son your mercy!"

The response was immediate. It came in the form of a voice in her head, too loud and clear to be ignored. "Confess your guilt," the voice said. "Tell the priest the truth." She rose from her seat obediently, cradling her son in her arms. She walked to Abba Tekle-Tsadiq and stood before him. The sudden change in Feleqech's demeanor alarmed the priest. His first thought was that the child was gone, and that his three-day labor had come to naught. He stared at her with questioning eyes before getting up from his seat and asking hoarsely: "What's the matter?"

"I have sinned Father. I have broken a silet," she said, and confessed her predicament in a barely audible voice.

Abba Tekle-Tsadiq didn't respond right away; he needed a few seconds to mull over what he had heard. Then he sank back to the chair as though Feleqech's offense had fallen on him and caused his knees to buckle. "Failing to keep a vow you have made to the saint is no trifle a sin," he said after closing his holy book. "I have no power to absolve you of such guilt." His words convinced Feleqech that she had reached the end. She sat back and began to wail. Then, like a specter out of nowhere, someone appeared at the door.

Be Creative
@ Your Library

Sé Creativo
en tu biblioteca

2009 New York Statewide Summer Reading Program

www.summerreadingnys.org

New York State
Library

She stopped her sobbing and blinked at the bent, shriveled figure, wondering if her eyes were playing tricks on her. But the man was not a vision and couldn't be blinked away. Abba Tafa had come. The half-blind medicine man stood there in the flesh although no one seemed to know how he had arrived. Who sent for him? Adde Argaatu had been with her all morning, and she was now busy in the kitchen relieving the distressed mother of the chore of making lunch for the family and for the ever-famished Soul Father.

"I hear your son is ill," said Abba Tafa in a voice like the rustling of corn leaves in the wind. The healer, a shrunken, leathery man of antiquity, had come to help. She stood up and began to cry aloud, while the priest knitted his brows at the sight of the medicine man and began muttering a prayer meant to fend off evil.

The woman who had told Abba Tafa of Tsegaye's illness and brought him to Feleqech's home was a neighbor, a good-hearted woman who couldn't bear to see the poor child slipping away. She had led him up to the door of Feleqech's home and discreetly stayed behind. And here he was, the healer and bonesetter, held in high regard by the villagers, come to tussle with death and deny it the life of an infant. Carrying a worn out goatskin bag full of medicinal herbs, roots and leaves, he stood leaning on a slender walking stick, looking at Feleqech with small, cataractous eyes, and waiting till her tears abated. Having been privy to the suffering of villagers young and old, he had learned to remain calm in the face of naked despair. His face, a tangle of wrinkles, remained serene.

"Come in Abba Tafa," said Adde Argaatu and ushered him in before going back to prepare the priest's lunch.

He entered and asked Feleqech to remove the clothes with which she had bundled the child. After a quick glance at Tsegaye's ailing body, "That is one mean looking tumescence I've ever seen," he said, as if talking to himself. He quickly untied the mouth of his medicine bag and fished out a tangled wad of roots, from which he snapped off a few pieces. He then extracted bits of dried leaves and crammed a handful of roots and leaves into his mouth. Solemnly, with a blank face that betrayed nothing of the taste in his mouth, he chewed the herbs into a pulp as his eyes roamed the small body of the child lying naked and still before him. He had noticed Abba Tekle-Tsadiq looking at him with thinly veiled disgust, but that didn't seem to bother him much. Ignoring the priest, he chewed, spittle the color of bile leaking out of the corner of his mouth and streaking over his snow-white beard. Under other circumstances, Abba Tekle-Tsadiq would have walked out right away. He wouldn't have allowed his eyes to behold such a sickening spectacle of the ungodly old man performing his satanic craft, but lunch was about to be served. He wouldn't leave empty bellied if he could help it. None of what the church offered equaled what he found in the homes of the flock. So he remained seated, muttering Ge'ez words, his defense against the enemy, and trying hard but failing to avert his stare from the revolting creature with the evil thing in his maw.

Abba Tafa spat the yellowish brown potion on and around the afflicted area of the child's body. Again and again, he chewed and drizzled Tsegaye's thighs, groins and belly with the juice. With his crooked knobby fingers, he gently spread the medicine, his lips whispering inaudible charms all the while, to no avail. It seemed nothing would rouse Feleqech's son out of his slumber at death's door. The bitter outcome of a Saint's grudge, it appeared, was to be undone neither by Bodda's ultimate representative of the Christian God, nor by the unsightly ministrations of a medicine man. And as the sun began its downward decent behind the horizon, the baby's life hung perilously over the precipice, and his shallow breathing grew ever fainter.

It was time for Adde Argaatu to act.

She had meant to let Feleqech have her way first; to let her do what she thought was best for her own son. But now that her friend had exhausted her options, it was her turn to try. So she went to fetch the old widow, an Amhara woman called Woizero Simeñ, the village midwife. Let her come and see what she could do to help the child she had lugged into the world. The woman claimed no higher calling than aiding women in labor or circumcising infants. But Argaatu had also been told of a few cases where Woizero Simeñ had applied her razor for purposes other than circumcision or midwifery and had gotten a few miraculous results.

In the end, Feleqech owed gratitude for her son's rescue neither to Abba Tekle-Tsadiq nor to Abba Tafa, but to the hag of a midwife who sliced open, with her sharp razor, the hardened, discolored skin on Tsegaye's groin, and pressing hard with her fingers, forced out a mass of putrid blood and pus. A risk worth taking, her remedy was so final and brutal that the child whose breathing had been faltering till then stirred suddenly and squealed weakly, causing Feleqech to shriek with a sob of joy. Abba Tekle-Tsadiq and Abba Tafa, the intercessor for divine favors and the healer with occult roots and herbs, watched with awed disbelief as the widow managed to drag Tsegaye back from the edge. The old surgeon who trusted no one or nothing beyond her earthly wits and razor cleaned away the mess, washed and dried the bloody infant. She then turned to Feleqech and said: "You can now feed him your breast milk." The mother did as she was told, and to everyone's relief, Tsegaye's fever-parched lips latched onto his mother's nipple and he began to suckle.

Chapter 4

THANKS TO WOIZERO Simeñ's remedy, the shadow of death had been lifted from Gabre-Medhin's home. A battle had been fought and won. But another bigger battle had been lost in northern Ethiopia. The Italians had invaded the country, and the Ethiopian resistance fighters, no match for the vicious might of tanks and bomber aircrafts, had been defeated. After slaughtering tens of thousands, the invaders declared victory in May 1936. Ethiopia, they claimed, was their colonial outpost.

The lingering shame of loss in this same rugged land in eastern Africa some forty years previously, and the humiliation that the Italians had endured at the Battle of Adwa, had been rankling them for decades. A formidable army of a proud European nation had been defeated by an army of barefoot Ethiopians wielding spears and shields. This ignominy had sent a dangerous message to other colonial subjects in the rest of Africa, jeopardizing European scramble for the continent. The Italians had now returned, four decades later in 1935, this time a hundred-thousand-man strong. Their attack was merciless and their rallying cry: victory at any cost. Benito Mussolini, orchestrating the invasion from afar, would accept nothing less. Determined to avoid another disgrace, he had given the army license to butcher and brutalize by using the most terrible weapons of mass murder: machine guns, artillery, and aerial bombardment with mustard gas and deadly chemicals. Whatever it took to teach Ethiopians a lesson.

The army was all too willing to oblige. It killed indiscriminately and unleashed terror. It burned homes, mutilated bodies of resistance fighters, and hanged the captives. It didn't take long to overwhelm the Ethiopian defense force. In just seven months, the conquest was complete and the five-year long occupation had begun. But even in the face of such a devastating loss and the enemy's unheard-of cruelty, resistance fighters had already organized counter-attacks. These dark-skinned, puny-looking spoilers of Rome's colonial dream in East Africa were proving to be a tough adversary to contend with. They were a defiant, hardy lot that no amount of European savagery could ever tame. Undeterred by the annulment of their government and the exile of their emperor, Haile-Selassie, they had been leaving their homes to join bands of guerilla fighters and to confront the Italians wherever they could. They carried out surprise attacks against enemy forces and displayed courage the like of which Mussolini's men had never seen. With their stubborn resistance, the Ethiopians were turning what should have been a peaceful plundering of their country into a nightmare.

❖ ❖ ❖

Following Tsegaye's birth and his brush with death three months later, Feleqech seldom saw Gabre-Medhin who was engaged in the mysterious activities of an itinerant businessman. What he did was too dangerous to be spoken of aloud, but she knew, as did his sister Adde Argaatu, that he was secretly commissioned to buy rifles and ammunition from some double-dealing *banda*—Ethiopian turncoats who had sworn loyalty to the enemy—and ferry them to freedom fighters via clandestine channels. It was a stint that could cost him his life if discovered, but the patriots were in dire need of supplies.

In Gabre-Medhin's absence, life had become dangerous for the family. The banda, armed with modern weapons given to them by their Italian masters, carried out frequent raids. With the pretext of hunting for guerilla fighters, they looted homes and killed civilians. But Feleqech's fear of a banda raid was second to her worry about the fate of her husband. What would happen to him if the Italians found out about his activities? What if someone tipped off the enemy that Gabre-Medhin delivered arms to the rebels? She had no doubt about the outcome of such a slip. The Italians had proven their appetite for sadism. There had been horror stories of flying machines disgorging weapons from their bellies that blew people to pieces or burned them alive. She had heard rumors of poison gas that rendered men deaf, blind and insane, and of bodies charred beyond recognition. The worst of it was that a good portion of those massacred were peaceful villagers that had done the Italians no harm. So it was not hard for Feleqech to imagine her husband's fate if, God forefend, he fell into the hands of the white-skinned devils.

Worry kept her awake at night. She was afraid that she may never see Gabre-Medhin again, although she did her best to keep her fear bottled up for the sake of the children. But there were moments when the thought of losing him would fill her with torment, and she would sing:

> *I hear of death from on high*
> *A roaring beast that can fly*
> *Like a demon in the sky*
> *And I long to see your eyes*
> *I long to see your face*
> *And your manly grace*

She sang and shed discreet tears. She missed her husband and fretted over his well-being so much that she had almost forgotten the other threat—the banda—when they finally arrived in Bodda. They had been pillaging nearby villages, she had been told, but never before had they set foot here. They came brandishing their guns, determined to ransack the town. And a few of the thugs were headed her way; they knew, thanks to their tipsters, which homes promised hefty loot.

Within a few minutes of their foray, the first cry of distress rang from one end of town, followed by several others. Something was awfully wrong, everyone knew, and most guessed what it was. The banda had come!

The screams multiplied, and even those whose homes had not yet been violated began lending the courage of their scream to their neighbors. "Oooooooo! Oooooooo! Oooooooooo!" they shouted until Bodda became a bedlam of wailing women and howling men. The Judases had to make off with whatever they had stolen before it was too late. They had gathered more than they had hoped to find, including the cows they had taken from Gabre-Medhin's kraal. But the victims were determined not to let them get away. In the midst of the shouts and screams, loud cracks of gunfire were heard. Emboldened by their outrage as well as their swelling number, gun-toting townsmen pursued the fleeing marauders and confronted them on the outskirts of town.

The banda quickly evaluated their predicament and knew that they were hopelessly outnumbered, if not outgunned. They could stand their ground and fight; they could kill quite a few of their pursuers with their superior weapons, but there was no doubt that some among them would perish. That was not a risk worth taking. Better to choose the sensible option and surrender the loot. They would return someday soon to make sure that the fools paid dearly for their temerity. Let the villagers take away the booty and swell with pride for standing up to the banda. They will be made to regret it later.

Owing to the courage of Bodda's men and women, the banda left almost empty-handed, but the rescue had come too late for Feleqech. One of the three men who had broken into her home had dropped a flaming twig on the thatch roofing out of sheer malice. Before she could run inside for water, the morning breeze fanned the flame and turned it into an inferno.

Later, standing bereft before a smoldering mound of charred wood and ash, she heard her neighbors saying again and again: "Thank God; the children are unharmed." "Thank God not a soul was hurt." "Your husband is a brave man. He'll build another fine home." It was all true, but she would be damned if she would let the banda find her in this town ever again. This was their first incursion into Bodda, but it wouldn't be their last, she knew. Especially after being forced to abandon their spoils, they would certainly return to punish Bodda's audacity. She had to take her family out of harm's way. There was a safe place for them to go, thank God, and it was only now it occurred to her that her husband must have foreseen such an incident when he told her to take the children and go to Goromti if Bodda became unstable. He hadn't said what could possibly happen; she hadn't asked either. But it was all clear now. "Go to Goromti; my brothers will look after you there," he had said. An out-of-the-way village made up of a few homes, Goromti was certainly safer. There was no threat of the banda attacking it; it was not the type of place to lure them. Feleqech could rest assured. The men, her brothers-in-law, would be keeping a watchful eye. Nothing was as comforting in such uncertain times as men in the house, men who would protect her family with their own lives.

When Feleqech gathered her family and broke the news of their impending departure, the children were not thrilled, but Adde Argaatu was delighted. She was born and raised in Goromti, had fallen in love and gotten married there, the land of her clan. It was the place she still called home. With the two women laden with the biggest bundles, Feleqech's eldest daughter, Askale, carrying Tsegaye on her back, and the three younger girls—Menbere, Tsedale, and Bogalech—each lugging a load to match her strength, the family began their trek, together with their livestock, along the rocky bank of Lake Dandi.

Feleqech's neighbors in Bodda had been right when they assured her that her husband would build a home finer than the one that the banda had burned. Gabre-Medhin did build a house in Goromti, and it was bigger and finer indeed. Sitting on top of a hillock called Gute Daña, the new house was big enough for Adde Argaatu to move in and live with her brother's family.

Chapter 5

L IFE IN GOROMTI was peaceful and placid although the man of the house was away most days of the year on that deadly business of his, while Feleqech wore herself thin with worry. The days went by while Tsegaye sat, crawled, tottered and toddled, and his mother thought "How time flies!" when she saw him playing out in the yard with little boys of his age. Her eyes shone with pride when he began following Goromti's shepherds and their herd to the grazing fields. Her own Tsegaye, snatched from the clutches of death at infancy, was now a healthy boy splashing about in the Bollo and Qersa Rivers. He climbed fig trees and stuffed his belly with yummy sticky figs. He gathered the incredibly bitter-sour-sweet koshim fruit, and together with the bigger boys, headed to the river edge—all of them carrying their harvest. Like his peers, Tsegaye crushed the fruit in the hollow of a rock, mixed it with water, and squatting with his head thrust forward, lapped it up till he was sick of it. Her Tsegaye, a bony little boy, crawled under the belly of a well-fed cow and drank milk by squeezing the dugs into his mouth, while older boys stood murmuring pacifying words to the gentle creature suckling a human calf. Tsegaye was happy. Life in Goromti was joyful, a magical world of bucolic bliss, until three men arrived from Menz. Like a rude jolt in the middle of a sweet dream, their arrival, brought an abrupt end to his joy.

As the Magi who arrived in Bethlehem guided by a dazzling star, these three elderly men from Menz had their sign to follow: a beacon of survival that led to Goromti. That ill-fated town of Menz, Ankober, had been burned yet again, this time by Italians. The Fascist invaders, furious when met by fierce resistance mounted by one of their fearsome foes Ras Abebe Aregay, had destroyed it with an avalanche of bombs and artillery. And the townsfolk who had survived the massacre had fled, as did these elderly priests who had traveled on foot for days to reach Goromti. They were Feleqech's relatives. Hungry and exhausted, they came empty handed except for the coarse woolen cloaks on their backs, a few bags of dried food that they had carried for the trip, and various holy books made of parchment. But they had brought a gift for Feleqech's male child, the gift of enlightenment, more precious in their eyes than myrrh and frankincense. In return for being taken in by Feleqech and saved from certain death, they would teach Tsegaye Ge'ez, the sacred language of the church. He would learn the alphabet and would soon read the holy books. Yes, they would sow in his heart the seeds of devotion to the Christian deity, the God of his mother's ancestors. What better way to repay a life-saving favor than to initiate the little heathen into a blessed way of life?

To Feleqech, though, it seemed as though there was more to the men's talk of saving Tsegaye's soul than a mere gesture of gratitude. Still laden with the guilt of a broken promise whose consequence had nearly killed her son, she saw Saint Abuye's hand in the matter. Ge'ez was the language of devotional rituals in the Orthodox Christian church. If her lambkin learned to read the sundry holy books that the elderly priests had brought with them, wouldn't that likely spark a pious flame in his heart? So, she wondered, could this coming of the refugees from Menz be a clever scheme laid out by St. Abbo himself? Were the guests unwitting instruments of a powerful being mistaking a divinely contrived purpose for a deed out of the goodness of their hearts?

Whatever providence might have had in store for Tsegaye, he learned to read Ge'ez while Gabre-Medhin was away smuggling supplies for guerilla fighters. The boy even committed a few short prayers to memory and recited them aloud. His mother was proud. She was happy, but he was not. Far from it, in fact. He was miserable. The lessons were tedious. The teachers were dull and severe. Tsegaye was the only pupil, but his tutors were three, and they took turns torturing him with their endless lessons from dawn to dusk. Having been compelled to seek refuge in the midst of Oromo folk with whom they had little in common, the stern Amhara men found the task of educating Tsegaye to be a welcome relief from the tedium of idly waiting for the end of their exile. But to him, the interminable lessons brought an end to his carefree days of fun. No more befriending unschooled shepherds for him. No romping about in the fields and crouching under the distended udder of a cow for a bellyful of fresh milk. Gone were the days of scaling fig trees and haunting the river banks to make the taste bud-tingling *koshim* juice. Instead of the mesmerizing tunes that the shepherds played on their bamboo flutes, he had now to listen to the endless drone of these gray-skinned men.

How bigoted they were, these survivors of Italian fury. How they tried and failed to conceal their disdain of the very people in whose midst they had found shelter from the firebombs of Mussolini; contempt so palpable that even Tsegaye, as young as he was, didn't fail to notice. They spoke Amharic, the language of the king and the nobility. They professed the Christian faith and led a life of rigorous piety—praying several times a day and fasting like hermits. But the Oromo, with their various gods and their strange attachment to their horses and cattle, were too consumed with worldly matters to take the hereafter seriously. They were too fond of singing and dancing. They gorged themselves with milk and butter. They swilled *tej* and brawled till blood was drawn. They loved with a passion and lived as though earthly joy was the single purpose of their existence. How could a God-fearing Christian who had trampled upon the flesh for the sake of the soul help being horrified at the Oromo's lust for life?

As the Italian occupation of Ethiopia was nearing its end, Gabre-Medhin came home bringing his own party of guests: a handful of Amhara men and women from Ambo. Now that the enemy was about to leave, lawlessness was sure to reign until authority was reasserted and order restored. The town was no longer safe for non-Oromos, and Gabre-Medhin had offered some of his friends and acquaintances in Ambo the shelter of his home in Goromti.

Feleqech was happy that her husband was unharmed. She was nervous too, wondering how he would take his son's transformation into a Ge'ez-parroting pupil of the Magi. Would he see it as a stumbling block on his son's path to worldly learning? Might he count Tsegaye's home schooling by these patronizing paupers as defiance against his wish by his wife? Would he evict her meddling kin and send them packing?

Gabre-Medhin did none of that, to her relief. As if he had been thoroughly transformed by what he had seen away from home, he didn't seem to mind what the priests had done to his son. In fact, he even appeared somewhat amused by the whole business. He smiled when he heard little Tsegaye reciting the holy passages in Ge'ez. Even the sojourn, in his own home, of not one but three of the priests he despised didn't seem to bother Gabre-Medhin. Feleqech couldn't believe it! To make her astonishment complete, a few days later her husband volunteered, with his son by his side, to accompany the priests to the church of Medhane-Alem— Savior of the World, in Goromti.

During the priests' stay, Tsegaye read and memorized various Ge'ez prayers, most of which meant nothing because he hadn't really learned the language. He heard his father's guests conversing in Amharic, which he himself knew a smattering of as he did his paternal native tongue—Oromiña. And this sudden transformation of his erstwhile monolingual environment into a polyglot den where the two widely spoken human languages in the land rubbed shoulders with the so-called Language of Angels, Ge'ez, sparked his enthrallment with languages. There was Soboqa too, the perennial jester, to encourage Tsegaye's infatuation with words.

Soboqa was Gabre-Medhin's older brother, who visited every once in a while, riding on his beloved horse, a piebald gelding he had named Chere after the very priest who had baptized him. Whether that was meant to mock or honor his christener remained unclear.

As Gabre-Medhin's house filled with guests who came seeking refuge, Soboqa's visits became more frequent. That was because he loved dialogue and debate, and he had discovered the ideal audience to impress with his linguistic finesse. His other motive for his regular visits, a reason no less appealing than his love for debate and a desire to show off his verbal agility, was this: he hoped to win the heart of an Amhara woman among those his brother had brought with him from Ambo. His first marriage had ended in a divorce when the wife had failed to conceive. Soboqa's tool being in good working order, he had no doubt that the fault was hers. No one disputed the fact. After letting the woman go, he married another and labored for three more years for a child, a son. There was none. Not even a daughter. He tried his luck with yet a third woman, but still there was no sign of a child. That was when he began to doubt himself. Could he be the cursed one? Was he infertile? He would have sought a fourth wife, but he had wasted time waiting. By the time he had parted from his wife, he was no longer young. He had lost his manly flame, and the damsels he lusted for had begun turning him down in favor of younger rivals. That was why Tsegaye saw more and more of his wordsmith of an uncle. Having been slighted by Oromo women, Soboqa now dreamed of a chance for fatherhood with an Amhara woman from Ambo.

Gabre-Medhin's home had room for all. A house made of mud-cemented walls and thatched roofing, it had space for every one of the eight guests to sleep on their beds of piles of hay covered with cow hide. It was big enough for Soboqa and his younger brother to sit at the fireside till late at night arguing before their entranced audience. Gabre-Medhin didn't enjoy the verbal jousts because Soboqa had a way of egging him on till he lost his temper. While the flicker-eyed spectators watched and listened, Soboqa assaulted his brother with his outlandish views on matters of justice, the role of tradition, and the right of land and cattle inheritance, prodding Gabre-Medhin into a heated exchange. Deftly whipping out an array of witty remarks, sprinkling his words with puns, adding a dash of bright couplets here, throwing in an apt saying there, polishing his speech with that inimitable touch of his till it shone and dazzled, he managed to draw one of his listeners close enough to earn her affection. One of his brother's guests from Ambo gave him a sign that she had been won over. She wasn't the type he would have looked at twice in former days. She was a flat-chested, spindle-legged woman with a long nose and a neck infested with tattoos of crooked crosses. But things were different now. An aging hunk confronted by the frightening prospect of lonely old age couldn't afford to be fastidious. He knew he would be lucky if this woman agreed to be his wife and followed him home, and luck was about to smile upon him, it seemed. Then one blighted evening he committed a grave error that ruined his plan. Emboldened by his success, he let his guard down too early and offended the Christian woman with a blasphemy of his tongue.

"There is something I don't get," he said in the heat of an argument, this time with one of the priests from Menz. "One thing that baffles me about your religion, which is also my religion, mind you, is this business of needing a go-between."

"What go-between are you talking about," asked his interlocutor.

"Isn't that what you say the saints and angels are for? To intercede on our behalf?"

"What do you mean?" asked the elderly priest, his voice betraying a mounting outrage.

"What I just said! Why must a Christian, in the hour of his need, go to a saint instead of to God himself? If an Oromo needs something from Waqa, the God of Earth and Sky, he needs no messenger. He can ask Waqa directly. You understand? Why bother with angels and middlemen as if they are more merciful than the one who made us?"

His profanity rendered the priest speechless. Like all the good Christians in the room, including the woman Soboqa was trying to impress, the priest crossed himself and scowled at the sharp-tongued reprobate. So incensed was he that he refused to eat dinner until Gabre-Medhin and Feleqech persuaded him to relent. "He means no harm," Gabre-Medhin told him. "He is just a blabbermouth with a good heart."

Chapter 6

THE WAR WAS certainly coming to an end. It was rumored that the British allies would arrive soon and that the Italians would leave. And now that things had calmed down somewhat, it was time for the Amhara guests in Goromti to leave, which they did, after thanking their hosts profusely and showering their blessings upon them. Soboqa returned to his home, cheerless and single, to chase the spinsters in his village with renewed vigor, and Gabre-Medhin resumed his clothing business. He was happy. After the misery and death he had witnessed throughout the Occupation, his appetite for the simple joys of life had reawakened. He was grateful for surviving the war unscathed. The breathtaking bravery of the freedom fighters who confronted the rumbling tanks of Mussolini armed with spears and rusty rifles had convinced him that his people were plucky men indeed. And he wanted his son, Tsegaye, to inherit this exceptional Ethiopian courage. Tsegaye, he thought, should grow up to be a brave man, and to that end, Gabre-Medhin decided to teach him how to fire a gun. Hearing the blast of the shot and getting a whiff of burning sulfur, the father believed, would give Tsegaye a taste of what it meant to be a fighter.

The chosen moment for his son's initiation into the world of guns was a quiet dawn when Tsegaye was enjoying his sweet early morning sleep. That didn't deter Gabre-Medhin from picking up his gun and approaching the sleeping boy. The sight of her husband hovering around Tsegaye with gun in hand alarmed Feleqech. She had heard of people returning from the battlefield unhinged by the horror they had seen there.

"What are you doing?" she asked Gabre-Medhin in a hushed whisper, careful not to wake up her son.

"I'm going to teach my boy how to fire a gun," he replied, shaking Tsegaye awake.

"What does he need that for? He is too young for a gun. Can't you wait until he is old enough?"

"He's not too young to try."

"Please don't wake him up for God's sake. He will be frightened when he sees you with your gun."

"That's what I'm trying to cure him of. Fear. He shouldn't be afraid."

Feleqech tried to stop him but Gabre-Medhin firmly moved her aside, and grabbing Tsegaye by the arm pulled him out of bed. Tsegaye opened his eyes and was petrified to find himself out of bed, naked and with his wrist in the grip of his gun-toting father. Too scared and confused to cry or scream, he let himself be dragged out to the front yard as Feleqech followed the two, pleading with her husband for sanity. Gabre-Medhin knelt down beside his son, and aiming the gun at a distant mound of hay, he ordered Tsegaye to fire. "Shoot!" he roared at the child. Tsegaye's little finger tried to pull the stiff trigger of his father's old gun, but failed. To make matters worse, his hand kept shaking. The father tried coaxing and urging him to fire, but the gun remained cold and mute. In the end, Gabre-Medhin grew impatient, and doubling his index finger on top of Tsegaye's, he pulled the trigger, crushing the child's finger as he did, and making him howl in pain. The blast ripped through the awakening village and the recoiling gun knocked Tsegaye off his feet. The target was missed, and Gabre-Medhin was disappointed.

"Get up!" he shouted, lifting his fallen son for yet another shot at the heap of hay, but then the loud report of gunfire had jolted Adde Argaatu out of sleep and sent her running outside in trepidation.

"What's going on?" she asked, hurrying over to where her brother had his son trapped between himself and a cocked gun. "Have you lost your mind, man?" she yelled at him angrily. No one else dared to chide Gabre-Medhin as fearlessly as Adde Argaatu. "Leave the child alone," she demanded and pulled the naked boy free.

Gabre-Medhin's second attempt at speeding up his son's journey to manhood occurred when he returned from Ambo once again to spend the Ethiopian New Year's day with his family in Goromti. As on other grand holidays, families celebrated the new year with feasts of raw beef and lamb stew. Gabre-Medhin, as head of his family, made sure that his household lacked for none of these.

He had gone to Gudar market and bought a big sheep, a ram with big twisted horns and spotlessly white wool. For Gabre-Medhin, slaughtering such a plump sheep on a high holiday was a solemn ritual that called for a medley of mystical rites. First of all, the sheep had to be white; no other color would do. Second, the slaughter had to take place at sunrise. Besides, the sheep's forehead had to be smeared with butter just before it was killed. With its four legs tightly bound with rope, the sheep had to be positioned facing the rising sun right before the knife was to slit its throat. And now that Gabre-Medhin had a male child he was proud of, he wanted his son beside him to witness this important moment.

The helpless sheep was placed before father and son while the patriarch, his eyes fixed on the only church of Goromti visible in the distance, offered a prayer to

Tsegaye with uncle Teklemariam (l) and father Gabre-Medhin (r), date unknown.

the Savior of the World. Gabre-Medhin was a Christian—his name, which meant "servant of the Savior"—testified to the fact. He had embraced the faith since the age of four, but he hadn't lost respect for the gods of his ancestors. After praising the Christian God, he also paid homage to the spirit of the hills of Goromti and those of the Qersa and Bollo rivers. Praise was also due to the exalted Waqa, the grandest deity of the Oromo. He too deserved glory for protecting the family, for letting the sun to continue to shine and for sending the rain to quench the earth's thirst. Once all the tributes had been paid, it was time for Gabre-Medhin to invoke the spirits of his forefathers by calling out their names one after the other. He had to honor his progenitors by declaring his ancestry as far back as he could remember. Like every man in his village who took pride in his lineage, Gabre-Medhin had memorized the names of his forebears. Reciting one's ancestry was a declaration of pride in one's identity, a legacy that Tsegaye too would have to pass on to his children in time.

Towering high above his son, his dark skin bathed in the fiery glow of the rising sun and a sharpened knife glinting in his hand, Gabre-Medhin raised his voice in exhaltation, and Tsegaye listened with awe.

"I am Gabre-Medhin Robale Qewesa," he declaimed. "I am son of the Marena clan. Son of the Metcha tribe. I honor you my ancestors." He cleared his throat and began calling their names, briefly pausing after each so that Tsegaye would remember. "Qewesa, Dabal, Daña, Awadi, Dandawo, Sinan, Jida, Elamu, Bonaya. Watch over my family," he said, and holding the muzzle of the struggling sheep, almost severed its neck with the knife.

Tsegaye hadn't seen much of his father till then. Gabre-Medhin had been away from home for many months until liberation in 1941. Sensing the child's yearning, the father seemed eager to make up for lost time which perhaps explained his quickened pace of initiation lessons. Gabre-Medhin later took Tsegaye indoors for morsels of raw beef dipped in fiery chili that he forced him to eat till he screamed in unbearable pain. It was then up to Feleqech to soothe the flames in Tsegaye's mouth with a bowl of yogurt while the father walked away with a contented smile on his face. Tsegaye had fired a gun, observed his father slaughtering a sheep, and eaten raw meat before he had turned five. He was well on his way to becoming a man.

In truth, though, no one would take Tsegaye for a man, whatever the father might have thought of him, until the boy partook, at the age of fifteen, in a grand rite of passage known as Buuta.

As laid down in the unwritten laws of the Gada, the foundation of Oromo social structure, Buuta was a consecrated day for Oromo boys. On that day, the village's 15-year-olds would elect a leader from among themselves and disappear into the forest along the Qersa River at dawn. There, they would be met by an elderly patriarch of the Gada. The patriarch would bless them and offer a long prayer before he signaled to the so-called Fuga woman to do her part.

Fuga was a name given to all members of her ethnic group. It was an appellation meant to signify the lowly status of her clan, for she belonged to a group of people despised by the Oromo and relegated to scraping a living as traveling artisans. An Oromo would be scorned for eating with a Fuga, and he would be cast out of his clan for marrying one, for the Fuga were considered inferior, endowed with the wondrous craft of molding clay and forging metal in return their lowly status. But why would the Oromo who would rather have nothing to do with the Fuga entrust the circumcision of their boys to a Fuga woman? Why would they let an untouchable touch their sons on such a grand event—the rite of passage? How could they submit the male organ of their sons, the very means of their clan's continuance, to a woman they considered unfit to eat with them? Well, that was because according to the Gada's inviolable rule of conduct, it was taboo for one Oromo to spill the blood of another with a sharp object. So said the edict of the Gada, and no one dared to defy it. The law gave clear instructions as to who would carry out the act of circumcision on Buuta: a Fuga woman. Let a Fuga wield a knife at the Oromo; her lowly birth had condemned her to be a fitting agent of such a sin. Or so it was thought.

After slicing off a dozen foreskins, the woman would accept a bagful of grain for her service and return to her people. The brave boys, wincing without a peep, would wait till the blood abated and return home where they would wait until late afternoon. Then they would be taken to a hill named Gute Daña, the place where they would gather together and wait for Jeti.

Of all the sacred rites of passage on Buuta, Jeti's appearance was the grandest. None of the other to-dos, not even the knife-wielding Fuga woman emerging from the bushes equaled the thrill of witnessing the spectacle of Jeti approaching the hill sitting astride a white horse.

She was an old woman, a blind septuagenarian who lived across the Bollo River. Taller than the tallest woman in Marena land, her snow-white hair glowing orange in the sinking sun, holding the rein in one hand and a sacred staff in the other, Jeti rode the horse with more grace and confidence than riders with their visions intact. The very sight of her struck young and old with awe. Jeti, they said, was endowed with the gift of the chosen. No wonder she was the spiritual leader of the Marena clan. Such a special day as Buuta called for the blessing of no less an imposing priestess than Jeti.

As her horse passed through the village, folks would stop and bow to her; each of them astonished all over again when she knew in an instant who they were by the sound of their voices. Those with no urgent chore at hand would follow her horse to Gute Daña, for Jeti was a sensation whose aura cast its spell even on the village idiot, the cowherd Wolde-Aregay. He too would find it impossible to resist her magnetism and he would bribe a dutiful shepherd to watch the cattle in his charge. He would then follow the old woman, gawking at her as spittle leaked out of his gaping mouth. Miraculously, even his signature yawn, his ceaseless, long-in-dying wail that sounded like the howling of a wolf, seemed to hold off in Jeti's presence.

Little boys in Goromti liked Wolde-Aregay, the Amhara herdsman, because he liked them too. Adults said he was possessed by bovine demons that were made homeless after being cast out of cattle. They called him a loony and treated him as one. But children were drawn to his harmlessly bizarre antics and his never-changing tune and moronic ditty: "There is a sky; for Wolde-Aregay." And most of all, they found irresistible the taste of his cherished tidbit: roasted sheep's testicles that he scrounged from homes where sheep had been slaughtered. He had no friends or relatives in Goromti. He was a lonely cattle herd who got through the days lowing like the cows he tended, munching on his beloved treat, and entertaining kids with the only song he knew.

Hanging around Wolde-Aregay had gotten Tsegaye in trouble more than once. Feleqech had warned him, time and again, to stay away from that demon-infested lunatic, but he had not complied. His defiance had earned him a few painful wallops, but Tsegaye, like many other boys, was unable to swear off the fun of watching Wolde-Aregay clowning in the fields or sharing his stash of sheep's testicles. And by the time Tsegaye's fascination with him had waned, enough of the herdsman's manners had been stamped on his memory to lie in wait and come to life years later in one of his plays, *A Mother's Nine Faces*.

Wolde-Aregay would follow Jeti halfway to Gute Daña before he returned to his cattle, and she would head to the place where the newly circumcised boys and two-dozen adults gathered waiting for her. As if the animal she rode were a magic horse that somehow knew where to go, it would take her to the big flat rock on the hill, the symbol marking the hallowed ground where the old woman was to meet the throng and bestow her blessing. Once there, Jeti would raise the staff above her head and bow to the sun. Sitting erect on the back of her white horse with a lush mane, she would turn to the four corners of the earth saluting land and water, and offering her gratitude for their gifts of life. She would then call out the names of Oromo heroes and mighty cattle lords who had conquered grazing land for her clan, the Marena, and sing paeans to them. At the end of the blessing, she would face the crowd before her and say: "*Marena Waqa yabulchisu!*"—May Waqa preserve Marena—to which all would respond in unison: "*Yabulchisu!*" Tsegaye, having come with an adult to watch the spectacle of the newly circumcised boys of his village, would beam in pride because Jeti was his father's aunt. Yes, it was this same Jeti, revered by young and old, who made him her exceptionally delicious *marqa*—porridge made of barley flour and spicy butter—whenever he went to visit her.

Chapter 7

GOROMTI WAS A small town, but it had more than its share of characters. There dwelled the sage and the simpleton, the sane and the insane, and every one in between. Tsegaye's loving and beloved aunt, Adde Argaatu, and the funniest man he knew, his uncle Soboqa, had their homes in Goromti. There was Wolde-Aregay, the perennial loony. There was Kodole too; another curiosity Tsegaye was drawn to. But unlike his attraction to Wolde-Aregay whose silly song and forbidden delight he truly enjoyed, his fascination with Kodole was mixed with dread.

For one thing, she was from far away, he had been told. Brought from the western border of the country, she did look different. Her skin was black as night. Her build was stockier, her lips thicker, and her nose flatter than most people's in Goromti. But what Tsegaye found disturbingly mesmerizing was the way she spoke and the gibberish that streamed forth from her lips, prattle so strange that one couldn't say for sure if it was her mother tongue or the language of her captors. Kodole was a slave, body and soul property of a well-known feudal lord in Goromti—*Grazmach* Chala.

Chala had as much property as befitted his status. Being a loyal servant of Fitawrari Habte-Girogis, Menilek's Minister of War, he owned land and cattle, together with a number of servants, including Kodole, the woman sold into slavery-unto-death under his yoke. So condemned, Kodole gathered firewood and dried cow dung for fuel. She fetched water in a big clay pot from the spring by the river. She ground corn, wheat, and sorghum hunched over a stone mill. She washed piles of dirty clothes on the bank of the Bollo River, and did it all bearing the satanic stamp of Chala, her owner, the man who had half of Kodole's tongue cut out so that she could be easily discovered if she tried to run away. There were other means of branding slaves or limiting their chance of escape, such as searing onto their skin their owner's name with white-hot iron. Some slave masters had even severed their slaves' Achilles tendons so that they wouldn't be able to run at all. The former didn't seem to Chala like a foolproof method of preventing a slave's escape, and the latter, he thought, slowed the slave down and made her sless of a workhorse. So he came up with his own clever scheme and chopped off the front half of Kodole's tongue, which he thought he had no use for. She wouldn't need her tongue to fetch wood and water; to cook, clean, and wash. It was her service that was needed, her endless labor, not her talk.

But that didn't stop Kodole from talking. Determined to defend this last shred of her humanity, her faculty of speech, she defied Chala's attempt to silence her and she talked and babbled and jabbered to herself. No one understood her chatter, but she went on unleashing her tongueless twaddle wherever she went, and good people shuddered at the evil in the heart of Chala.

Chapter 8

ADDE ARGAATU HAD a mule given to her by her brother, Gabre-Medhin. She had named the mule Beletech. She was a gentle brute, Beletech, and served her owner devotedly, carrying her up and down the hilly land of Goromti and Bodda, carefully picking her way along treacherous paths.

One day, Adde Argaatu, together with her nephew, Tsegaye, set out on a trip to Ambo. He sat behind her on the mule's back and ambled on until they reached town at noon. The noise and clamor in the bustling town was more than Beletech could stand. She grew edgy and skittish, just as frightened as the five year old Tsegaye sitting on her back.

Tsegaye's mother, Feleqech, had fallen ill and she had been taken to Ambo for treatment by modern Italian medicine. Her grave illness had made her doubt if she would ever be well enough to go back to her family in Goromti. Her daughters had visited her earlier, but she hadn't seen her son, and she had asked for him to be brought to Ambo for a chance to hold him close to her bosom and kiss him. And once again, it was Adde Argaatu who had volunteered to fulfill her wish.

The ride from Goromti to the outskirts of Ambo on the back of Beletech was peaceful, although a bit bumpy, owing to the rugged terrain and the jerky steps of the short-legged mule. But when they arrived in Ambo, the bedlam there perturbed beast, woman, and child. From his perch behind Argaatu, clinging to her waist with all the strength of his arms, Tsegaye heard people speaking in a babel of motley tongues: Tigriña, Gurageña, Italian, Arabic, Wolayita, Oromifa, Amariña. He saw strangely attired folks milling around in the open-air markets and chattering incessantly like a flock of geese. He heard townsfolk gabbing in disturbingly loud voices and laughing without reserve. He saw an endless array of big bright houses swarming with people who were too loud and hurried. Nothing in Goromti could compare to this. Tsegaye was terrified.

He had heard much about Ambo but had never seen it. Goromti's grownups went to sell their wares there. The men bragged about the delicious *tej*—potent alcoholic brew made of hops and honey—that they drank in Ambo, and the peerless songs of the crooner, Nigatwa Kelkaly, that they had heard on the wondrous phonograph. He had heard them spinning their yarn about the sweetly perfumed beauties they had met and the white-skinned Italians that they had seen, but none of this had prepared him for the day he would face it all himself. There was nothing for him to hold on to as noise assaulted his eardrums and grated on his nerve, and the teeming multitude closed in on him till he was short of breath. Overwhelmed, he tightened his grip on his aunt and became rigid as a plank. To top it all off, there was a strange looking thing with shiny glass eyes massively squatting in their path, snarling like a mean-tempered beast and belching plumes of smoke from its rear end. Sitting inside it was a creature like out of a horrid nightmare barking at a man on the street. The sight of this apparition with skin like that of a scalded chicken was the final straw. Tsegaye was about to leap off the mule and flee when Beletech gave way to her own terror and reared dangerously in an attempt to jettison her load and bolt out of the commotion. It was time for Adde Argaatu to rein in boy and mule.

Her one hand pinning her nephew down to the saddle, Argaatu lashed at

Beletech's rump and thighs with a whip made of hide strips. Cursing the animal for making a fool of her before many watching eyes, she whipped furiously at the mule's haunches, unaware that the lashes were landing on Tsegaye. His legs, clinging to Beletech's flanks, had caught half the brunt of Argaatu's wrath. They too were flogged till welts appeared on them. His battered legs twitched at every sting and he winced, but he bore it all in silence. Now that he was in the land of the surreal, he took his auntie's attack on

Feleqech Dañe, Tsegaye's mother.

him as one more instance of the mayhem all around.

In the end, Beletech gave in and brought her forehooves back down to earth.

❖ ❖ ❖

Feleqech had grown thin and sallow. She said she was better but looked far from it.

"Go give your mother a kiss," said Adde Argaatu and thrust Tsegaye forward when she saw him hesitating. Still shaken by the riotous events moments ago, he was in no state to be the loving son. To make matters worse, he had never seen Feleqech looking so weak and helpless.

"What's the matter with you? You don't recognize your mother or what?" said Argaatu smiling nervously. In the bright

Tsegaye with siblings and other family members (Addis Ababa, ca. 1988). Standing (back row, (l) to (r): Nigatu and Kidane (brothers); Seated (l) to (r): Tsegaye, Menbere (sister); Gonfa Deqissa and Chimsa Debissa (cousins); Front row (l) to (r): Digafe Aweke (nephew) and Meseret Bayisa (nephew).

daylight outside, she had seen what her whip had done to his legs, but fortunately, it was dark here inside the house.

"Don't be afraid. I'm okay. Come and kiss me," cajoled Feleqech, in a voice so unlike hers. The aunt, propelling the reluctant boy to his mother, was annoyed by his chilly demeanor. The way he was behaving would make one wonder if Adde Argaatu had usurped Feleqech's place in his heart.

Tsegaye didn't like Ambo one bit, and he was happy when, two days later, Argaatu said it was time to go back to Goromti. Ambo had greeted him with a nightmarish hullabaloo that had scared him, and he had had no single moment of joy in the two days since. He was bored and lonely. There was nothing here but the dull chatter of old men and women in the house, punctuated by his mother's moans. Noise and dust outside, and a bunch of snotty kids playing strange games and trying to make fun of him. He hated the town and was glad his stay there was over. "Back to Goromti" he shouted in glee, and this time, his mother didn't have to sweet-talk

Gabre-Medhin Qewesa, Tsegaye's father.

him into giving her a kiss. Excited by the prospect of leaving soon, he ran to her for a farewell hug, but Gabre-Medhin had another plan. "You're not going back to Goromti," he said, and Tsegaye's exuberance dissipated at once. He looked at his mother, then at his father's stern face, and turned pleading eyes to Adde Argaatu. She was no less disheartened by what her brother had said, for she loved the boy with all the affection of a childless aunt. During Feleqech's illness the two had become very close, so close that Adde Argaatu had even fancied herself to be his true mother.

"You'll stay here. It's time you started school. You're old enough," said Gabre-Medhin, and Tsegaye began crying.

"What do you want to go to Goromti for? What is there for you to do? Do you want to be a shepherd all your life, you fool?" Gabre-Medhin shouted at his son.

Chapter 9

THE Italians had built a modern grammar school in Ambo. It was a beautiful compound where about two dozen of the town's children learned reading and arithmetic. Gabre-Medhin had heard some fathers bragging about the wonderful things their kids were being taught at the so-called *ascola*. They said that their boys came home carrying books written in strange letters and confounding their parents with unheard-of notions that their Italian teachers had been filling their heads with.

Gabre-Medhin hated the Italians. They were the enemy—monsters who had treated his countrymen barbarously. He wanted them to leave, and he had done what he could to hasten their downfall. Their days were numbered; those loud-mouthed aliens from far away were on their way out. But he also knew that this place of learning they had opened in Ambo, the ascola, was the future. Even the hated banda who had sold their loyalty to the enemy had acquired skills from the Italians; craft that they would exchange for piles of money. The ascola was home of the modern education he imagined for his son. Let Tsegaye learn what he could there for as long as the occupiers lasted. That would be a good start.

A few days after Adde Argaatu had dolefully returned to Goromti leaving behind her heartbroken nephew, Gabre-Medhin took his boy to school.

Tsegaye looked his best for his first day at the ascola. He was scrubbed clean and dressed in a new pair of shorts and a shirt. His hair was combed, and his fingernails trimmed. The Italians had a reputation for tantrums at the slightest sign of scruffiness, Gabre-Medhin knew. He had been told that the headmaster himself inspected children's heads for lice.

Students in the school were divided in two; those who started earlier and learned a smattering of Italian were "advanced", and latecomers like Tsegaye were "beginners". The beginners' class, a roomful of demure, barefoot boys, learned the Latin alphabet by parroting their teacher as she read out letters from the blackboard. Following her cues, they chanted: *ah bə čə də*. She was a nun, and to prove it, she wore a habit and a necklace with a pendant of Saint Mary's image, but townspeople rumored that she was the headmaster's wife.

Tsegaye as a young man in Ambo

Tsegaye liked the new school. It was nothing like schooling that he had experienced Goromti. Not at all like the nauseating ordeal he had suffered at the hands of those tedious priests. The Italians, whose bizarre looks and manners he found fascinating, did a far better job of teaching. Their lessons were not hard to follow because there was method in them; no mindless rote learning here. The teacher paid attention to the students and made sure they understood what they learned. And best of all, there was time for fun, time for songs, and for a healthy dose of horsing around. There was time for playing *corda*—a crude merry-go-round— Tsegaye's favorite. There was even time for pleasure trips once or twice a week.

The Huluqa River was the destination for the first outing that Tsegaye took part in. The headmaster and the nun, assisted by two monitors, put students of both classes in two single-file formations and led them marching to the river. Once there, the kids happily splashed around in the shallow water before they ran to the top of the steep river bank on the other side. It was a bright day. The teachers strolled blissfully, basking in the sun and keeping an eye on students darting up and down the slope across the river.

Then suddenly, the river began to swell. The headmaster was the first to notice it. He saw the water surging, growing wider, murkier, and noisier by the minute. He called the monitors with a shrill blow of his whistle and signaled them to quickly gather the children. He didn't want them to be stranded on the wrong side of a rising river. Huluqa was not big enough to be called a river. It was a brook that at times grew angry and caused trouble after feeding on flashfloods spawned by a downpour further upriver.

The monitors shouted the order and the boys returned obediently. The bigger boys had no problem crossing; even a few kids slightly bigger than Tsegaye safely waded through, immersed up to their navels. But Tsegaye wouldn't dare take the plunge. The fast moving water scared him. Standing alone on the brink, he remembered horror stories of death in the river, frightening tales of people swept away and drowned, and later spat out still and bloated somewhere downstream. And he began to cry. He yowled wringing his hands till the director heard him through the din of Huluqa's fury. There was no one among the students big enough to carry him across, the headmaster knew. He made his way carefully across to Tsegaye's side of the river. He was a tall, strong man with a big belly. Jabbering his annoyance in his tongue, he picked up the weeping boy, cradled him, and walked back through the muddy water. The rescue was quick; Tsegaye's glide across the river in the arms of the Italian headmaster lasted no more than a minute, but it was long enough for him to observe the man in naked amazement and to examine his strange features. With unblinking saucer-eyes staring out of his tear and mucus stained face, Tsegaye studied the headmaster's tawny hair; the startling size of his nose—prominent as an eagle's beak– and his eyes, like those of a cat's. He marveled at the giddying fragrance of his cologne.

Tsegaye did enjoy the ascola, but the fun didn't last long. Italian occupation came to an end with the arrival of British liberators, and the ascola closed its doors. And once again, he had nothing to do. The boredom of his first days in Ambo returned. But there was no hope of returning to Goromti, the place that was still close to his heart, for by the time Feleqech had recovered, Gabre-Medhin had decided to settle in Ambo. The rest of his children had come from Goromti, and the family had found a home in town.

There was talk of a government school soon to be opened in Ambo. Gabre-Medhin had heard that the building that housed the office and residence of the ousted Italian governor was to be converted into a modern school, and he had made up his mind to take his son there when it opened. But in the meantime, he wanted to spare his son the tedium of idleness and asked his wife to take him to the village reading teacher, Abba Wolde-Mariam.

Abba Wolde-Mariam was blind, but you wouldn't notice that when you first saw him. His eyes were big as eggs, and they darted from face to face of those he conversed with. When he got angry, they bulged even further from their sockets. The teacher didn't do much of the teaching himself. Perched on a stool surrounded by a flock of students sitting on bare earth, he fixed his unseeing eyes on the distant horizon and wallowed in his private thoughts, listening to this or that child every now and then. The students, newcomers paired with seniors, tutored each other. With a wide range of literacy among the children, there was no shortage of tutors and pupils. As for the blind master, he mostly paid attention to the bright students, those who read the Psalms of David, the acme of learning under Abba Wolde-Mariam's tutelage. The teacher knew the book by heart and could easily catch a student if he skipped or misread a word.

"He has learned to read; unless he has forgotten it," Feleqech told the teacher when placing her son in his charge. She then tenderly stroked his head and left. Tsegaye watched her receding figure as far as he could, and shuffled closer to Abba Wolde-Mariam to read a test passage from the Psalm. But when he began to read, his voice began to quaver, and the teacher knew that the boy was on the brink of tears, as most were on their first day there. So he slid a hand into his pocket, to fish something out and place it in Tsegaye's mouth. A magic lump flooded his taste buds with such incredible sweetness that the sadness left him instantly. He had never tasted candy before; never held anything so sweet in his mouth. "Eat your candy first and you will read afterwards," the teacher said, and Tsegaye sucked on it blissfully. He took it out every now and then and saw it getting smaller while enjoying envious glances from many in the room. Every student had tasted of that special treat. A candy had been inserted between the trembling lips of every one of them on their first day with Abba Wolde-Mariam, but no one had ever gotten a second piece of candy. The candies in the teacher's pocket were strictly for the purpose of comforting new arrivals.

Rumor had it right after all. What used to be the Italian governor's office and dwelling was now partitioned in two. One half was fenced off to serve as the emperor's vacation resort, and the other half became a school. Named Haile-Selassie I Primary School, it was free and open for all those who wanted to attend. Not many parents sent their children there, however; some because they needed them to help around the home while others were not yet certain as to what this new school was all about.

The school kept its doors open nonetheless, so much so that Tsegaye didn't even need to be accompanied by a parent to be admitted. He enrolled himself and walked into a classroom of his choice where his playmate, Belete, a boy a bit older than he, had been placed in the third grade. The teacher didn't seem to mind but he wanted to find out if the boy could read. He scribbled a few Amharic words and sentences on the blackboard and asked Tsegaye to read, which he did without difficulty. Then he wrote an English word, *other*, and turned to him. "Oh…te…cher" read Tsegaye. The way he said the word made the teacher laugh. "That's not how it's pronounced," he said. "Listen and repeat after me. Oh…zer" Tsegaye repeated: "oh…zer" and was officially accepted as a third grade student at Haile-Selassie I Primary School.

The students of the new school had a funny way of addressing their all-male teachers. Each was called with the prefix Moosie the French honorific, Monsieur, distorted into something that sounded like the name of the Hebrew prophet, Moses, in Amharic. Moosie Kinfe-Mikael was Tsegaye's English teacher, the one who taught him how to say "other" properly. And there was Moosie Habte-Wold—the math teacher, and Tsegaye's favorite. Unlike his English teacher who made teaching sound like an onerous due he had to pay in order to survive, the Math teacher enjoyed teaching and vibrated with his enthusiasm for it. Students liked him because he never failed to arouse their rapt attention. Tsegaye sat in Math class for one hour every day, a whole hour that passed like a minute and became the highlight of his school days. Sitting in the front row and soaking up his ardent educator's sundry wisdom, he wondered how it was possible for one person to know so much, and why the school wouldn't hire more teachers like Moosie Habte-Wold.

Moosie Habte-Wold was paid to teach the handy science of numbers, but he imparted a lot more than that to his students. After meandering through a slew of his adult thoughts, which he shared with the kids as though they were his equals, he would bring up a subject that was closer to his heart: theatre. His face glowed whenever he ended the day's lesson and announced what he called "theatre time". From then till the bell rang, he would have students entertain him and themselves with role-plays and impromptu performances that depicted life in Ambo. Moosie Habte-Wold enjoyed watching them impersonate the various characters of their town. Tsegaye lived in Kolfe Arada, right by the open-air market where theatre-worthy events in town occurred, and he was never short of material for performances.

Ambo's Kolfe Arada was the place where things were bought, sold, and traded. Folks engaged in noisy haggling there and money changed hands. It was the center of action where disagreements became squabbles and then turned to scuffles and full-blown fights. That was where drunks made fools of themselves and pickpockets caught in the act were thrashed mercilessly. No one bothered to call on the police. Justice was served right at the crime scene. Whenever a thief was caught stealing, the victim would shout *"leba!"* and anyone up for the task of trouncing a leba would run to the spot. Leba meant thief, and the call, more than a signal of distress, was an invitation to partake in doling out punishment. Fists and sticks would rain on the captured desperado till he was reduced to a bloody pile. Or if the fearsome Abba Qemera, the self-appointed scourge of thieves, happened to be nearby, he would come running, his eyes glinting in bloodlust to handle the offender all by himself. A tall, broad-framed, muscular man with a passion for violence, he lived for the thrill of chasing, capturing and walloping pickpockets and petty thieves. No one else, not even the hysterical crowd, did as thorough a job as Abba Qemera.

Moosie Habte-Wold lived in a quiet part of town, a gloomy corner of Ambo known as Yegzer Dildiy—God's Bridge, and he was often captivated by Tsegaye's enactments of what went on in Kolfe Arada. Whenever the boy acted out a drunk swaying on his feet, or a thief sneaking up on an unsuspecting prey, or Aba Qemera serving up corporal punishment to a pickpocket, the teacher watched in absolute delight, and his lavish praises sparked a deep interest in Tsegaye for performance.

Moosie Habte-Wold was a popular teacher indeed. Students adored him, and their parents respected him. But his brother, Moosie Gebreyes, was a pariah, outright disliked and looked down upon for the guilt of practicing the Catholic faith. As the director of the school he should have been esteemed no less than his brother, but having embraced a religion that the Portuguese had tried and failed to impose on the Orthodox Christian people of Ethiopia in the 16th and mid 17th century, he was branded a heretic. To a God-fearing Christian in Ambo, the very mention of the word Catholic conjured up horrors of hellfire and brimstone. Children learned of the director's despised faith from the lips of their self-righteous parents, who accused him of gorging himself with meat and eggs on fasting days. And whenever the kids passed by the director's home on a Wednesday or Friday, they held their noses to protect themselves from being defiled by the smell of roasted meat or fried eggs. In the end, Moosie Gebreyes got tired of the shabby treatment. He asked for a transfer to a less intolerant part of the country and left town for good.

The person appointed to fill in the departed director's shoes, Arafat Musaid, had even less in common with the people of Ambo. He was a foreigner. He neither looked like them nor spoke their language, but he was a Coptic Christian, a subscriber to the same brand of faith as the official religion of the country. He came from Egypt bearing the commendation of the Pope of Alexandria, and was assigned Headmaster of Ambo's primary school by the emperor himself.

A stocky man with an aquiline nose and a shiny bold patch on his head that he tried to disguise by plastering across it wisps of hair from his temples, Musaid ruled by the stick and quickly became the terror of every student. Prowling in every corner of the school ground in search of mischief to punish, Mr. Musaid seemed to enjoy most of all his role of a ruthless disciplinarian.

"Hey you! I've seen you. Stay right there! Don't move!" he would roar if he saw a student misbehaving. He always carried a slender tree limb freshly cut and handed to him by the school's custodian. Strangely, once Musaid started thrashing the cringing urchin squealing at his feet, he never said a word. With his lips sealed tight, he would lash and lash until he got tired, and then walk away, composed while his victim writhed in the dirt.

Tsegaye too had once been at the receiving end of Mr. Musaid's fury. His offense was a case of unpardonable tardiness. Earlier that morning, he had gone to school wearing a tattered pair of shorts, and his classmates, who had seen his buttocks winking through ripped patches, had laughed at him. When he could no longer put up with their mockery, he had decided to run home during recess and change into his better shorts. But he had to sprint all the way home and back in the fifteen-minute break. By the time the stick-brandishing director found him, recess had been over for about ten minutes.

"You're going to get it today, boy," the guard at the gate somberly warned Tsegaye when he came running in. He was right. After barking at him to stand still, Musaid grabbed him by the arm and gave him a flogging, good and proper, till he begged for mercy. As was his wont, the director didn't even bother to ask why Tsegaye was late or where he had been.

Two years after it was opened, Ambo's primary school was moved into a new building, and the old complex that was once the Italian governor's office and residence became an agricultural college.

Chapter 10

HINGS WERE A lot more organized at the new school. For one thing, students didn't just wander in without registering, or join whatever class they wanted. Teachers were chosen with care and they taught what they were hired to. There was a curriculum as well; there were quizzes and exams. There were homework assignments. And like in the old school, Tsegaye had found a favorite teacher here in the fifth grade: *Aleqa* Me'amir, the man who taught composition. No one called him Moosie because his own title—Aleqa—was grander than a paltry Moosie. It meant 'head' in Amharic; a top ranking personage. There was an Aleqa in every field of work. None, however, had the lofty ring the title acquired when it referred to a person of high ecclesiastical learning in the Ethiopian Orthodox faith. Aleqa Me'amir was that; a luminary in his calling. "The king himself had him brought from Dima," people said in reverence. Dima was a prestigious place of learning for Ge'ez poetic arts in northern Ethiopia. And if one were to judge its caliber by Aleqa Me'amir, a Dima graduate, one would agree that it was a gem of a school indeed. The man was a brilliant poet who could compose divine verses, in Ge'ez and Amharic, without pen or paper.

Like many a gifted man, however, Aleqa had his flaw. He loved tej and drank it with abandon. Whenever he had that mighty potion in his blood, he forgot the wisdom of his age and learning, and competed against much younger colleagues for the town's most sought after prostitutes. He was old—nearing fifty—and lost the contest more often than not. Yet, there had been times when he prevailed, for what he lacked in youth and vigor, he more than made up for in wit and charm. Aleqa was well liked as he was admired.

He taught composition and poetry, subjects that Tsegaye enjoyed the most because the teacher warmly praised his gift. Especially after reading the lines that Tsegaye had composed about the school's windows, Aleqa had become convinced that the boy was the best of all his students in the entire school. The assignment was to write a short something, prose or doggerel, describing some part of the new school where Tsegaye was now a fifth grade student. On his way home that afternoon, Tsegaye had turned back and seen the many glass windows of the school glittering in the late afternoon sun and was struck by an idea. Once home, he filled his empty belly and while the inspiration was still fresh in his mind, scribbled a page-long poem about the dazzling windows he had seen earlier.

"Did you write these?" asked Aleqa, jabbing with his finger at the two lines that he found impressively poetic:

> *Glittering with borrowed light*
> *As if it were their own*

"Yes Aleqa Me'amir," answered Tsegaye. Who else could have written that for him? Tsegaye was the most literate in his home.

"Quiet, you nitwits!" Aleqa ordered the chattering boys of his class to hush. "Sit still and listen to the poem Tsegaye has written," he said and asked him to read it aloud. "This is poetry. You understand?" said Aleqa to the students. "Next time, try to create something half as good as this." Then turning to Tsegaye, "You are a gifted Oromo[2] boy. You whipped these Amhara knuckleheads, by God! Good job, Tsegaye. You can go back to your seat."

The truth was, to Aleqa Me'amir, Tsegaye's Oromo-ness was part of the wonderment in the beauty of his impressive verses. That's not to say the teacher wouldn't have been impressed if one of his Amhara students had done the same, but perhaps not with as much fervor as in the case of Tsegaye.

From then on, Aleqa made no secret of his admiration, which at times bordered on partiality in the eyes of the less-gifted students. "He is a bright Oromo," the teacher told one and all. Tsegaye basked in his teacher's genuine affection for him and beamed in the glory of being called the most gifted, though perhaps a bit less brightly than he would have if Aleqa had dropped the slur.

---

2   Aleqa Me'amir would have used the word "Galla" in place of Oromo. We have substituted the word Oromo here and elsewhere in the text in recognition of the negative connotation it invokes.

Chapter 11

MBO WAS A metropolis in its own right, and it housed the good and bad that came with being a thriving town. It had its share of misdemeanors and grave cases of felony. Those were times when the emperor was still reasserting his authority over the land after his stay abroad during the Occupation. Things had gotten out of hand in his absence, with some crowning themselves governor of this or that province while others maligned the emperor's name. Haile-Selassie's emphatic protest of Italy's colonial ambition at the League of Nations and his plea for justice on the international stage was being eclipsed locally by the perception that he had deserted his people in their time of desperate need for leadership.

As elsewhere in the country, there were those who ran afoul of the law. Here in Ambo, these outlaws were called *shifta* by the locals. Some among them were mere villains, thugs who kidnapped people and sold them into slavery long after the slave trade had been declared illegal. There were those others as well who, outraged by unfair land ownership matters, had decided to take the law into their own hands. To capture these brigands and kill or bring them to justice, law enforcement personnel made frequent forays into their lairs in the environs of Ambo. Occasionally, the confrontation with armed marauders and underground human traffickers became such a momentous0 standoff that even Ambo's governor, Fitawrari Tsehayu Enqo-Selassie, joined the skirmish in the company of police officers.

He was a humble man, Fitawrari Tsehayu, not half as thick-skinned and conceited as most of the minions in Ambo's government machinery which he oversaw. Being an avowed enemy of slave traders, he would put his own life in danger and risk becoming a target of the vultures who dealt in human chattel. More than his outrage about the slavery business, however, it was his simplicity that endeared him to the people he governed; his humanity and humility, uncommon in a land where most in authority treated those below with unadulterated contempt.

When folks saw him on his way to the battlefield with a squad of armed officers, "There comes the Governor," they whispered affectionately. Deferentially.

"Good morning, Fitawrari," Gabre-Medhin would greet him, hat in hand and bowing low. His greeting was heartfelt, and his obeisance genuine. Clad in shorts and sandals, with a pistol in a holster and a rifle slung on his shoulder, the governor would warmly return the greeting.

"May the good Lord protect you! May Saint Gabriel be your shield!" Feleqech would pray aloud watching the receding figures of Fitawrari and his men. The good man needed a prayer. Those bloody ruffians wouldn't hesitate to murder anyone getting in their path. They had proven it; they had slain scores already, and they would go on killing without remorse. These showdowns were no joke; everyone knew. Tsegaye, barely even ten years of age, had been horrified when he saw Fitawrari Tsehayu returning with only four of the twelve police officers he had left with one morning. It was a miracle that the governor survived the carnage perpetrated by a notorious Oromo rebel known as Qoritcho.

Qoritcho had disavowed allegiance to the king and submission to the law to become an outlaw—a shifta. And what drove him to such folly of becoming a one-man combatant against the might of a state was this: settlers from faraway had dispossessed him of his land; the land of his forefathers. He had tried, by legal means, to recover what had been his, but his efforts had come to naught. He had thus concluded that if the law was powerless against outlanders usurping his property, he might as well refuse to abide by such a law. And he had become a shifta and disappeared into the bowels of the Wadessa Forest.

Rebelling against authority was nothing new in Ambo. Of course some of the rebels were miscreants who thrived on the misery of their people, slave traders who deserved harsh punishment. But a few of the outlaws were helpless victims of the dual tyranny of iniquitous authority and their own conscience; brave men with the inflexible cast of a born non-conformist. What made Qoritcho's saga unique, however, was that he outwitted his pursuers for longer than expected.

Qoritcho knew the town and its surroundings well and had a few discreet sympathizers who provided him with intelligence and supplies. Several attempts were made to capture him, but he escaped and continued to defy the law, breaking into stables and granaries of the rich, and at times even going after the police unprovoked. People said he had uncanny gifts; they spoke of the unearthly power he possessed. He was aided by a mighty ally, the rumor went, and he was shielded with potent magic. Adults whispered of his immunity to bullets, and fearless shepherds sang of his valor aloud. And soon, stories of his superhuman feats circulated in taverns and around fireplaces.

"The man can make himself invisible, becoming flesh or phantom as it suits him. When they go to kill him, he vanishes into thin air, and when they let their guards down, he becomes Qoritcho in the flesh and shoots them all in the back."

"He can turn bullets into cotton balls that bounce off his body. A police officer I know told me. Saw it with his own eyes."

"He spawns multiple specters in his image. Dozens of apparitions in his likeness. Scares the police into shooting madly till they empty their magazines. Then he picks them out one by one."

Qoritcho, a feared foe for too long, had fast become a living legend until one day he was caught after a brief fight. He was captured alive, and people said he had finally lost his magic. Upholders of the law sighed in relief.

News of his capture spread like wildfire, and townsfolk young and old gathered to see the mighty Qoritcho in shackles being escorted at gunpoint into a well-guarded jail. That was it for the bullet-proof shifta, they said. It was now time for him to atone for his colossal guilt. Then the very next day, he made an utter mockery of his captors by snapping off his shackles and running away. Unscathed by the barrage from the watchman's gun, he escaped as he was being led away to the urinal that evening. He clambered up the jail's fence and dove into the Huluqa River below. Bullets sent to stop him failed. Being a skilled swimmer, he slipped away unharmed. And this time, even those who scoffed at the rumors of Qoritcho's occult powers began to doubt themselves.

That was when Fitawrari Tsehayu realized he had a serious problem on his hands. The shifta he was dealing with, the invincible Qoritcho, was beyond the power of Ambo's police force to contend with. This, the governor believed, was a brazen affront to law and order that called for the involvement of higher authority. It had taken Fitawrari quite some time and cost him the lives of his bravest men, not to mention the embarrassment of failure and the folk hero status that Qoritcho was acquiring in the eyes of the people, but in the end, he saw the matter for what it was: a crisis. So, he swallowed his pride and asked for help.

Help arrived soon enough. The capital sent its best trackers and marksmen, who got to work as soon as they slipped into town in the cover of darkness. Two vanloads of the elite police force came and divided the task of chasing after Qoritcho. Half of them were in charge of intelligence; theirs was the task of turning the rebel's own weapon against him by paying his least devoted informers to switch sides. They would then relay to the pursuing squad information about the whereabouts of the outlaw.

Darkness had gripped the land when Qoritcho, already tipped about the strangers in town, snuck into the home of one of his mistresses secretly, or not so secretly, for word of his location got out to the competent hounds from Addis Ababa.

Qoritcho had just had dinner; the best of his paramour's kitchen, and was warming himself seated before a fire. He chatted amicably with his woman—the fearless man—without letting his guard down. On his lap was a loaded gun ready for any urgent action.

"Bang!" the deafening blast of gunfire shattered the stillness, followed by a volley of automatic fire. His mistress screamed and fell as a bullet grazed her shoulder while two bullets almost simultaneously plunged into the back of Qoritcho's head and ripped his forehead open, spilling his brain. He toppled without a sound and fell on his face into the roaring fire. What bloody mess was left on his shoulders was roasted like a chunk of flesh in a bonfire.

The men from the capital wanted to send a strong message to the people of Ambo, some of whom, to their alarm, sympathized with the dead shifta; a dangerous state of affairs if not nipped in the bud. To stress their warning, they hanged the almost headless Qoritcho in the center of the open-air market, and left the body on display for hours.

Wriggling through a hushed crowd for a better view of the spectacle, Tsegaye saw something dreadful—a man with a charred face hanging suspended by the arms—a sight that would be etched on his memory and haunt him for years to come. And like other scenes from the days of his childhood, this grisly image would be rooted in his psyche and color his worldview. It would be as much the stuff of his universe as other realities of his boyhood, a legacy of his early life out of which his literary voice would emerge. Instances of Ambo's law enforcement in action and the meting out of brutal justice by callous executors of government authority would be conjured up years later in Tsegaye's play *Enat Alem Tenu*, his adaptation of Bertlot Brecht's *Mother Courage*, featuring Gerafi Gebreyes, a famously merciless court-appointed flogger in Ambo.

Flogging was Gebreyes's calling. Employed to carry out court-sanctioned corporal punishment, Gebreyes stamped welt signatures on the backs of Ambo's hoodlums, bandits and burglars. He was the man in charge of dispensing sentences of lashings handed out by the tens: forty, fifty, sixty, or as many as the offense warranted.

A tall burly man with a face as blank as a wall, Gebreyes carried his whip in the crook of his arm, coiled like a long black snake, as he approached the cringing offender waiting for him stripped to the waist and tied to a post. He would glance at his victim like a lion eying a crippled prey and slowly unwind his tool. Then he would roll up his sleeves, positioning himself before the bared back of the accused, and nonchalantly proceed with the task at hand. He would lash with the full force of his muscular arm, swinging the whip and bringing it down mercilessly on the quivering back before him. Most of the guilty were destitute. They stole grain or livestock because their children had nothing to eat. They were malnourished; they didn't have much flesh to stop the tip of Gebreyes's whip from sinking down to the bone. By the time the flogger was done, the accused's back was a gruesome sight of tattered skin drenched in blood. The unfairness of it all was that the end of Gebreyes's punishment didn't spell release for the accused. If the plaintiff, often a land and cattle owner, felt that he too had his own score to settle he would be given his wish. And there were some who eagerly seized the chance and added their own evil torment and humiliation by forcing the bloody wreck to crawl around town confessing his guilt aloud. If the offender was too ashamed or weakened to shout out his mea culpa, his pursuer would force him to scream it by stinging his mangled back with a horsewhip. Some passersby would stand and watch, calm in their certainty that it was all good and fair; justice was being served. Some winced at the sight and turned away, while others cheered the outraged plaintiff and flung curses at the sinner. There were also a handful who followed the procession, unable to tear themselves away. But none came to the staggering man's rescue; not a soul took his side, or gave him comfort to help him get through the medieval torture, except for his wife, or his mother, or some other female kin. Always a woman.

Carrying chicken eggs in a basket, she would follow the suffering man, urging him to be brave, to clench his teeth and bear it, while her own guts twisted in pain and tears streamed down her face. Sometimes a victim who still had some pride left would beg the woman to roll a piece of cloth and stuff it into his mouth to spare him the shame of his animal cry.

Once the ordeal was over, the woman would break the eggs one by one over the man's quivering back, her first act of ministration to nursing her beloved back to being a man again. The cool viscous content of the eggs was meant to soothe his pain and abate the flow of blood, but the sting, the burn, and the unbearably painful rub of her hands on his flayed skin would fry his nerves and make him howl till he foamed at the mouth.

Years later, moments of inhuman torture perpetrated in the name of justice would also appear vividly in Tsegaye's plays, so vividly that at times some simple souls in the audience would lose their grip on what was real and wholeheartedly enter the make-believe world of the stage, as did the bodyguards of Colonel Mengistu, the authoritarian dictator of Ethiopia.

Among the local colors and characters that Tsegaye had added to *Enat Alem Tenu* was the story of a dead hero by the name of Belay Zeleqe. Upon its debut in Addis Ababa, Colonel Mengistu, the supreme leader who had allegedly killed Emperor Haile Sellassie with his own hands and later buried his body underneath his office, had expressed his intention to view the play. Accompanied by fanfare of wailing sirens and a long trail of station wagons carrying his doubles, Mengistu arrived at the Ethiopian National Theatre surrounded by the best of his bodyguards. Several armed guards took their position outside around the theatre hall while half a dozen bodyguards with unconcealed weapons entered with the colonel. The leader sat next to Tsegaye in an emptied front row area and the gunmen took their seats at strategic locations around him. As deferentially as he could, Tsegaye oriented his most important guest on what he was about to see. The lights dimmed, then turned off completely. The protectors of the supreme leader became noticeably nervous. They fidgeted incessantly and their eyes darted about in the near-total blackout of the hall. How were they supposed to guard their master in the dark?

The play began.

When Tsegaye first saw him, Belay Zeleqe was a prisoner, chained to another prisoner—an important person who had fallen out of favor with his masters. They were both awaiting sentence in Ambo's jail, hobbling around in the backyard. Belay was a hero, Tsegaye had heard, a peerless nemesis of the Italians whose name had become synonymous with patriotic valor. Even to those who had never laid eyes on him, Belay was a towering embodiment of unbreakable Ethiopian resistance against Italy's colonial rule. Tales of his heroic feats in the battlefield had traveled far and wide. Idolized as he was by his compatriots, Belay was feared and hated by the enemy because he fought with breathtaking bravery and had the audacity to hang the Italian soldiers he had captured.

Then liberation came, and like many a hero before him, Belay committed the tragic mistake that caused his own downfall. The man who had outfoxed the wily white men failed to divine the folly of antagonizing his own king, and paid with his life.

After his return, the emperor recognized Belay's service to his country, with an honorary title Dejazmach, and he was made governor of a small region in Gojam province. Belay disdained the reward. He thought his service deserved more and angrily took up arms against the regime. Unhappy with the way things were being done in the newly liberated Ethiopia, Belay soon became an outlaw. But Haile-Selassie, who was struggling to regain his own position, seemingly had little patience for the insubordination of praise-fed patriots. His power depended in part on establishing that, despite popular perception, they remained his subjects. He pinned medals and empty titles on the true patriots while bestowing wealth and power on those who, as far as the embittered were concerned, had never fired a shot at the enemy. The emperor was cunning; he knew that fame had the power to intoxicate and lead men to forget who they were. So when fame emboldened Belay Zeleke to challenge Haile-Selassie's authority, Haile-Selassie acted quickly and sentenced him to death by hanging.

Tsegaye didn't know what crime had landed the legendary man in a squalid jail. He wasn't old enough to fathom the deadly game of politics behind Belay's captivity. What struck him the most was not his well-known bravery, but his simple kindness. It was Belay, not his mean looking chain-mate, who returned the rag balls that Tsegaye and his friends accidentally kicked into the prison yard. If the ball landed anywhere near the other man, their hearts would sink because he would keep it out of spite, as if to say: "How dare you be having fun when I'm suffering?" Belay would ask him to give it back, but the man would refuse vehemently. "No!" he would say angrily. "Never!" He would then clutch it close to his bosom and glare at them with jaundiced eyes. But if Belay got the ball, he would do whatever it took—even drag the other man along if he had to—to throw it back to them.

"There he is. Go get him! Catch him quick! Don't let him get away! Don't let him escape!" The din of stamping feet and noisy scrimmage filled the stage in the darkness. The audience waited in hushed anticipation to see what the melee was about, while Mengistu's armed bodyguards crowded around to shield him with their bodies, ready to unleash a barrage from their machine guns if necessary. They had never seen a play. Most of them were handpicked recruits from remote parts of the country, strangers to aspects of city culture.

Tsegaye saw the nervous shadows of Mengistu's protectors holding their guns at the ready—muzzles pointed at the stage—and he panicked. What if one pulled the trigger? The rest would follow and that would spell sure disaster. But he could do nothing, except hope that they would remain calm. With his heart in his mouth, he waited. Incredibly, the guard's agitated action seemed of little concern to the leader.

To Tsegaye's relief, stage lights shone and illuminated the scene, and Colonel Mengistu signaled his protectors to relax. As it was, the opening act of the play was ample cause for commotion. The patriot, Belay Zeleqe, was being captured by government soldiers.

Chapter 12

Emperor Haile-Selassie liked Ambo for one reason: it had heavenly weather. For one like him who spent his days in the stone and marble edifice of his palace in Sidist Kilo, Ambo's balmy weather was a welcome relief. It warmed his bones and awakened his zest for life. The town became his tropical paradise a mere four hours away, and to return the favor, he wished to bestow upon it a name to match its glory. So he called it Hagere-Hiwot: Land of Life. Not such a glorious name for a place that he adored so much, one would think. Land of Life! A good part of the country was just that—land swarming with life, unless he meant the other kind of life, the life one felt bursting inside one when one found oneself in a place like Hagere-Hiwot. But the new name didn't catch. The strange Ge'ez phrase stumbled on the tongues of Oromifa speakers. So, they went on calling their town what they always had: Ambo.

The retreats offered the emperor days of peace and agreeable weather, but other essentials for his wellbeing, such as food, protection, and skilled service had to be brought from the capital in a convoy of cars and trucks that would enter town a couple of days earlier. Teams of cooks and cleaners came together with security personnel and their canine assistants: half a dozen German shepherds.

Tsegaye had never seen the emperor in person until he turned thirteen, but from the ripple of excitement that spread through Ambo on the eve of his arrival, he had gathered that Haile-Selassie, also respectfully called Janhoy, was indeed a supreme being. From his parents' gestures of reverence to the unseen presence of the monarch, and from his mother's prayer for the sovereign, "May the Ambo Eyesus protect you! May the Savior give you a long life!" while Gabre-Medhin stood quietly with bared and bowed head, the boy had figured that the emperor was the most exalted mortal in the land. That was why the moment of finally seeing Janhoy thoroughly shocked Tsegaye.

He saw him first when he was a student of Ambo's primary school. Standing among students, all dressed in their best, Tsegaye waited impatiently. Haile-Selassie was going to visit this particular school, which like hundreds of other institutions throughout the country, was named after him. Fidgeting in anticipation, he searched the open field for signs of the emperor's arrival. He stood on tiptoe to look over the shoulders of taller boys and peered, but all he saw was a man on horseback galloping ahead of the commotion behind him. "That's Danfa!" "Yes, that's him," Tsegaye heard people whispering all around him. He saw folks kowtowing to the man on horseback. None of them looked up at the rider, but at the hooves of his prancing stallion. *Danfa* meant boiling water, you could be burned if you gazed directly into the man's eyes, or so it was said. A wealthy man who owned a large number of cattle and a battalion of servants, Danfa was the grand spiritual leader of the Oromo in the Metcha region. He led the way on horseback, and the emperor followed in a Rolls Royce.

Tsegaye didn't look at the hooves of Danfa's horse. He stared the man in the face without being burned and saw Danfa smiling at the bowed heads of the multitude. There was nothing special about his appearance, except that he looked well-fed and very pleased with himself. Then the boy turned his gaze to the more exciting spectacle in Danfa's wake: Haile-Selassie arriving in a slow-moving parade of motorcars flanked by big armed men trotting along on foot. As Danfa rode away on his cantering horse with the glossy rump, the emperor's party got closer, and the motorcade crawled to just a few yards from the gathered students. Then the cars came to a stop. An attendant opened the door of the shiny car in front, and out came a small man in a flowing cape. Despite seeing all eyes fixed on the man, Tsegaye kept searching for a figure to match the image in his head of a mighty being called Janhoy. That man in a billowing cloak couldn't be Haile-Selassie, he thought. But then a slight wave of the man's hand, a gesture of greeting or blessing, set the women ululating and the men genuflecting, and Tsegaye realized that he was in fact the emperor. No less astonishing to Tsegaye was the size of the emperor's cherished pet, a tiny Chihuahua named Lulu—the Pearl, or the Prince, depending on how the name was pronounced. Any one of those massive German shepherds could gobble up three Lulus for lunch.

He was the ruler nonetheless, the monarch whose very name conjured up all the formidable might of the law, and to whom Tsegaye's parents paid taxes and obeisance due a sovereign. Eventually, the shock left Tsegaye and his thoughts wandered off to the glory of capturing the emperor's attention. What would it be like to be recognized by such a personage? There was no way Tsegaye could ever stand out here in the midst of his peers. If he wanted to shine enough to be noticed, he would have to do something special. Something different from the usual tedious affair that towns put together to impress the emperor. And a daring thought entered his head, a notion so bold and farfetched that he dismissed it as a mere fantasy at first. But it refused to go away, and the longer it lasted, the less improbable it seemed.

"I've got something to tell you," he said to his friends, Melaku and Deressa, as soon as the emperor left and the students were dismissed for the day.

"What is it?" they asked him, intrigued by his excitement and the sparkle in his eyes.

"I can't tell you now. You'll have to wait till later. But first you have to agree to spend the night with me at my father's store. We need to work for most of the night, and we need the store's electric light for that," he said.

Deressa and Melaku exchanged glances.

"What are we going to do?" Melaku asked.

"You'll find out," he said and smiled. Tsegaye's air of secrecy piqued their curiosity. Torn between their eagerness to find out and the daunting prospect of sacrificing a night's sleep, they were unable to accept or reject the idea.

"We'll have dinner there, and as much yogurt as you want," Tsegaye sweetened the deal and they acquiesced. Not for the dinner, they had dinner in their own homes, but for the yogurt. They both loved yogurt, and would gladly agree to forfeit sleep for an ample supply of it.

Reader Six of the English textbook at Tsegaye's school had an abridged, simplified version of Tsegaye's favorite play, *King Dionisiyus and His Two Brothers*. He had read it several times and memorized many lines of it by heart. He had even wished that the teacher would ask students to perform the play; he would have jumped at the chance to play the role of king. But now that Tsegaye had seen Emperor Haile-Selassie, the happy thought had struck him that a performance of the ancient Greek play would be the perfect gift for him.

"We'll rehearse *King Dionysus and His Two Brothers*," he revealed the big idea to his friends.

"For what?" Deressa asked.

"To perform it for the emperor."

The two boys, loaded with yogurt, looked at him with disbelieving eyes.

"We can't memorize this in one night. We need more time," Melaku protested.

"We can do it. You'll see. We have to try," Tsegaye insisted.

"They won't let us perform it for the emperor," said Deressa. "They won't even let us go near him."

"We'll tell our English teacher, Mrs. Hutchings, and she can ask her husband, the Director. He can help us do it if he wants."

Tsegaye wasn't sure if Mr. Hutchings would be willing to help, but he had to feign confidence before his friends, and they agreed to try.

"Deressa, you are the older brother, and Melaku is the younger one. I'm the King," he told them, and the three got to work.

Melaku and Deressa didn't have much to memorize. Their parts weren't half as challenging as Tsegaye's, who would have had a hard time if he had not read the play many times before and committed quite a few lines to memory. Within just a couple of hours, each of them had learned his lines by heart, lines whose meanings they only half understood.

Tsegaye appointed himself as director, and they rehearsed the play till their eyelids began to droop and they lay down to sleep.

"My friends and I prepared a play for His Majesty," Tsegaye announced to Mrs. Hutchings as soon as the English class began.

"What play is it, Tsegaye?" she asked.

"*King Dionysus and His Two Brothers.*"

Her eyes wandered away from Tsegaye's as she thought of a way to decline his offer without sounding dismissive. "Uh... that's very thoughtful of you... I must say... uh..." she began, but it was clear she was less than enthusiastic. The only way to capture her interest was to give her a taste, Tsegaye thought. That might change her mind. And before she was done mumbling the longwinded rejection, he signaled to his pals and they rose. Then without delay, they began reciting what they had memorized the night before. Each of them reeled off his part as their classmates gaped in astonishment and Mrs. Hutchings' eyes twinkled in pleasant surprise. She was impressed. She then sent a student to bring her husband.

The Director came, his face a mask of concern, asking: "What is it Winnie?"

"Tsegaye and his friends have a surprise for us," she told him and nodded to Tsegaye to begin.

Now that Winnie had thought it was worthy, at least, of the Director's attention, the boys became more alive and confident. Their voices acquired gusto.

"Oh gosh!" Mr. Hutchings exclaimed when the actors were half way through. Their performance wasn't bad at all. With a little coaching by his wife, it would surely be better. And if Janhoy was to see it, there was much to be done in a short time, but first, Mr. Hutchings had to contact the governor as soon as possible. No such event as staging a performance for the emperor could be planned without his knowledge and his help.

Meanwhile, Winnie embarked on the difficult task of preparing the stage, grooming the boys for the event, and giving them proper direction. She was an Englishwoman; flesh and blood of the post-Grecian theatre buffs in the land of Shakespeare. She grew up watching plays, mediocre and good ones. As a girl, she had even acted in a few school performances herself.

"We need to go to the school auditorium. We need to do more rehearsals," she said and took the boys. She got a pair of scissors, sat each one of them on a chair, and sheared their hair. They looked better with their hair trimmed, but they were still far from show material. Even in Ambo, a barefoot King Dionysus in shorts wouldn't do. She had to think of ways to turn the shabbily dressed boys into something Haile-Selassie would be pleased to see. For that, she sent someone to buy a roll of white fabric and had the town's notable tailor brought to the school. She gave the sartor instructions, with the help of a translator, to make togas.

"I can do that in a jiffy," the tailor assured her.

Next was the matter of the footgear for the boys. Their mucky bare feet needed to be shod, and Winnie's clever solution was to order three pairs of rubber sandals, the ubiquitous footwear of the masses, cobbled up with strips of rubber from discarded car tires. They would go splendidly with the togas. For a crown, she crafted headgear from wires and colored threads and put it on Tsegaye's head. It made him look kingly and set him apart from the other two.

Clad in his costume, Tsegaye was told to sit in the Director's revolving chair hauled to the stage to serve as a throne.

"Sit here, Tsegaye," ordered Winnie.

"Me sit on Mr. Hutching's chair? No, Madam," he refused. The ruler of the land was coming to see the show, true, but that didn't mean Mr. Hutching's rule over the school had ended. Any other time, a kid like Tsegaye wouldn't dare to get close to that chair, let alone to sit in it.

"It's absolutely alright by Mr. Hutchings. Don't worry; he wouldn't mind," Winnie reassured Tsegaye. "Go sit in the chair now; let's not waste time."

He squirmed and dragged his feet, but finally obeyed and sat perched on the edge with a look of guilt about him like one forced into committing sacrilege.

"Show me a king's poise now. Sit straight. Look proud; kingly. Like this. Acquire a dignified air," Mrs. Hutchings babbled excitedly, fussing all around him. She pushed him this way and that, prodded and nudged him until he attained just the right posture and she smiled. "That's it!" she approved delightedly.

The following day, minutes before Haile-Selassie's arrival at the auditorium, Tsegaye noticed with surprise that the event he had made possible had turned things upside down at the school. This sudden seismic shift had now relegated all important school functionaries from Director to teachers and administrators to a dark back corner of the hall. In contrast, Tsegaye and his friends, unknown students till then, had been placed on a pedestal, and were basking in the glory of the spotlight. He couldn't believe it.

The audience was seated: the students sitting behind the school's staff, and the staff behind Ambo's most notable personalities. Then the emperor walked in surrounded by a tense circle of bodyguards, all tall and fierce looking. Their hawk eyes scanned the people in the hall, now on their feet in deference to the king. They escorted him to his place on a garishly decorated high chair in a cleared area. With a gesture of his hand, Haile-Selassie asked the crowd to be seated. He then turned to one of his aides and signaled for the show to begin.

The play in the sixth grade English textbook would have taken a mere fifteen minutes if the three boys had zipped through it as they had originally intended to under Tsegaye's direction. But Mrs. Hutchings had told them to slow down.

"You've got to make sure that every word is heard. You've got to stress. You've got to enunciate," she had told them, stopping them whenever they failed to keep pace, showing them how to say it, modeling it to them and praising them when they got it right. As they listened and repeated after her, the clutter of hard-to-make-out words began to acquire life and the performance stretched to half an hour.

Haile-Selassie was impressed. He was moved. Having heard what he could, seen what he did, and guessed the rest, he applauded the boys who had given him a treat unlike any he had ever gotten in Ambo. He nodded approvingly and shone his brightest smile at Tsegaye. Then with a flick of his finger, he called a burly aide-de-camp who came bowing low to receive orders. The emperor whispered something to him and the man hurried to the stage.

He caught Tsegaye as he and his fellow actors were being escorted away by Mrs. Hutchings and *Ato* Eshete Bayuh, the geography teacher and the darling of students whom he treated as his friends.

"What would you like to get from the emperor?" the Titan asked Tsegaye.

"Who? Me?" Tsegaye asked back.

"Yes, you. What would you like His Imperial Majesty to do for you?"

He didn't know what to answer. He had never thought of that. How would it ever have occurred to him that the most powerful man in the country would one day be willing to fulfill his wish? And that all he had to do was just say the word, name his fancy—a royal favor—and do it at once before a sea of watching eyes.

With a look of a cornered quarry, he turned to his trusted Geography teacher, "What should I say?" he asked.

In response, Ato Eshete tore a page out of his notebook, and after thinking for a second, he scribbled a few sentences and handed it to Tsegaye. The request, written by the teacher on behalf of the tongue-tied Dionysius, was a touching one. Stripped of the courteous claptrap and its florid diction, it asked for a small budget for food for those out-of-town kids who attended school without lunch because their homes were far away. "To traverse the very long distance to school," the teacher had added to tug at the emperor's heartstrings, "these lads have to leave their abodes at the crack of dawn, risking death in the terrifying jaws of rapacious hyenas and other dreadful beasts of the wild."

"Do you agree with this?" the Aide asked Tsegaye.

"Yes," he answered in relief, and the message was given to the emperor. Haile-Selassie glanced at the paper, called his aide again and said something to him. The Goliath quickly returned to the stage. "Not for the other students, but for you!" he fiercely whispered to Tsegaye. There was complete silence in the hall; the ongoing exchange between the King and Tsegaye had the audience captivated.

If Tsegaye was nervous at first, he was positively flustered this time around. So unnerved was he that he felt the halo of his glory dissipating. The man who stood towering above him was vexed, and Tsegaye, unable to think of a proper response, felt like a fool.

"You can ask for school uniforms for every student at the school," the Geography teacher came to the rescue once again in a meek, hesitant voice.

"Yes," Tsegaye approved.

"What do you mean 'yes'? You have to say it. Tell me in your own words," ordered the messenger.

"My request to His Majesty the Emperor is for a school uniform for every one of us," said Tsegaye, and the aide relayed the message.

Things were getting nowhere. Tsegaye wouldn't name a prize for himself, nor would the goodhearted teacher stop thinking about the rest. In the clash of values between Ato Eshete and the Emperor, the teacher's advocacy for the common good won the day, and Haile-Selassie relented.

"A uniform for every student as you wished! Two uniforms for your partners, Melaku and Deressa and three uniforms for you! The emperor has granted your request," the aide announced in a voice loud enough to be heard by all.

"Bow to His Majesty," Ato Eshete whispered to Tsegaye and nudged him as the hall erupted in applause.

"Emperor Haile-Selassie Attended a Play Presented by a Very Young Actor and Director at Ambo's Primary School" the newspaper headlines announced the following morning. Copies were put on display at the director's office and in the teacher's lounge.

Tsegaye became an instant sensation in the school—a celebrity. "Bravo Tsegaye!" cheered even those teachers who until then hadn't noticed him. "You made us proud," they told him. And no one was prouder than Aleqa Me'amir. Having been a lone singer of Tsegaye's praise thus far, he was finally proven right in the best possible way. "You showed them what you are made of! Now they know who you are; the dimwits, hee hee! You are a gifted Oromo destined for high places."

Gabre-Medhin was the only person for whom Tsegaye's fame and glory didn't mean much in light of his imbecilic response to the emperor's offer of a favor.

"You could ask for land, or obtain a promise for a worthy government office for when you come of age. What possessed you to ask for miserable uniforms? Is that a thing to ask from a king, you fool?" he chided his son.

Chapter 13

WHEN TSEGAYE GRADUATED from the eighth grade and passed the school leaving exam, Gabre-Medhin swelled with pride and knew that the life path he had envisioned for his son was indeed the wisest of choices he had ever made. Tsegaye would soon leave for Addis Ababa; he had been accepted at a the prestigious General Wingate Secondary School. News of his impending departure for the capital spread in the neighborhood, and all lavishly congratulated him. The men shook his hand and patted his head while the women kissed his cheeks and showered him with blessing. "You will soon be a student of Wongel!" envious fathers said to him. With their knack for finding a sound-alike for a foreign term that they were unable to pronounce, Ambo's folk called Wingate by the same word that meant *gospel* in Amharic: *Wongel*. Wongel and Wingate: repositories of heavenly wisdom and earthly learning.

It was a happy occasion indeed, this turning point in Tsegaye's education, and it called for a celebration. Gabre-Medhin slaughtered a fat sheep and Feleqech brewed *tella*—homemade beer—in an enormous clay pot. Neighbors and relatives were invited, and Tsegaye, dressed in a white shirt and new khaki trousers, sat among the guests beaming in their praise and listening to sundry words of advice.

"Be a good boy and make your parents proud. What haven't they suffered to raise you and your siblings!"

"Watch out for those foxy city boys. Don't trust any of them. They'll ruin you if you don't know how to keep your distance."

"May the Ambo Eyesus watch over you!"

"May Waqa pave your path to the top, and may you never forget who you are and where you come from!"

They ate and drank. They praised Feleqech for her cooking and Gabre-Medhin for being a wonderful father. The tipsy ones sang and some danced capering as in their younger days, while the sober ones watched laughing and clapping. All had a merry time in the name of giving Tsegaye a festive sendoff to Addis Ababa.

His heart brimming with blessings of kith and kin and his pocket carrying what his parents had given him of their hard-earned cash, Tsegaye arrived in the capital together with a few other students who, like him, had passed the school leaving exam. They had been told to report at the office of the Ministry of Education early the following morning. There would be a long line, Tsegaye had heard. The best students of every school in the country, all those who had won admission to secondary schools in Addis Ababa, would be there.

The lines were very long indeed. After completing the registration form, Tsegaye took his place in the winding queue, and when his turn came, he handed the form to a stern looking official of the Ministry at the window. The man inspected the paper, his eyes darting back and forth, and he was about to put it away and give him the admission slip when something caught his attention and he frowned.

"There's incorrect information," he growled. "You haven't answered one question correctly."

"Which question, sir?" asked Tsegaye.

"The one about ethnicity. You have answered Ethiopian. That's not ethnicity. What's your ethnicity?"

"We say we are Ethiopian, sir."

"What's your father's name?"

"Gabre-Medhin."

"And your grandfather's name?"

"Qewesa."

The man rudely returned the form and told him to cross out *Ethiopian* and replace it with an epithet that denigrated the Oromo. Tsegaye had never winced at the slur before; no one had ever called him that except Aleqa Me'amir, whose fondness of Tsegaye was the envy of his classmates. But the venom of bigotry from this official stung him and darkened his spirits.

Tsegaye did as he was told: crossed out Ethiopian, replaced it with the offensive epithet and returned the form.

❖ ❖ ❖

British 'liberators' who had expelled the Italians had established General Wingate Secondary School. In return for their assistance they were granted the license to spread their influence in the country mainly by means of educational and cultural institutions. Built in the chilly, windswept neighborhood of Gullelle, Wingate had all the makings of a British boarding school. And its rigorous discipline, more in keeping with a boot camp than a school, proved challenging to Tsegaye in his three months there.

The day at Wingate began at 5:30 a.m. on weekdays, when Mr. Casbon, an insomniac in charge of physical education and overall student discipline, would wake the students up with an infernal sound of his whistle. After being wrenched out of deep sleep, the boys would have to quickly make their beds before being herded into the shower rooms for a three-minute splash in ice-cold water. Gasping and shivering, they would then scamper to the yard in front of the flagpole where they stood in formation for the flag-raising routine. Once the tri-colored piece of cloth hung high up in its place trembling furiously in the wind under the bloody-hued sky of dawn, the students would march to the cafeteria to have breakfast. But even in the cafeteria, there was yet one last torment waiting for them. Each student's breakfast, a mug full of steaming hot tea and a goodly hunk of white bread, would be already laid out on the dining table when they got there, but no one would dare to touch it before first the school's chaplain, an Orthodox priest holding a bronze cross in his hand, offered a long prayer in Ge'ez, followed by Mr. Casbon who would do his turn of a prayer recital in English with students repeating after him.

Tsegaye soon realized that he didn't enjoy being a student at Wingate. He got tired of the long gray days, the unfriendly staff, the tedious lessons and the wearisome rigmarole that he, like the rest of his schoolmates, was subjected to by Mr. Casbon. He had a plan to organize a theatre group, to write a play and to have it performed, but the person in charge of the performance arts club didn't sound excited by the idea. He was busy coaching a few students for a production of *Romeo and Juliet*, an Amharic translation by a popular Ethiopian author, Kebede Mikael, and wasn't interested in indulging a novice.

In the monotony of life at Wingate, watching a soccer game became Tsegaye's only escape. A match between his school team and that of Medhane-Alem Secondary School was the perfect antidote.

The students of Medhane-Alem were a unique bunch. Unlike the students of other high schools, they didn't have to pass a test to be admitted. They were children of wealthy folk for whom the emperor had built an exclusive school as a favor to their parents. Accustomed to getting what they wanted, they played soccer to win at any cost and to wreak havoc if they lost. As a result, a game between the teams of Wingate and Medhane-Alem promised an impending melee where unruly fans taunted players, fights broke out in the field, and noses were bloodied. And from a safe corner somewhere in the midst of less agitated spectators, Tsegaye watched the skirmish and savored the thrill.

Chapter 14

G RADUATES OF THE Commercial College in Addis Ababa were in high demand in the 1950s and 60s. The country was embarking on a path to modernity, and it needed a workforce equipped with the crucial skills of accounting, shorthand writing, typing and business management. A person trained in these fields was eagerly courted and recruited for a well-paying job at such coveted places as the national bank or Ethiopian Airlines.

Tsegaye had a good friend, Gelagay Zewde, who was enrolled at the Commercial College, and he had told him that his was the best college in the country.

"Can you guess how much a Commercial College graduate makes?" he asked Tsegaye.

"How would I know? One hundred birr a month?"

"A hundred? Hee hee hee!" Gelagay laughed contemptuously. "That's the salary of a school teacher in Ambo. Try again."

"One hundred fifty?"

"Three hundred birr, my friend!"

Tsegaye was stunned. He had never heard of anyone making that much money in just one month.

"That's a lot of money, man," he whispered. "You're not kidding me. Are you?"

"I swear I'm telling you the truth. If you have a Commercial College diploma, you make even more than three hundred a month. Guaranteed. What do you think of that?"

Tsegaye was in the ninth grade at General Wingate Secondary School. He would have his chance to try to get admission to one of the colleges in Addis Ababa when he completed the tenth grade and passed the college entrance exam. That wouldn't be until a year later, but in light of what his friend Gelagay had told him, one more year at Wingate appeared to be a senseless waste of time.

"What do they teach you there?" he asked Gelagay.

"Lots of things. I had a shorthand class this morning."

"What's shorthand?"

Quietly, Gelagay wrote his name on a piece of paper and showed it to Tsegaye.

"That's my name in shorthand," he said.

Tsegaye took the piece of paper and stared in amazement at the strange writing. He tried to make sense of it by looking at it from various angles, but couldn't. He then asked his friend to show him how to write his own name in shorthand.

Wingate's tenth graders were to take the college entrance exam in less than a month. The best of the seniors would then say goodbye to gloomy Wingate, spend the summer with their parents, and join a college of their choice in September. But Tsegaye felt he couldn't wait that long. "I have to do something," he said to himself again and again. He tossed and turned in his bed that night, too anxious to fall asleep, until with the audacity of despair he decided to go to Mr. Hairring the following morning and ask him for a favor.

Mr. Hairring was the much-respected Headmaster of Wingate, and his authority was beyond question. But would he bend the rules for Tsegaye, and allow him, a mere ninth grader, to sit for a tenth grade exam? Tesgaye knew the headmaster liked him. After reading the glowing recommendation letter his compatriot in Ambo had written, Mr. Hairring did treat the boy differently than he did most other students in the school. "I'll go and ask him to help me. If he does, I'll be very happy. If not, I won't lose anything by trying," reasoned Tsegaye.

The following morning, he went to Mr. Hairring's office and told the secretary that he needed to see the headmaster.

"What is it you want to see him about?" she asked him.

Cringing in discomfort, he answered that it was a private matter. She sneered, but let him into her boss's sanctum nonetheless.

"What brings you here, young man?" asked Mr. Hairring.

"I would like to take the college entrance exam, Sir."

"But you're in the ninth grade, aren't you?"

"Yes, sir."

"So what makes you think you can take it now? You have to complete the tenth grade to be eligible for that. You'll take it next year," said the headmaster. He nodded, smiled briefly and turned his eyes back to something on his desk that he was reading.

The message was clear, but Tsegaye wouldn't budge. He remained where he was as if he understood none of what he had heard. The silence grew awkward and Mr. Hairring fidgeted in his seat. He waited for a few seconds and looked up.

"Why do you want to take the test now anyway?" he asked, sounding annoyed.

"I want to study at the Commercial College."

"I beg your pardon?"

"I want to join the Commercial College."

"Why Commercial College? Why would you want to do that?"

For a job right here in the capital, and the goodly pay that comes with it. Three hundred birr a month! That is why. But Tsegaye wouldn't say that, of course. It wouldn't sit well with the headmaster, although he hadn't prepared a proper response either. He would have whipped out a seemlier reason for such a drastic decision, had he trusted his English. In the meantime, Mr. Hairring ignored him and went on reading the paper on his desk. There was nothing more to discuss. It was time for Tsegaye to leave, but he had to say something in parting. A line from King Dionysus's play he had memorized long ago came to mind. He shuffled close to the headmaster's desk and said: "This is my last request. I beg of you to grant it."

The headmaster's brows flew up and a faint smile broke on his face. The solemn way that Tsegaye spoke, like one pleading for a favor from his deathbed, amused the director.

"Okay," he said. "If that's what you want, you can take the test. You can try."

Tsegaye tried and passed the test. His excellent score pleased Mr. Hairring and guaranteed his early transition to an advanced stage of his education.

Before being admitted officially, candidates of the Commercial College had to be interviewed by the college's screening committee, which was made up of faculty and some prominent members of the community. It was a big day for Tsegaye, a culmination of his ambitions and a step towards a rosy future whose visions he had held on to since his conversation with his friend, Gelagay. He was excited. He was nervous. Dressed in his best, his hands in his pocket, he stood at the fringe of the throng outside the hall where the committee conducted the interview. A good looking woman dressed in formal attire came out every once in a while, called out a name from a list and ushered in the interviewee.

It was a bright, warm day, a bit too warm indeed for Tsegaye who, coming from a nippy part of town, was bundled in triple layers—an undershirt, a shirt and a jacket—and the full assault of the sun through hours of waiting had made him overheated and restless. Seeking a respite from the heat and the mounting unease of wondering if his name would be called next, he tried to start a conversation with a serious looking young man next to him, but the man rebuffed Tsegaye's advances with monosyllabic grunts and turned away. As the crowd thinned without the pretty woman calling his name, a hint of boredom crept into Tsegaye's agitation and sent him sauntering over to a cluster of poorly tended rosebushes in front of a closed window of the hall. There was nothing there to attract attention, except a loose electric wire dangling from a jutting rafter.

Electricity had always fascinated Tsegaye. He grew up in a small town where very few homes had electric light and some folks believed that electricity was the work of the devil. Marveling at the dazzling light it gave and the flouring mills that it powered, they said it was unearthly. Tsegaye knew better than that, but his astonishment at its invisible reality was no less.

Looking at the shiny copper threads at the split end of the wire, he remembered something his elementary school science teacher had said: that one of the twin strands was neutral—no electricity flowed in it. "Which of these two could be the neutral one?" Tsegaye wondered, staring at the bright threads sticking out of their insulation. There was no way he could tell by looking at them; they looked exactly alike. If he really wanted to know, he would have to feel with his finger. Seized by a mounting curiosity, he stood transfixed for a while and then furtively turned to see if he was being watched. He wasn't. The few students waiting to be called stood wilting in the sun and were oblivious to the risky experiment that Tsegaye was about to conduct. He knew there was a fifty percent chance of touching the wrong wire, but even if that were the case, he would only feel the jolt for a split second before he withdrew his finger, he thought. He glanced at the waiting crowd one last time and carefully sticking out his index finger, brought it in contact with one of the strands. A paralyzing tempest of electric current zipped through him to satisfy his curiosity—an angry torrent then flooded his limbs and churned his innards till he howled. Rescuers came running to help, but he somehow managed to free himself and collapsed to the ground.

He was safe; those who came to save him with panic in their eyes could see that, and they began to laugh. Tsegaye staggered to his feet cursing himself for being such a fool. He was shaken but grateful that he was alive. Just then, "Tsegaye Gabre-Medhin!" he heard the woman calling his name.

The interview went well and Tsegaye's questioners were satisfied with his test scores. Despite having just escaped electrocution, he was able to make an impression by demonstrating, when asked, the three ways of writing his name that he knew: Amharic, English, and shorthand. After conferring in subdued voices, one of the committee members, the wife of a press secretary for the American Embassy, told him the good news. "Congratulations Tsegaye! You've been accepted."

Chapter 15

The Commercial College was first opened in Sidist Kilo, in the same place where the Nazareth School stands today. The city was in its youth then, and the environs of Sidist Kilo and Piazza were the early bustling centers of the young city. They were home to newly established schools, the parliamentary building, and Haile-Selassie's palace. Prominent churches, restaurants and coffee shops were located there, as were the first movie theatres and theatre halls. There was daytime glamour embodied in the glitzy boutiques and trendy cafés, and bawdy nightlife in popular bars tended by sought after women of ill-repute.

Tsegaye loved his new station. Ensconced in the well-tended compound of the college right in the heart of affluence, he pondered his good fortune and smiled. A simple boy from far-away Ambo now living a stone's throw away from the emperor's palace! His wildest fantasies could not have conjured this up. And in four years' time, God willing, he would graduate and plunge into the razzmatazz of the high life that went on in the vicinities of his school. But first, he had to focus on the task at hand and do well in his studies. Having been granted his last request by Mr. Hairring and skipped the tenth grade, he had to quickly fill the gaps in his skills. Even his urgent desire to put together a theatrical performance group would have to wait.

As demanding as his freshman year was, however, it didn't deter him from writing a play that he had been mulling over for a while: *Yedem Azmera* (*Harvest of Blood*). He might have lacked for time, but not for inspiration. Along with the wealth of stories and images he had brought from the world of his childhood, the localities of his school proved to be a perfect macrocosm for the social realities of the country. The rich flaunted their fabulous wealth there, and the poor came to pick crumbs. That was where the first generation of the foreign-educated, sons of the affluent, came to visit Wube Berha, a cluster of brothels where whiskey flowed and phonographs blared till cock crow. Wube Berha was the center of tabloid-worthy scandals where monstrous egos collided on account of prized prostitutes, shots were fired, and young lives were cut short. There was the lure of Hager Fikir Theatre too, a short walk from the college, to keep Tsegaye's fire burning. On his strolls along the streets to Piazza, he saw the stage photographs of popular actors and actresses, and colorful posters advertising ongoing plays and other artistic events that took place in the theatre. He envied the well-dressed people flocking there for the latest shows. On the rare occasions that he could afford a ticket, he sat in the audience, entranced as the folks around him. Somehow, he knew it was only a matter of time until his work would be performed on this very stage of Hager Fikir.

Tsegaye had never attended a proper play till then. The only stage performance he had ever seen was a crude burlusque presented by the students of Ambo's Agricultural College. He was a young boy of eight, and the guard at the door of the auditorium had rudely turned him away, along with his friend Belete. The two had remained nearby until the door was closed right before the show began. They had then dolefully wandered around the hall searching for some crack or hole to peek through. There was none except an open window at one end of the hall, but it was high above their heads. How would they be able to reach it?

And then, "I have a solution," Tsegaye said to Belete, his eyes shining with a foretaste of mischief. "Let's take turns carrying each other. You carry me till you get tired, and I'll carry you afterwards."

"What if they find us?" asked Belete.

"We'll run. They can't catch us."

He agreed and Tsegaye stood on his shoulders, and propped himself on the window frame to watch the spectacle on the stage. The play was a crude farce by all accounts, one that ridiculed a peasant who was utterly confused by the modern ways of a big city. He didn't know how to use a fork or what to do with a pair of undershorts. The audience couldn't contain its laughter.

Tsegaye and his friend watched different portions of the play, and later pieced it together on their walk home.

In his third year at the Commercial College, Tsegaye was finally ready to recruit actors from among the students for the play he had completed. Luckily, most of those he asked were willing to participate. The older actors were reluctant until he let them read pages of the handwritten manuscript. He wanted the play to be ready by Parent's Day, he said, and they began preparations. There was a problem though: he didn't have a single girl in the cast, not because there weren't any in the school but because they seemed remote. How would a bashful small-town boy dare to converse with a city girl? To make matters worse, the girls were kept under watch by matronly chaperones who followed them around and made sure they didn't stray.

The Commercial College had broken from tradition by being among the first to admit women, and by way of reassuring many concerned parents, it had taken the unusual step of assigning dignified middle-aged escorts to watch the girls. The chaperones accompanied the girls back and forth between the college and their dormitories in *Etege* Menen School, a half hour walk. They also instructed them in proper ladylike decorum and taught them those feminine virtues that they wouldn't be taught in a modern school. But more importantly, the chaperones were there mainly to ward off unwanted attention. Their job was to make sure that the damsels in their charge wouldn't fool around with smooth-talking nobodies and ruin their chances of catching worthy suitors. At a time when very few girls got even a high school education, many a wealthy bachelor would vie for the rare chance of marrying a college-educated woman. So even if Tsegaye had plucked up the courage to try to recruit a female for his play, her no-nonsense chaperone would prove to be a formidable barrier to contend with. He had no choice but to make do with an all-male cast.

Then to his pleasant surprise, a girl appeared of her own accord during rehearsal and expressed interest to join. He had seen her before, and noticed her beauty and her uniquely outgoing demeanor. Most of the girls in his college, groomed by severe chaperones, were distant and reserved. But this sprightly thing was a free-spirited soul who wouldn't be tamed by convention. Undeterred by her keeper's objections, she became the only girl in the cast.

"I heard you have written a wonderful play, and I'd love to join your group if you have a role for me," she said, dazzling Tsegaye with a bright smile.

"Of course! Yes. I'll be uh…happy to have you," he mumbled and assigned her a role.

The play, based on Fascist Italy's occupation of Ethiopia, was an instant success. Parents who saw it spoke about a gem of a play written by a young playwright by the name of Tsegaye Gabre-Medhin. Important persons picked up their phones and rang Dr. Nagib, the director, asking if there would be more of Tsegaye's *Harvest of Blood*, so that they would come to see it. The director obliged by extending the show dates, and notables of Addis Ababa flocked to the Commercial College on weekend afternoons. Many took the trouble because of their genuine interest in art, but there were a few well-placed bachelors who had gotten tired of wasting their years with the fallen beauties of Wube Berha that they would never marry. They were in trouble, these foreign-educated men with their outlandish notions of matrimony. They sought for more than a demure housewife in a spouse. Not a practical fancy in those days unless they frequented places like the Commercial College where they would have a better chance of finding a modern woman of their ilk. So when they heard of Tsegaye's much-talked about play, they were quick to seize the chance, and they kept coming, bearing gifts of perfume, scarves, and handkerchiefs; hoping that they wouldn't leave the school without presenting it to a lovely maiden.

One such man was a prominent journalist, Ato Ahadu Sabure, who instantly fell for the bright star and only girl in the cast of *Harvest of Blood*. Unfortunately for him though, she was the fancy of a more powerful personage—a prince—and she would break his heart in the end by tying the knot with his rival.

As bitterly disappointing as Ato Ahadu's visit to the college was to himself, it was a godsend for Tsegaye, for it gave him the publicity he needed. The journalist wrote a gushing review of the play in the major papers. He even had Tsegaye summoned to the director's office just to meet him and shake his hand. Ato Ahadu Sabure was an influential man, and it was quite an honor to win his praise.

Once Tsegaye had felt the thrill of watching adults riveted by something he had created, once he had heard their hearty laughter at his funny lines and seen the outrage in their faces at the distressing scenes of his play, once newspapers lauded his work and called him a gifted young writer with a bright future, his life-long commitment to theatre and poetry was irrevocably charted.

He was progressing in his studies as well; he was in his third year of college. When he graduated in one year's time, he would get a full-time job. He might even be able to immerse himself in his first love, writing plays, in his spare time. A career in business administration no longer seemed compatible with the life of a writer, though. The consuming world of modern bureaucracy outside the college campus, he thought, could be detrimental to his true calling. The diploma of business education, which he was to receive soon, and the financial reward it promised, had already lost their appeal. What he needed, he believed, was to engage in something less demanding of his time and energy; something that would leave him room to indulge his passion. For that, he had made up his mind to ask the Director, Dr. Nagib for a job as a librarian. But he knew he still needed a college degree of some sort, something to fall back on if, God forefend, his pen ran dry. He had thought of that too, and had applied and been accepted to Chicago's Blackstone School of Law for a correspondence degree program in legal studies.

Dr. Nagib was quite surprised when Tsegaye told him that he wanted to be a librarian.

"You are a great student and a promising artist. You can get a much better job when you graduate. Why would you want to waste your talent by taking a job that doesn't suit your talents?"

"I don't think any other job would allow me to continue to write plays."

"Do you know how much you would be earning as a librarian?"

Tsegaye didn't know for sure, but he had guessed it wouldn't be that much.

"Less than half what you would be making elsewhere."

"That's alright," answered Tsegaye.

"That doesn't seem alright to me. What you're about to do doesn't make much sense. You really have to give this serious thought," Dr. Nagib voiced his concern, leaving Tsegaye no choice but to divulge his other secret.

"Well, Sir, the other reason why I wanted to get this job is because I've enrolled in a correspondence program at the Blackstone School of Law. So I thought that if I worked here as a librarian, I'll have access to the study materials that I need."

That was credible enough, and a more prudent reason.

"You never cease to amaze me, Tsegaye. You're about to graduate in business education; you have proven yourself to be a talented playwright, and now you are telling me that you're studying law. You're incredible!" Dr. Nagib expressed his astonishment and fulfilled his request.

At twenty years of age, Tsegaye was hired for his first job as a librarian.

He was right in hoping to get enough idle time for writing. There wasn't much to do at the library. He had an assistant who did most of what needed to be done, while he sat at his desk surrounded by shelves stacked with books. Wisely enough, he made the most of this boon by writing, in quick succession, two more plays. The first one, *Lelaw Adam* (*The Other Adam*), was an angry indictment of the tribal divisions of his society, and the many injustices that the poor were subjected to. He submitted the play to the curriculum department at the Ministry of Education to be considered for a school textbook, and was promptly rejected. Without being explicit, the Ministry made it clear that it wouldn't serve as a conduit for such a brazen social critique written by a student. Tsegaye didn't lose heart; he finished his second play, *Yeshoh Aklil* (*Crown of Thorns*), and presented it to wide acclaim at the college. Soon afterwards, the new complex for the Commercial College was completed in the Senga Tera neighborhood, and Emperor Haile-Selassie came to inaugurate it.

Chapter 16

AILE-SELASSIE WAS UNIQUELY charismatic in that he owed his charisma not to the man-of-the-people type of humble leadership that had endeared other leaders elsewhere, nor to crowd-electrifying oratory that had enabled some heads of state to hypnotize the masses and lead them into fulfilling their calamitous whims. He didn't even have the imposing physique one would expect in an emperor. His charisma emanated from the "Elect-of-God" mystique and from his aura of majestic grandeur—stately air and carriage—all products of royal etiquette bred into the bone. Groomed since childhood for the prize of lifelong monarchy, he had mastered his role and played the part well for decades.

The emperor's visit to any public institution, be it in Addis Ababa or in the provinces, was a momentous occasion that caused quite a stir. No person in charge of hosting such an event wanted to incur Janhoy's displeasure. Plans for a royal visit would thus often be accompanied by frantic ado to put things in perfect order before the king arrived with his entourage of important persons, armed guards, newsmen, photographers, and the indispensable Lulu, the Chihuahua dog.

A meticulous schedule of events had been drawn up at the Commercial College, complete with a list of dos and don'ts, and distributed among the staff, faculty, and students. Tsegaye, now chief librarian at the new campus, had been instructed to close the library's main door during the visit and to stand outside. Things were still a bit messy inside the new library, so the director had designated it off limits for the visit.

Tsegaye had accepted the order, but he had also taken the liberty to lighten the bare front wall and closed doors by posting a large piece of paper bearing a quote that he had taken out of a book written by the Prime Minister, *Bitwoded* Mekonnen Endalkachew. The quote, printed in beautiful calligraphy, read: "Books sweeten the bitterness of life." To Dr. Nagib's dismay, however, Tsegaye's attempt at adding a cheerful touch had the unintended consequence of attracting Haile-Selassie's attention. After standing before its door and quietly gazing at the words of the quote while the throng waited in hushed anticipation, the emperor signaled to one of his bodyguards to open the library door. The man threw the door open and barged in, followed by his master.

The Director's fear was in vain, or so it seemed. To all appearances, the emperor didn't seem unhappy with what he saw inside. He scanned various areas of the new library's interior, and turned to Tsegaye. Quietly, he looked at him for a few seconds, and then: "Have you abandoned it?" he asked.

Tsegaye hesitated, unsure if he was the one being addressed. The question hung in the air as all eyes watched him, leaving no doubt that it was indeed to him that Janhoy had spoken. He gathered his thoughts and responded: "Is Your Majesty asking me?"

"Yes. Have you abandoned your craft?"

Wonder of wonders! The emperor hadn't forgotten! He had remembered Tsegaye from what he had seen of him six years ago: the little boy in a crudely stitched toga who, together with two of his classmates, had regaled him for half an hour in Ambo's junior school.

"I haven't abandoned it, Your Majesty," answered Tsegaye.

"So what have you done since then?"

"I have been writing and producing plays. In fact, I've just finished writing a new play."

"Where is the new play you have written?" asked Haile-Selassie.

"Right there in my drawer, Your Majesty."

"Go get it and read it."

"Right now?"

"Yes."

He went to his desk and pulled out the handwritten manuscript of his play, *Crown of Thorns*.

"It is made up of five scenes, Your Majesty. Which of the scenes would you like me to read?"

"The beginning," answered the emperor.

In a subdued voice, Tsegaye began to read. Haltingly, he read the opening scene of the play, while an aide anxiously pulled up a chair for Haile-Selassie, which the emperor pretended not to notice. He stood just a couple of paces before Tsegaye and listened. The hallway was packed with the school's staff, faculty, and students, and inside the library were crammed the armed guards and the high-ranking personages of the country's educational affairs. The assemblage was sizeable, but not a sound was heard except Tsegaye's reading, punctuated by the rustle of paper and the occasional pattering of Lulu's tiny paws on the floor. As the minutes ticked by, the young playwright's voice gained more confidence and rang louder. On and on he read as the sovereign hearkened and the crowd stood motionless.

Haile-Selassie didn't respond right away. As if he needed a few moments to reflect over what he had heard, he mutely looked at Tsegaye with thoughtful eyes. Then he stepped a bit closer and said: "This is your first; it shouldn't be your last. Don't abandon your pen." He smiled at him and walked out, leaving Tsegaye wondering if he was awake or dreaming.

What message did Tsegaye mean to convey through his play? What was it about the opening scene of *Crown of Thorns* that captured the king's rapt attention for over an hour? Like his other plays, this one too had a theme that was foremost on Tsegaye's mind: the iniquitous social mores of his society. It was the best developed yet and the most well written; a testament to his maturing intellect and wordsmithery. It told the story of a love triangle between the young daughter of a feudal lord, a youthful military officer who is her social equal, and another—her childhood playmate born of her parent's servants. When the play nears its denouement, it is clear that the girl cares about her nameless suitor who, to improve his lot and his prospect of winning her hand, had put himself through college. But in the end, he is not her parents choice of a son-in-law. So she is compelled to marry the officer. It was a piece of writing dripping with the author's outrage at the fact that in his Ethiopia, a person's humble birth was a stigma that no amount of later success could wash away.

The emperor might have grasped as much from the pages Tsegaye had read. If he was troubled by the message, he didn't show it. That was what royal aplomb was for.

Chapter 17

O F ALL THE SCHOOLS that Tsegaye attended, the Commercial College transformed him the most. That was where he embarked on a path to becoming a member of the educated class in a country of non-literates. It was there that he matured into adulthood and arrived at a welcome convergence of his passions that would in turn form his intellect. Interestingly, more than the formal education he got there, which earned him a diploma he would have little use for in his single-minded devotion to his art, it was the informal learning that would turn out to be crucial. The lessons he soaked up without books or teachers—the art of communal living, the challenges of being in complete charge of himself away from home, the feat of juggling his artistic pursuit and his studies, the wisdom to keep his poise in the precarious glory of fame—would all prove to be vital. Certainly, this portion of Tsegaye's education had not been all smooth and painless. Unlike his studies where he had no trouble excelling, this other schooling—intense, complex and bewildering—had been interspersed with many rude jolts and low moments.

Tsegaye grew up in Ambo, whose ways had more in common with rural Ethiopia. He came to the capital steeped in a small town brand of manners and speech that some sleek city boys found worthy of mockery. His missteps gave the snobs reason to insult him; his blunders were fodder for jokesters to deride him for a laugh. Of course, many at the college were above the folly; they had more respect and admiration for his other virtues, his academic caliber and his art, than contempt for his lack of the urbane touch. Even when they couldn't resist the urge to laugh, they were quick to make it up to him with fond remarks afterwards. But there were those like Abdoñaw, a fiercely competitive soccer player for a second-tier team of Medhane-Alem Secondary School, who couldn't put up with Tsegaye's rough-edged conduct and plotted a vicious act of retribution to punish him.

Tsegaye dabbled in soccer in his junior year at the Commercial College. Having acquired the taste for it from when he and his friends kicked about a rag ball on the dusty roads of Ambo, he had joined the college's lower team and was assigned to play in the position of a defender. He was chosen for that role for good reason. He had proven, at other minor matches on campus, that he had a knack for defense. He was a mighty human bulwark who would do anything in his power to stop the ball from getting past him. His trick was simple but effective. He ignored everything around him: turned a deaf ear to the noise in the field or beyond; paid no attention to scurrying players, and kept his eyes on the ball alone. He watched its movements with unwavering attention; followed its rolls and bounces. He then stood a few yards in front of the goalkeeper and waited. When it came dangerously close, he made his move. He kept his eyes glued to the ball and charged with his head down like a raging bull. He flew at top speed to stop it with whatever it took, be it shoving off the trespasser or kicking his foot together with the ball.

After suffering Tsegaye's painful kicks a few times, Abdoñaw, the battered midfielder of the opposite team, one day decided he had had enough. It was time to teach the crude defender a lesson. So he devised a brutal scheme. Halfway through the game, after Tsegaye executed his foolproof defensive maneuver and knocked out a player in the process, Abdoñaw picked up the ball and without Tsegaye noticing, carefully put it on top of a wiry clump of crab grass. Then turning to him, "Bravo Tsegaye!" he shouted. "That was a clever move, man! You're the best!" Tsegaye wasn't sure if the praise was genuine. "You deserve a free kick for that," said Abdoñaw, aching for vengeance inwardly with a smile on his face. "Show us your mighty kick one more time," he urged him, pointing at the dangerously placed ball that was waiting like a well-concealed trap.

Abdoñaw was no referee, Tsegaye knew that. He had no right to call a free kick. Yet, what he said flattered his ego and he fell for the ruse. For momentum, he backed away a few paces and, pausing to sharpen his focus, he ran full tilt and whacked the ball together with the knotty, unyielding tuft of wild grass. Just as Abdoñaw had imagined, he smashed his big toe against its earth-gripping roots.

Tsegaye would have quietly limped away, or lunged at his foe and trounced him if he could, but the agony was excruciating. He sank to the ground and began writhing like one bitten by a deadly snake. The impact had peeled off the nail of his big toe, and blood spurted out of the torn canvas shoe. The painful mishap signalled the end of Tsegaye's days on the soccer field and Abdoñaw's visits to the college.

Tsegaye knew what set him apart from most of his city-bred schoolmates. He was aware that his speech and mannerisms at times irked some thin-skinned grousers and caused outrage and resentment. He did his best to blend, to adapt and change as much as he could, but he was no zealous disciple of citified manners; no blind devotee of everything metropolitan. Having embraced what he accepted and rejected what he despised, he evolved into a product of two worlds. Sleek and suave like some of his detractors, he was not, but he shone brightly in his studies and in his creative pursuits. He had taken multiple challenges and achieved great success in each. He had proven himself to be an astute student and an accomplished playwright with a precocious awareness of the fair and unfair realities of his world. By the time he graduated from the Commercial College, he was on his way to earning a law degree. He had fared exceedingly well indeed; his lack of polish had not deprived him of much. Yet there was one thing that remained elusive; he hadn't found a sweetheart.

He couldn't blame his failure on those invincible guardians and their unflagging vigilance. Some wily fellows had actually managed to snatch their future mates from under their noses. Neither did Tsegaye have the excuse of not finding a girl that had stolen his heart; there was one, a coy dainty thing who was the top student of her class. Unable to resist her dual charms, her delicate femininity and her academic excellence, he had followed her about nervously, stalking her from a few paces behind whenever he saw her alone. He had been too timid to say a word and could only summon what courage he had to throw pebbles at her back. By way of announcing his presence, he carried little bits of stone in his pocket and lobbed them, one at a time, when he was sure no one was watching. What would he have said if she had turned and asked him what he wanted? He had no idea. He might have fled or stood there defiantly and said nothing. How could he possibly have explained such a loutish act? Thankfully, she had simply refused to turn around as if it were beneath her to acknowledge his existence.

Tsegaye graduated from the Commercial College at twenty. By then, he had learned things that his friends in Ambo hadn't even heard of. His head was filled with notions that his folks wouldn't be able to fathom. He had acquired a foreign tongue. He had written and directed plays. He held a respectable job and was preparing to lay roots in the capital. Yet, not once in his twenty years had he lost his head in that intoxicating emotional tempest known as romantic love. The only time he had a vague taste of this enchantment and pain was through a brief spell in his boyhood, when he was only ten.

❖ ❖ ❖

Her name was Abeba, and she was a neighbor's daughter. A bony, light-skinned, fleet-footed girl who danced like a gypsy and sang like a bird, Abeba had a thousand and one ideas for imaginative plays. She had a knack for crafting wonderful playthings with her bare hands. With bits of rags and straw, she made twig-limbed dolls that looked like miniature scarecrows. She created a musical instrument made of twines strung on a stick inserted into rusty cans. She sang strumming her crude lyre and whirled around Tsegaye, her mesmerized audience. She placed a piece of broken pottery on three stones and lighted a small fire beneath it to make her stew, a concoction of leaves, roots and ground red clay for pepper. She spread a piece of cloth on a circular structure of twigs that she had him drive into the ground, and called it their home. "You're my husband," she told him. "I'm your wife," and Tsegaye felt his knees buckling as blissful warmth flooded his heart.

Abeba was an only daughter to her single mother—a kind woman who made a good living brewing and selling tej in her home. And like any mother of an only child, she doted on her daughter and did all she could to make her happy. If Abeba wanted Tsegaye to share the *chechebsa*—freshly baked flat bread soaked in peppery butter—that her mother had made for her, so he would. If she asked for another glass of *birz*, a non-alcoholic brew sweetened with honey, for her playmate, her mother would gladly oblige. Sitting crouched in their little home, the small flimsy tent they had pitched in the backyard, they sipped birz while Ababa babbled and giggled, and told him one of her inexhaustible stories. Abeba knew fairytales galore.

Then one day, Abeba said her mother had told her that they would be moving to Addis Ababa. They were leaving in two days, she told Tsegaye, and his blissful world began to rock. His lips trembled and tears welled up in his eyes. No less distressed herself by the imminence of her departure and separation from her friend, Abeba did her best to make the most of what little time they had left together. She made her stew of leaves and clay, and later tried to sing and dance, but none of it was half as magical as before. In the end, she gave it all up and they quietly crawled into their tent where she held him close and kissed his cheeks till he purred in delight. They embraced and kissed each other, neither of them certain what it was about wrapping their scrawny arms around each other and kissing that they couldn't get enough of.

On the day that Abeba and her mother left Ambo, Tsegaye walked along with her, both carrying small bundles, while their mothers led the way to the bus depot. Feleqech too had come to see her neighbor off. The adults conversed, but the kids were speechless because the ever-talkative Abeba had nothing to say that day. Every time she tried to speak, a lump swelled in her throat and choked the words before they left her lips. Tears clouded her eyes, but she bravely refused to let them flow.

At the bus station, the two friends shook hands and said goodbye. They would have loved to hug and kiss, but they didn't have the cheek to do that in front of the adults.

Abeba followed her mother into the bus and sat by the window. As soon as she took her seat, her eyes searched for Tsegaye and saw him standing where she had left him. He had refused to leave until the bus pulled out of the station. Then she saw him looking at her with mournful eyes, and she could no longer hold down her grief. She dissolved in tears. Taking his cue from her, Tsegaye too bawled loudly. Feleqech didn't know what to make of her son's copious weeping. She knew Tsegaye liked

Abeba, but didn't fathom the depth of his affection, whereas Abeba's mother, who had a better sense of what went on between the two, told her daughter to quickly hop off the bus and give Tsegaye a goodbye hug and kiss.

Chapter 18

FOLLOWING HIS GRADUATION from the Commercial College in 1956, Tsegaye continued to work in the library for one year before he was hired as a deputy to the chief librarian at University-College of Addis Ababa. His new position had more pay and prestige than the old one at his school, but his elevated status brought him little contentment, possessed as he was by his latest obsession: his dream of winning a scholarship and going abroad to study theatrical arts. He had been searching for such a chance and one had finally come his way. Sponsored by UNESCO, the cultural and educational arm of the United Nations, the scholarship was to be conferred upon one deserving candidate with exceptional grades and extracurricular achievements. Forty hopefuls competed for the opportunity and Tsegaye won the prize.

Modern education had begun to take root in the early 1960s as people were slowly coming to terms with the fact that education was a way out of a life of ignorance and poverty. With schools proliferating in the provinces, college education had come within reach of thousands of high school graduates, whereas the government's ability to meet the rising need lagged far behind. There weren't enough colleges to take in the masses of students who had passed the college entrance exam, but that didn't stop the students from coming to the capital hoping to be admitted into the colleges there. They bade farewell to their family and friends and arrived in Addis Ababa with expectations of a warm welcome. A multitude of young men from the provinces swarmed around the building of the Ministry of Education and Fine Arts asking for support before their meager supplies ran out. Their demands were impossible to meet and no one was brave enough to admit the truth. "Please be patient. We are working hard to resolve the matter," a notice on the bulletin board said, and the students continued to wait for days.

The Ministry, being the sole authority on matters of education, was in charge of processing college placements, and foreign scholarships, as well as handling issues of salary, promotions, and transfer of teachers. In the midst of the teeming crowd of college-bound students, there were also disgruntled schoolteachers who had come from faraway places with complaints such as overdue transfers and unfulfilled promises of pay raises. Things were nearing a crisis point when Tsegaye arrived there carrying the congratulatory letter he had received from UNESCO to get his scholarship approved. Something needed to be done or there was no telling what the ill-treated mob from out of town would do out of despair. Haile-Selassie wanted quick action, but that the head of the Ministry, Ato Kebede Mikael, was a wise man of letters with little inclination for harsh measures. As luck would have it though, Ato Kebede left the country to attend an international conference in Paris. His departure made it easier for the emperor to replace him, and he tapped Lij Endalkachew Mekonnen, son of the Prime Minister, to assume Ato Kebede's place in his absence. The emperor knew Lij Endalkachew well and reckoned that he would quell the trouble at the Ministry.

The new head made his first move as soon as he assumed control: he retroactively raised the passing score of the college entrance exam, and instantly disqualified half of the eligible students. The underhanded scheme sent a shockwave of anger and disbelief through the weary crowd. Some howled in rage and pulled their hair. Many were struck dumb and stood frozen as if the news had turned them to stone. Others paced, seething with impotent rage, cursing the new boss and their fate. There were a few who broke down and wept inconsolably while a handful charged at the closed main door of the office, determined to knock it down, and had to be driven away by armed policemen.

A few held on to their optimism, convinced that they had a uniquely compelling case that would move even the most callous bureaucrat. Out of sheer despair, they believed that if only they could somehow meet the minister in person, they would prove to him that theirs was a special case. They would confide in him their heartbreaking stories; yes, pour their hearts out and win his pity. He wouldn't turn them down, they figured, and they hung around at a safe distance from the policemen and their clubs and guns. Eager yet inconspicuous, they waited for their moment, while rehearsing their messages for quick delivery. A few got their chance; they accosted the minister and submitted their plea.

"I decided to leave it all, Honorable Minster. I even refused to marry a girl my parents had chosen for me because I want to be an educated man."

"You are a fool! Go back and marry her before you lose her to someone else," the minister would retort brusquely as he walked away.

"My parent borrowed money to slaughter a cow for a sendoff party, Your Excellency!" confided another.

"Let them slaughter another cow for a welcome-back party because you are going back."

And there was an exhausted-looking middle-aged man, a gangly schoolteacher with a balding head, who, unlike the supplicants before him, had the nerve to be longwinded.

"I've been in Addis Ababa for twenty days, Your Excellency. I have no one here. I have no money left for another day."

The minister, about to get into a car, asked: "What's your complaint?"

The teacher's face brightened up. "I'm a Math teacher from Wello, but because there's a shortage of teachers in our school, I've been teaching Geography as well."

"Get to the point," the Minister said, peevishly.

"When I was hired, I was told that my monthly salary would be 120 birr, but I've never been paid a cent more than 82 birr in the last six years."

"So you want 120 birr a month?"

"Yes. I have a big family, and 82 birr isn't enough to feed us all."

"Is your father alive?"

The question startled the man; he had no idea what the minister was driving at, but he answered it nonetheless. "No, Your Excellency. He passed away when I was young. My mother is old and bedridden. She is living with me. I'm taking care of her."

"What did he do?"

"My father? Uh … he was a farmer. He worked on the land."

"And you, the son of a poor farmer, are turning up your nose at 82 birr a month! You are ungrateful," said Lij Endalkachew. He got into his car and drove away.

It was quite brave of Tsegaye, in light of the minister's foul treatment of students, some of which he had witnessed, to persist and ask him to approve the scholarship he had won.

His moment finally came on the eighteenth day of his wait when an assistant called him in and escorted him into the spacious office of the Minister.

"Your business, briefly," the minister asked gruffly.

"My name is Tsegaye Gabre-Medhin, Your Excellency. I'm a playwright. I competed for a scholarship offered by UNESCO and I'm the only one of forty applicants to win the prize. I have chosen a school, the Royal Court Theatre in London, and completed all the preliminary procedures. I only need your signature to get a passport and a visa."

The minster quietly perused the contents of the paper on his desk and turned to his aide.

"How much is the regular monthly stipend for Ethiopian students in Britain?" he asked.

"Thirty five pounds," the assistant answered.

"Then why is this a hundred and thirty four pounds—more than three times what other students are paid? What are you? A diplomat?" he jeered at Tsegaye. "This is a lot of money. We'll try to find another scholarship for you," he said and signaled his aide to show Tsegaye the door.

"UNESCO is paying the stipend, Your Excellency," Tsegaye countered. "My scholarship won't cost our government a cent. Countries from all over the world will be sending students abroad through this scholarship. Why should I miss such an opportunity given to me by an international organization?"

The aide knew his boss; there was nothing to be gained and perhaps everything to be lost by bravely talking back to him. So he tried to take Tsegaye's arm and lead him out, but Tsegaye pushed him away.

"What's this?" yelled the minister in disbelief when he saw Tsegaye resisting. He jumped out of his seat and angrily picked up a long, thick ruler rumored to have been used against those who had crossed him, but the guards quickly grabbed Tsegaye by the arms and hustled him out.

For averting a riot and sending home thousands of heartbroken students with their deflated hopes, the minister was appointed ambassador to Britain while a new Minister of Education was appointed to take his place.

The new minister was *Blaten Geta* Mahteme-Selassie Wolde-Meskel. His title signified a distinguished man of learning. Despite the formidable length of his name and the grandiose sound of his title, however, the new minister was a humble, genial man, quite the antithesis of his predecessor. Maybe because the emperor felt some qualm or perhaps because he paid heed to the counsel of some farsighted advisor that running afoul with so many of the country's brightest youth was asking for trouble, he chose an upright man to make amends.

Blaten Geta was horrified at the mountain of unresolved cases he found at the Ministry. In a dramatic reversal of Lij Endalkachew's policy of wholesale rejection, he accepted as many applicants as had been turned away. He promptly signed their papers and directed his staff to expedite their cases.

Tsegaye had by then given up hope of studying at the Royal Court Theatre in England. He had been resigned to the sad fact that his scholarship was a lost opportunity. Sorely disillusioned and powerless to do anything, he continued working as a librarian at University-College of Addis Ababa. Then a phone call came one day and a woman informed him that the new minister had signed his papers. "You can come and pick it up. Congratulations!" she said.

Chapter 19

HERE WERE TWO groups of Ethiopian students attending schools in England. One was a handful of students like Tsegaye, who had competed for and won coveted scholarships. The other group, larger than the first, was made up of children of the power elite. Unlike their less privileged compatriots, the highborn didn't have to prove their academic worth. The gift of foreign education, bestowed on them by the emperor, was a token of gratitude for the devoted service of their parents. They were sons and daughters of the nobility, and were treated as such even in a foreign country; social distinctions were strictly maintained. The chasm that divided the students, the highborn and the rabble, was evident in the disparity of their stipends, the quality and prestige of schools that they attended, and the services made available to them by the Ethiopian consular office.

When Tsegaye arrived in London, a stern, portly English gentleman who introduced himself as Mr. Kendal met him at Heathrow Airport. He had been assigned as his guide to help him get acquainted with the ways of the great metropolis. From the first day as Tsegaye's cultural mentor, Mr. Kendal made it clear that his authority was not to be disputed, and proved it through the half-caring, half-imperious ways he told him where to shop at a bargain, where to have fun, what to eat and what to wear. He accompanied him on his shopping trips and made him buy drab looking clothes in keeping with his own taste. Tsegaye felt slightly suffocated by Mr. Kendall's closeness. There were times he got tired of the eccentric man and his quaint manners, but he was not ungrateful for having him as a companion. Having just arrived in a bewilderingly strange world, he was quite overwhelmed.

Within a week of his arrival, Tsegaye reported at the Royal Court Theatre dressed in a gray three-piece suit of Mr. Kendal's choosing. Later that afternoon, on his way to the Ethiopian consular office, he found himself standing in an elevator next to Lij Endalkachew, by then the Ethiopian ambassador to the United Kingdom. The encounter made him shrink as he recalled their last meeting and the ugly confrontation that ensued after the man had rejected his scholarship. But he still greeted the ambassador with a polite bow and a grin.

"So you are here, young man. Well, I'm glad," said Lij Endalkachew, smiling and offering a handshake. "Congratulations!"

His cheerful congeniality, his let-bygones-be-bygones attitude, took Tsegaye by surprise.

"By the way," the ambassador went on, "I'm on my way to a dinner party. Most of the guests are Ethiopians. Why don't you come with me? You'll meet your people there," he said and took Tsegaye along.

The Ethiopian Embassy in London hosted frequent social gatherings and whenever news of such an event reached the small Ethiopian community, it was received with glee. Coming from a land where the sun shone most days of the year and where homes bustled with large families, the students found life in cold, wet England unbearably lonesome, and longed for these festive gatherings where they relished the joy of belonging. Tsegaye too enjoyed mingling. Carrying a bottle of gin or whiskey as he had seen others doing, he went to the embassy's reception hall to see familiar faces and to speak Amharic for a change.

But these festive occasions were not wholly fraternal; the usual divide held fast even here. Commoners like Tsegaye mixed with their kind on one side of the hall, while those of exalted lineage kept to themselves on the other. There were several girls too, but none of Tsegaye's ilk. Very few girls ever attended schools then, the true scholarship awardees often being men. The lovely Abesha ladies in London were all of the privileged class whose hefty tuition fees were paid by the government. Each of them was married or engaged to a bright-futured son of the nobility, which left the likes of Tsegaye with little hope of striking an amorous liaison with any of them.

That didn't mean he couldn't lap them up with his eyes and praise their beauty. The good-looking women might be out of reach, but they were not out of sight. He could stare to his heart's content and admire them from afar, and he did. He watched and admired and daydreamed until one evening he decided to go and ask one of the young ladies for a dance. He wouldn't have dared had he been sober, but having downed a few drinks, he was now filled with devil-may-care audacity that seemed to miraculously erase the yawning gulf between himself and the girl.

He had been eyeing her for a while because she was so good looking and there was something touching about the way she gazed at the whirling couples on the dance floor. She sat with other women, all watching the dancers and chatting amongst themselves every now and then, but none betrayed the naked longing for a good time that Tsegaye thought he saw in the eyes of this particular girl. In his alcohol-clouded vision, he saw the sad figure of a dark-skinned beauty, her girlish limbs aching to dance, sitting spurned by Abesha men who were busy wagging their bottoms with *ferenji* women and the unfairness of it filled him with outrage. He

Tsegaye in May 1959.

picked up his glass, tossed off a mouthful, and wiping his lips, marched up to her purposefully. The spurned beauties saw someone approaching, a swaggering drunk from the wrong side of the hall. His intention was clear, and they were alarmed.

He headed straight to the sad-eyed girl and bowed like the gallant gentlemen he had seen in Western movies. "Let's dance" he said, holding out his hand to take hers.

"I'm sorry, but I don't feel like dancing," she declined, softening it with a smile.

"Why not? We're here to have fun; aren't we? They're enjoying themselves." He said, pointing at the Abesha men jigging with white partners.

"I'd rather not, please," she pleaded, her eyes worriedly wandering off to a particular spot on the dance floor.

To Tsegaye, a product of a culture where a girl was expected to play hard to get, her refusal was simply for form's sake. It was a charming prelude to surrender, and he knew what a man was supposed to do in such cases: persevere! Since words had failed to do the job, he grabbed her arm firmly and tried to drag her out of her seat. The girl resisted by holding onto the edge of a table laden with bottles of alcohol. But Tsegaye had reached the do-or-die phase of his resolve to dance with her and wouldn't let go. So he gave her slender arm one last mighty tug and the force of his pull wrenched her loose, upsetting the table. A loud glassy clatter and the sound of smashing bottles rose above the din of loud music and the buzz of revelers, attracting attention. Someone stopped the music and the room turned silent as heads turned to where Tsegaye stood gripping the arm of a woman with the look of a frightened gazelle on her face. Then from somewhere in the midst of the dancing crowd, a man strode towards Tsegaye with a gun in his hand and shoved its muzzle in his face.

"What do you think you are doing? Who are you?" he roared, breathless with fury.

He was Jarra Mesfin, son of Shewa's governor, Ras Mesfin Sileshi, and unbeknownst to Tsegaye, the husband of the young lady he was trying to haul to the dance floor. Of course Jarra never gave his woman a chance to dance with him; not once had he waltzed with her since Tsegaye began watching. He was busy cavorting with blue-eyed women, but that was beside the point. A trigger-happy man known for his violent temper, Jarra was the wrong person to cross.

The sight of Jarra's loaded gun aimed at Tsegaye at such close quarters terrified onlookers. Women screamed and men shouted admonitions to cool him down.

"Come on Jarra. Take it easy for God's sake!"

"Calm down Jarra. You don't want to go to jail for murder."

His friends tried to take him and his gun away from Tsegaye, but he kept pushing them aside, while Tsegaye refused to be cowed, daring him to pull the trigger. It was a deadly standoff that no one knew how to diffuse until a thirteen-year-old girl weaved her way through the tense crowd and approached Tsegaye. Her name was Rahel. Seeing his little sister close to his loaded gun had a sudden calming effect on Jarra: it sobered him at once and he removed the gun from Tsegaye's face. Rahel then looked up at Tsegaye and asked him: "Do you want to dance with me?" He stared at the smiling little girl dubiously, searching for any hint of mockery in her eyes. But it was clear that she meant it.

"My pleasure," he answered and took her hand. The clamor subsided in an instant, and Jarra, taken aback by his sister's action, quickly simmered down, while Tsegaye, saved from a suicidal face-off by a girl almost half his age, headed to the dance floor. All sighed in relief, and the merrymaking resumed.

Chapter 20

SEGAYE STUDIED THEATRICAL arts at the Royal Court Theatre and at the Royal Windsor Theatre of London for four months. Then he went to Paris for a three-month training at the Comédie Française, the national theatre of France. He spent the final three months of his scholarship in Europe at the Rome National Opera in Italy where he studied the origin and development of the opera. He returned to his country in late December 1960.

He was happy to be back, but shocked at what had taken place in his absence. He had heard tidings of the trouble while in London but hadn't realized its magnitude nor its implication.

An attempt had been made to overthrow the rule of Emperor Haile-Selassie. Unthinkable as it was, a coup had been launched to oust the monarch while he was on a royal visit to Brazil. The man at the helm of the treasonous movement was the commander of the Imperial Guard, Birgadier General Mengistu Neway, assisted by his brother, Germamme Neway. The two, together with a few security officials, the police chief and several radical intellectuals intent on freeing Ethiopia from feudalism and autocracy, had come close to toppling Haile-Selassie's rule, but failed miserably in the end.

General Mengistu's promise to establish a government that would improve the economic, political, and social lot of the people had appealed to many at the start. Even university students had rallied to show their support, but the group with the might that mattered—the army and the air force—remained loyal to the emperor. To the coup leaders' undoing, one other formidable force they had thought little of, the Patriarch of the Ethiopian Orthodox Church, also supported the loyalists and denounced General Mengistu and his allies as traitors that the God-fearing people of Ethiopia should condemn. His repudiation was the final condemnation and the coup d'état turned into a debacle. When their failure appeared inevitable, Mengistu and his men panicked and shot more than a dozen government officials and nobility they had detained, including Ras Kasa, and the popular patriot Ras Abebe Aregay. Then they fled.

Upon Haile-Selassie's return to Addis Ababa on December 17, 1960, the renegades were hunted down and hanged for the crime of high treason.

It was in this grim aftermath of an averted disaster that Tsegaye and six other young men, who had been attending schools in Europe, went to appear before Haile-Selassie. On the surface, there was the semblance of normalcy at the palace where the king's trusted men had been murdered just days before. But beneath the calm facade, the horror of what had and could have taken place had put everyone on edge.

Ato Ketema Yifru, the emperor's personal secretary, was the first to meet the seven men. He had just been released after being jailed wrongly suspected of sympathizing with the traitors. "You must bow before the emperor," he ordered them and demonstrated how low they were to stoop before handing them over to yet another dignitary—Ato Million Neqniq, head of the foreign scholarship office at the Ministry of Education, who escorted them to the emperor's sanctum.

Haile-Selassie looked sickly and frail. The events of the past days had obviously taken their toll. Having reigned for decades in a peaceful Ethiopia over docile subjects who prostrated themselves whenever he appeared in their midst, he was unnerved by the specter of an upheaval. Just as it had sown the malignant seeds of dissent and proved to the long-suffering people of Ethiopia that one could attempt to dethrone the emperor without causing the stars to shatter and the earth to crack at the seams, the coup had lifted the veil of complacency from the emperor's eyes. It had roused the beast of mistrust in him and awakened his much lauded instincts for sniffing out betrayal and treachery; a quality that would serve him well until age would slowly erode it. But for now, he seemed alert and in command of his faculties, albeit sour and exhausted.

Tsegaye and his fellow returnees had elected a German-educated man called Eguale Gebre-Giorgis to give a short address of gratitude to Haile-Selassie. The speech, which was delivered without prior consultation with the group, was faintly smiled at by Janhoy, while Tsegaye cringed inwardly at its abject tone. Particularly the final words of the address, spoken in Ge'ez, struck him as absurd. "Use us as you see fit, Emperor Haile-Selassie," was what Dr. Eguale said.

Haile-Selassie inquired after each young man's career interests. "What do you want to do?" he asked Tsegaye in turn.

"If it is your wish, Your Majesty, I would like to be assigned to work at the Haile-Selassie Theatre," he answered.

"We expected that," replied the emperor. "It will be done."

All bowed low in parting and left.

Tsegaye was bothered by what Dr. Eguale had said on their behalf. The use-us-as-you-see-fit ending of his speech irked him. "How could you say that? What do you take us for? Slaves?" he fumed at Eguale as soon as he knew they were out of the emperor's earshot, but someone had heard the angry outburst. Ato Bekele Aberra, the deputy Minister of Education, was nearby.

"Listen you fool!" he snapped at Tsegaye. "Just because you come with a degree from overseas doesn't mean you know what life is all about. Wait till you grow up, okay? Just hold your tongue for now and drink your milk!" He stood for a moment staring down the upstart to emphasize his point and walked away. Tsegaye was speechless. The outrage was gone, replaced by panic, and then by an overwhelming sense of relief. He was glad that the man left things where he did. He could have done worse if he had wanted to. Those were dangerous days. The slightest sign of insubordination could cost a man dearly.

❖ ❖ ❖

The emperor kept his word. Tsegaye became the Artistic Director of Haile-Selassie I Theatre. The position was prestigious for a young man newly graduated from college; it promised a life of relative comfort.

He rented a house in Arat Kilo, close to the busy Saint Mary's Church. The neighborhood was safe; no miscreants roamed its streets at nightfall. No burglars dared break into homes there. Tsegaye liked it; it was conveniently located. His room was big enough for him. It was bright. But the landlord was unbearable. Unlike his former landlord who visited his property only once a month to collect the rent, this other landlord lived in one of the many rooms he rented out to his mostly bachelor tenants with reliable incomes.

He was a well-off middle-aged man without a wife or family. His single status was almost scandalous for a man of his age and means. The sassy youngish woman who lived with him, he claimed, was his maidservant hired to cook and clean, but his tenants suspected otherwise. Some even flirted with her while he was watching just to prove their hunch by the way he reacted. None of the landlord's foibles and bizarre behavior irked his tenants more than the way he sat outside in a folding chair, watching the activities on his property while turning page after page of an old Bible. He would sit there on most mornings reading aloud, his singsong voice bothersome as the nagging of a meddlesome mother-in-law. In between verses, his beady eyes would quickly scan the surrounding in search of a misstep, a breach in the unwritten rules that he expected lodgers to observe. When he did, he would promptly close the holy book and start hurling abuse at the offender. He got away with it most of the times, not because the carefree young men who lived in his rental units were afraid of him, but because they liked the place and didn't want to risk losing it by insulting him back. But not all were willing to meekly suffer the tireless wagging of his tongue for fear of forfeiting their rooms. And one such rebel was Tsegaye, who cut the landlord to size on the day he saw him maltreating one of his tenants—the only woman among a dozen or so men.

She was a young woman in the full bloom of her charms, a mother of three little boys. Her single-motherhood outraged Tsegaye, not because she lacked the means to raise the boys—one could keep a family of eight on an income like hers—she was a college graduate after all, and an employee of the State Bank, later renamed National Bank—but because he imagined there was some swine somewhere that had turned his back on a woman like her.

She had hired a young woman to help with the housework, to cook, clean, and do the laundry. One busy morning, the housemaid put a large bucket under a running tap in the front yard, but was late in returning. The landlord saw the pail overflowing, an infraction he would not tolerate. He could get up and shut the tap himself, but that would deprive him of the joy of pointing at the spilling water and unleashing his harangue.

As soon as the water's flow ceased, the man's tirade began, directed not at the housemaid, but at the woman who hired her. "What's wrong with you, woman? Are you trying to ruin me? Do you think I get this water for free from the Qebenna River?"

"I'm sorry. She didn't think it would fill up so soon," she said. She dreaded his tongue, and had managed to avoid crossing him thus far.

"She didn't think it would fill up so soon, she says," he mocked her in an appallingly shrill mimicry. "How long does it take for a bucket to fill up? An hour? A whole day?"

Tsegaye had been watching through the window of his room and listening to the landlord berating the woman. Several times before, in his broodings over his loneliness that ended up in fantasies of this woman sharing his life, he had imagined various scenarios of how that might all begin. He had pictured a magic instant when eloquent messages were poured into each other through the eyes, and all that would follow would be a mere formality. Or another when he would somehow find the courage to bravely walk up to her on the road somewhere and confess his old crush. But none of his fantasies had cast him in the role of a hero saving her from the tongue-lash of a tyrant.

"It won't happen again" she said to the landlord.

"Listen to me carefully now. If I ever see that knucklehead servant of yours wasting my water again…" he didn't have the chance to finish before Tsegaye came rushing out of his room and stood looming over him.

"Didn't you hear her say that she was sorry?" he thundered with glaring eyes, his finger pointing at the woman standing just a few paces away. "What else do you want her to do? You disgusting, miserable creature! What gives you the right to treat us like this? Do you think we live on your charity here? We pay our rent. Show us some respect for God's sake!"

Windows flew open and heads stuck out to witness the tyrant's humiliation, while the woman Tsegaye came to protect stood, unable to move. She was relishing the storm while hoping the two wouldn't come to blows. Tsegaye's eyes quickly caught hers and turned to the cowering man before him. "If I ever catch you talking to her like that again..." he began, but left the rest unsaid. The bible-thumping landlord who had been mercilessly berating the woman was now speechless. His lips kept moving but no sound came out of his mouth.

Within a few weeks of the confrontation, Tsegaye proposed marriage to the woman and she accepted.

Later, when they were reminiscing about life at Commercial College, Tsegaye posed a question that he had wanted to ask for a long while.

"What did you think of me when I followed you around throwing pebbles at you?"

"I thought maybe that was how courting was done where you came from," she answered.

Within a year, Tsegaye and Lakech had their first child—Yodit—in 1965.

Chapter 21

T HE BIRTH OF a child is a life-changing event. It is a miracle that has the power to transform.

Tsegaye welcomed the change that fatherhood had brought and greeted his altered self at the moment a woman relative took the baby from his wife, Lakech, and put her in his lap. The tiny, feather-light bundle wriggling in its swaddle, that helpless bit of his flesh carefully cradled in his arms, ushered in a wondrous stage of his life as a parent. And the earliest signs of his surrender to the tyrannical might of fatherhood came just a few months after Yodit was born.

She had been left under the care of a nanny while the couple went to the cinema. When they returned, the house was peacefully quiet. The nanny, having lulled the infant to sleep, was herself snoozing on a mat in a corner. Tsegaye lounged in the living room while Lakech sneaked into the room where her baby slept, and saw something odious. "Tsegaye!" she called out to her husband. Her horrified voice was a stifled shriek; a panicked whisper louder and more urgent than a scream. Tsegaye came running with a look on his face of one about to hurl himself at a mortal enemy or down a precipice, and saw a rat slithering along the sill of a closed window just above the sleeping child. Yodit seemed alright, but that didn't stop something insane and bloodthirsty from bursting forth out of Tsegaye and driving him wild for a few frightening minutes. Even Lakech herself, who was no less terrified at seeing the rat skulking just above her sleeping baby, was not prepared for what happened next.

He chased the gray-furred creature with the ineptitude of a furious but ineffective predator. Knocking down the furniture on his path; stumbling over obstacles and falling; hurling whatever he could grab: shoes, books, glasses, ceramic mugs; shouting obscenities Lakech had never heard him utter before; he turned the house into bedlam in his murderous pursuit. His eyes blazed like a maniac's. He shook. He ranted. He panted. But he didn't get the rat.

His failure to capture the repulsive creature and rip it apart with his hands or crush it to a bloody mess under his feet devastated Tsegaye. "I missed it!" "It's gone." "It escaped," he said, again and again. He was unusually quiet that evening. He thought of nothing else that night but the horror of what would become of him if he

At home with family (Ginfille, Addis Ababa, 1968). Standing from (l) to (r): Bitew Delelegn (father-in-law); Lakech Bitew (wife); Aynalem Bitew (sister-in-law); Tewabech Woreta (Lakech's aunt), and Gabre-Medhin Qewesa (father). Front row: daughters Mahlet (l) and Yodit (r); and Tsegaye.

and his wife had arrived home a bit later to find that the rat had in fact … A shiver ran down his back and he tried to banish the dreadful thought.

Later, soberly reflecting on the incident, Tsegaye realized that the awful event was an intense right of passage to fatherhood, and the force that had swept through him was the firestorm of initiation. It was the transformative magic of parenthood whose mystery would be a fascinating subject of reflection for the remainder of his poet's life, as would be other ancient riddles, such as religion, and how it can turn one into a saint and another into a demon. Or the thirst for power and all the horrendous evil committed in its quest. Why does the victim, when given the chance, become a perpetrator? How does the descendant of a slave become a slave master?

❖ ❖ ❖

After Yodit was born, Lakech and Tsegaye's sought a bigger house and found it in Qebenna, at the foot of a hill across Ginfille. Their new home was bigger, and it was close to the Sandford English School that their daughters would later attend.

Lakech had three boys—Ayenew, Estifanos and Hailu—from a previous marriage that had ended while the children were very young. By the time Tsegaye returned from his studies abroad, she had been raising the boys as a single working mother with assistance from her parents. At the start of Lakech and Tsegaye's life together in Qebenna, the boys lived with their grandparents. When a few years later the couple moved into a home they had bought in Qera, Lakech's eldest son, Ayenew, moved with them while Estifanos and Hailu remained with their grandparents, visiting on weekends and holidays.

Chapter 22

SEGAYE WROTE TWO short plays in quick succession soon after he returned from London in 1960. The first, a one-act play that he called *Ign Biye Metahu (Back with a Grin)*, was a sarcastic piece meant to satirize the ubiquity of lifeless smiles that had baffled him London. "Why don't you smile?" "Why the long face?" "You should smile," people used to pester him often. At first, he found it impossible to smile when he didn't feel like it, but with patience and practice, he learned and began to grin. But that had come at a price: he had lost his gift of genuine smile, or so he thought. And now that he was back in his homeland where a person would be seen as wrong-in-the-head for baring his gums for no good reason, he felt he would poke fun at the charade through his art.

His other short play, produced in 1959, was called *Joro Deggif (Mumps)*. Like most of his earlier plays, it was accusatory, and meant to reveal the muck lying beneath the clean façade of fairness.

The main character in *Joro Deggif* is a poor laborer, a tanner who makes a living by transforming the freshly flayed pelt of a goat into the most durable of grain bags. Throughout the play, he is hard at work mounted on top of an inflated goat hide and stamping on it with his bare feet. Holding on to a strap attached to a wooden post, he bounces up and down on the taut, smelly balloon, trampling it beneath his feet to remove the hair and to stretch the bag to its limits. And he converses with himself as he does. It is *Fasika*, Ethiopian Easter, the day of feasting and merrymaking. From the opulent home that hired him, sounds of talk and laughter, the clinking of glasses and silverware spill into his soliloquy. Wafts of buttery spicy lamb and chicken stew make his mouth water. His stomach growls, but he ignores it all and carries on with his monologue. He talks about his sundry woes. To the audience watching in the darkened expanse of the hall, he unfolds a tale of his pauper's lot: his life of endless toil with no respite just to barely stay alive. To worsen his misery, he has mumps, and a large swelling of the salivary glands beneath his right ear has disfigured his face. At times, his rant of self-pity causes him to forget his swollen jaw, and he tramps hard on the goat hide. When he does, the pain darts across his face and makes him wince. Then he turns his face to the left and keeps it that way to lessen the pain.

To the people at the censorship bureau, the fact that the miserable tanner sought and got relief by turning his face to the left was cause for concern. What could this mean? Why was the pain located on the right? Why the relief on the left? What transparently coded subversive message was Tsegaye trying to convey with his *Joro Deggif* in these uncertain days following a failed coup?

The person who unwittingly passed along troubling details of the play to the censorship bureau was none other than the prompter. It was the so-called *souffler* who blurted it out in a bar one night. He was the one whose job it was to stand in a dark corner of the stage, unseen and unheard by the audience, to cue actors when they failed to recall their lines. Eventually, the prompter had fallen in love with the script and committed every word to memory. Whenever the chance arose, he regaled whoever would lend an ear with portions of the play. But the man seated next to him at a popular bar one night was more attentive than most. He listened to the recital of lines from *Joro Deggif* with undue eagerness bordering on the suspicious even to the befuddled souffler. He then asked a few insistent questions and left. The following day, a messenger was sent to Tsegaye's office to summon him for questioning.

Tsegaye denied harboring seditious motives in placing the tanner's pain on the right; he said he had no leftist-rightist agenda, but his questioner was unconvinced.

"You must think we are stupid if you thought we couldn't see through that," the literary police rebuked Tsegaye.

"That's a mere coincidence, sir, and nothing else," Tsegaye replied. "If it's absolutely necessary, I'll change the details that you find objectionable. I will place the inflammation under his left ear."

The official left Tsegaye's suggestions unanswered; instead, "I have to leave right now. I'm needed at the palace for an urgent matter. Wait for me here," he brusquely told him and left after locking the door from outside. He returned six hours later and released Tsegaye from what turned out to be a short detention, with a warning to "place the swelling on the left."

Tsegaye was relieved, though tired and hungry. He went home to eat and rest and reflect on what had happened. But trouble awaited for him there, too. His wife, Lakech, was livid because he hadn't shown up for lunch at the usual time. He had never done that before without her knowing where he was.

Spousal infidelity was nothing new. It was rife among the educated folk of those days, as if a lesser regard for matrimonial integrity was an inevitable product of their education. Lakech knew of marriages that ended and homes that were broken because the husband, as was often the case, had been involved with someone else. She had no reason to suspect Tsegaye, but as she waited for him while his lunch

Tsegaye Gabre-Medhin (ca. 1965)

sat cold on the table, she couldn't help wondering.

Given the events of the day, Tsegaye had little energy to spare, but Lakech was his wife. He owed her an explanation. The explanation, however, brought her no peace of mind. When he told her where he had been, she began to worry. Could this be the beginning of many more collisions with power in store for her husband? His plays, she knew, increasingly dwelled on matters that the rulers found irksome.

Tsegaye belonged to a group of writers who pioneered socially conscious literature that grappled with questions of a new generation. Most had been educated abroad where they had observed fairer social orders. They had been acquainted with notions of human rights and democracy. When they returned home and saw a yawning gulf between the affluent and powerful on the one hand and the helpless poor on the other, they believed it was their duty, as enlightened Ethiopians, to be the agents of change; to channel their talents and craft to stir awareness. Unlike their predecessors who mostly remained in the good graces of the emperor by writing moralizing pieces and inanely amusing skits, writers like Tsegaye chose to use their voice to shed light on the hidden tales of their land.

Lakech's fear wasn't in vain. The masters of censorship, already incensed by Tsegeaye's earlier plays, took issue with yet another one of his works—*Askeyami Lijagered* (*Ugly Maiden*).

The girl in *Ugly Maiden* is an orphan. Her father is the only parent she has left when the play begins, and he dies before she is old enough to get married. Anxiously, the father summons his bachelor brother to his deathbed in an attempt to arrange a safe future for his daughter. "You are all that she has now. Be like a father to her. Find her a good husband, when the time comes, and she will inherit this house." he says, meaning the fine house from which his body would soon be carried out.

"You have my solemn word," his brother tearfully assures him, and the girl's father dies in peace.

Soon after, the uncle promptly abandons his bachelor's hovel and moves into his dead brother's house where he turns his niece into his slave. She is kept in the confines of her own home where she spends her days laboring for him. She cooks and cleans from dawn to dusk. She scrubs the floor and washes his clothes. She is not allowed to step outdoors for fear that she might attract attention that could lead to some besotted fool sending mediators on his behalf to ask for her hand in marriage. To the uncle, that would mean losing his good fortune, and he is determined to prevent it at any cost. So he keeps her in confinement. Filthy, dejected, and alone, she wastes away her youth baking bread and cooking stew for her uncle.

To the watchful officers of censorship, the slave girl was Ethiopia, and her dead father, they suspected to be Emperor Menilek. This led them to the conclusion that the cruel uncle had to be Haile-Selassie. Tsegaye's message, they divined, was that the emperor had neglected his subjects and hadn't lived up to his responsibility as Menilek's successor.

The harassment was relentless, and it troubled Tsegaye just as much as the audience's praise delighted him. But neither the trouble nor the kudos held lasting sway over him for long as he continued to seek and express his artistic inspiration.

Following subsequent productions of his next plays, *A Mother's Nine Faces*, and an adaptation of Moliére's *Tartouf* which Tsegaye titled *Awonabaj Debtera*, he wrote *Yekermo Sew*.

Chapter 23

COMPARED TO HIS light sketches of various societal ills in his earlier works, *Yekermo Sew* was a broader portrayal of Ethiopian realities. The play depicted the apathy of subservience and the deadly thrill of defiance. By juxtaposing the untamed spirit of the rebel with the docility of the conformist, *Yekermo Sew* was sure to raise eyebrows among the authorities.

Protocol dictated that the play had to be reviewed by *Blatta* Wolde-Giorgis Wolde-Yohannes, the emperor's trusted literary critic, before Tsegaye was given permission to stage it. And while he was waiting for an answer from Blatta, Tsegaye was asked to present a debut performance not at Haile-Selassie I Theatre, but at an entertainment hall in the emperor's palace. The audience, he was told, would include Janhoy himself, as well as princes, princesses and other notable personalities.

Loosely translated as "The Seasoned," *Yekermo Sew* depicts the life of a government clerk, a hardworking man who ekes out a living earning a measly wage that barely feeds and clothes his family: a wife, a son, and his brother, a high-school student. After laboring all day in a dingy back office, he trudges home in the evening where the gloom of his cramped house offers no escape from his wearisome life. His wife toils ceaselessly and tends to their little son. She performs daily miracles to put food on the table. In the couple's shadowy existence, it is the clerk's brother, a quintessence of fiery youth, whose presence is the most conspicuous. He is a hot-blooded young man seething with discontent and full of irreverent talk. His association with student anarchists worries the older brother who keeps nagging him to stay away from the troublemakers. "Those rich kids have someone to bail them out if something happens," he warns him. "You are poor. Who do you have? Nobody! They will break your bones and lock you up in jail, if not worse. They will crush you."

As the play progresses, it becomes apparent that the clerk's wife who had vowed her devotion before God and man to sharing his fate, in sickness and health, for richer or poorer, has had enough of the gloomy life. She had been pondering her fate, her own endless labor to barely stay alive and the bleak future of her malnourished son. Her life is half-wasted, she knows it, but why not spare her son's lot by taking him away from this dismal den of destitution? Why not give him a better chance? Why not jump the doomed ship—her marriage to a weakling of a husband—and seek refuge elsewhere? She is still in good health, and in the afterglow of her fading good looks. She could sell her labor to a well-off bachelor and provide for her son's needs with her wages. She could feed and clothe him. She could send him to school. She knows a certain bachelor who will be happy to take her for a salaried housekeeper. There is just such a man, her husband's own boss who has been to their home a few times. He has eyed her covetously, and said that he was looking for a good housemaid to set his house in order.

She leaves and takes her son with her. Her cruelty devastates the clerk, but he does nothing about it except mope and curse his fate. Years of servile drudgery has endowed him with a bottomless capacity for suffering.

Into this broken home of a lonely clerk and his embittered brother comes their uncle, a sick old man from the country. He used to be a brave soldier in his youth; he had fought against the Italian invaders during the Occupation, but now he is ailing. There are no doctors and hospitals where he lives; a gravely ill man has to get to the city to find treatment. But he is lucky to have a nephew there with a government job. He has no worry about a place to stay; he is offered the young student's bed to sleep in. As for the treatment fee, that's none of his concern either; there is St. Paul's Hospital where, he has been told, a poor farmer like himself can be seen by a doctor for free as long as he submits a written testimonial declaring his poverty. The doctor examines him and prescribes medication, but the poor man can't afford to buy it. So he asks his nephew for help. The clerk is mortified by the request; he rummages through his pockets, turns them inside out. Then twisting in pain, he confesses to the old man that he has no money. "I have nothing to spare," he says in a voice barely audible from under the crushing weight of his shame. Admitting his indigence breaks the dam of his reserve and he weeps bitterly. In the grip of self-pity, he pours out his grief to his uncle. He tells him the truth about his wife's absence. "She left me because I'm poor. She took my son away and went to work as a hired housekeeper for my boss."

As suddenly as it has come, the pain subsides and his old forbearance returns. "I'm sure you're thinking what a saintly soul your nephew is," he smirks, sniffling and wiping away the tears with the back of his hand, "Thank God I haven't forgotten what my mother taught me. I could have done something reckless and ended up in more trouble otherwise. She used to tell me, God rest her soul, that if a stick doesn't bend, it snaps! Do you hear that? That's my mother's wisdom, the magic mantra that saves me from my folly. I have to bend or else I'll snap! It hurts to have my wife abandon me, but at least, my son has a better home now. He'll be well taken care of there. I hear he is attending a fine school, and even has his own tutor at home. He'll have a good life. What do you say, uncle? What do you think? Isn't it better to bend than to snap?"

The uncle hoists himself up on his withered arm and looks at his nephew with infinite pity. "You ask me what I think is better, and I'll tell you," he says. "I think it's better to die than to see your wife sell herself to your boss and take your son away to raise him with a man who is not his father."

Nursing a worsening illness, the uncle had been quietly taking it all in: the noise and clutter of the city, the loneliness and despair in his nephew's home. It had saddened him greatly, and the clerk's pained outburst had struck a chord that warranted a response. "You think we country folk live in filth, ignorance and poverty. There is no worse poverty than this," he says. "Our life is thrice richer. Leave this misery and go back to the land of your forefathers. This is no life for a human being. Go work on the land and build a family there. Go and till the earth; it will nourish your soul," he tells his nephew with his fading breath.

❖ ❖ ❖

At the royal entertainment hall in the palace, Tsegaye guardedly watched Haile-Selassie, wondering what he would think of *Yekermo Sew*. Would he like it or would he not? Would it move or annoy him? Would he read into it something that Tsegaye hadn't meant? And would something about him betray what he felt, or would he keep it masked behind that serene exterior? The emperor sat in the front row as the play began. From an ornately crafted silver tray placed on a small table next to him, he picked pieces of cheese and bread, and nibbled on them.

The play continued with Tsegaye furtively peeking at the emperor in hope of catching him unawares, and often getting distracted by the sight of His Imperial Majesty snacking. He was mesmerized by the way Haile-Selassie transformed the mundane act of feeding into an elaborate act worthy of wonder. He watched his punctilious table manners. The elegance of his gesture as he impaled a lump of cheese on his fork. The graceful economy of his movements as he tore off a piece of bread and put it into his mouth. The slow measured rhythm of his close-lipped chewing. The way he sipped his drink and dabbed at his lips with a napkin, all done with studied finesse. Lost in this sideshow, Tsegaye was taken by complete surprise when, well before the end of the play, Janhoy abruptly rose to his feet. With a sweep of his arms, he gathered his loosely donned lustrous black cape close to him and walked out of the hall. The sudden departure of the most important spectator sucked the wind out of the actors, and they faltered, but Tsegaye signaled for them to continue.

The moment the emperor chose to walk out was when the clerk's brother, having gotten tired of sleeping on the hard floor while his uncle slept in his bed, exploded angrily. "When is he going to leave my bed and go home?" he shouted, and lights were dimmed to signal the end of the scene. When the lights came on seconds later, the emperor had left, followed by other eminent persons who were seated nearby.

What could the young man's words have meant to Haile-Selassie?

The play ended; what was left of the audience mutedly applauded, and Tsegaye stood chatting with lingerers, trying to appear unperturbed but failing. He was more offended than alarmed at Janhoy's dramatic exit, for contempt was contempt whether it came from king or pauper.

Then came the emperor's messenger and Minister of Information, Dr. Minasse Haile, followed by two young attendants, one carrying a bottle swathed in a piece of cloth and another pushing a trolley laden with canapés.

"His Imperial Majesty sends you his congratulations. Here is a bottle of champagne to celebrate your achievement," he said. The cork was popped open, and the bottle's content poured out into slender flutes.

"Was His Majesty displeased with *Yekermo Sew*?" Tsegaye asked.

"The emperor will see the play in its entirety someday soon," answered Dr. Minasse.

Two days later, someone called from the palace and demanded to speak with Tsegaye.

"Are you Tsegaye?" an obnoxious voice asked him when he picked up the phone.

"Yes," he answered.

"Do us a favor for God's sake. Come and collect your army of bedbugs. Rid us of that squalid mattress you left here, okay?" the voice barked and then the line went dead.

For the sake of authenticity, Tsegaye had asked Birhanu, the stage manager, to find an old mattress made of sackcloth stuffed with straw as prop for the dying old man in *Yekermo Sew*. The mattress had been found in one of the shabby homes in the slummy part of town: an old tattered palliasse, the genuine article for a home like the clerk's. And it was properly infested with bedbugs, although Birhanu hadn't noticed that when he had it carried to the palace for the show. The little nocturnal vampires had no difficulty burying themselves inside the straw to hide from daylight and wait for nightfall when the lure of a warm body would rouse them out of their slumber and they would flock to the feast. Nightfall at the palace, however, brought no such promise to the displaced army of bedbugs. Left cold and hungry inside a deserted backroom of the hall, a horde of them poured out of the mattress in search of blood and swarmed into the lushly carpeted hall, to the cleaners' dismay. A reddish brown rustling mass of blood-seeking creatures were seen scurrying over Persian rugs and darting across exquisite upholstery. Bedbugs at the emperor's palace! That was simply scandalous. An abomination! "Track down the source!" the head servitor had ordered, and it didn't take long to identify the culprit: that dirty, dilapidated mattress where the old countryman lay dying and begging his nephew to return to the land.

After considering his dual offense, the vermin he had unwittingly smuggled into the palace and the back-to-the-land message of his play which was open to interpretation by the emperor himself or by one of his close associates, Tsegaye grew anxious. Was he pushing things a bit too far? With his misdeeds and blunders, was he putting himself on a collision course with the might of authority? He wanted to find out, and the best person to see to gauge his predicament, he thought, was the Minister of Information, Dr. Minasse. If the emperor was unhappy with the play, he would let Tsegaye's superior know.

That Minister Minasse had received an earful was apparent from the way he scowled as soon as he saw the author of *Yekermo Sew*. When Tsegaye walked into his office, he gruffly motioned him to take a seat. "Was His Majesty displeased with the play?" Tsegaye asked. The question sounded superfluous even to him, for the answer was already written on Dr. Minasse's face, more eloquent than words. The minister didn't bother to respond. He wasn't going to answer questions; he had a message to deliver, and he was biding his time thinking about how best to word it. But the silence stretched on and Tsegaye became impatient. "Well, what can I do?" he barged in "I can't be what I am not. I write serious plays. I can't write comedy. I'm not a humorist," he said. The scowl lifted from Dr. Minasse's face, and he burst out laughing.

"You a humorist? Hee hee hee heee!" the minster's eyes welled with tears of laughter. "You can make people weep. You can sow discontent by raking muck. But you can't make them laugh. There is no humor in you, Tsegaye. You can't write comedy. You are too bitter for that, man. Comedy! Hee hee hee!"

Then in a surprising twist, a month after *Yekermo Sew* debuted at Haile-Selassie I Theatre, Tsegaye was told that the emperor would attend. He came, and this time, he watched the play to the end.

❖ ❖ ❖

Haile-Selassie loved literature. An avid reader and a critic, he relished good writing and analyzed what he read with the sharp insight of a connoisseur.

Petros Yachin Se'at actors (l) to (r): Tesfaye Gessesse as Graziani; Wogayehu Nigatu as *Abune* Petros; and Haimanot Alemu as *Shum Basha* Abagirsha (Haile Sellassie I Theatre, ca. 1973).

He had been raised with *Negadras* Tessema Eshete, the protégé of the emperor's father Ras Mekonnen. Just a few years older than the young prince, Negadras Tessema was variously talented. He was a vocalist, a musician, a sculptor, a poet, and a court writer. Of all his marvelous gifts, however, it was his passion for the power and beauty of the written word that influenced young Teferi Mekonnen and gave birth to his life-long love affair with good prose and verse. But alas, this childhood friendship, this bond cemented by their shared love for literature, was not meant to last. It would be broken irrevocably when Negadras Tessema sided with Teferi's arch rival and favored the wrong man for the throne. When Emperor Menilek died and both Lij Iyasu and Teferi Mekonnen vied for succession, Negadras Tessema chose to support the doomed contender, Lij Iyasu. And when Lij Iyasu, allegedly having committed various sins heinous in a candidate for the monarchy, was locked away in jail while Ras Teferi Mekonnen became Emperor Haile-Selassie, Negadras Tessema would be cast out of the royal circle. For supporting a rival, he would be regarded as a betrayer and an enemy until the end of his days. Haile-Selassie would keep him at a distance, but he would hold on to his ardor for good literature, the relic of their childhood intimacy.

As much as he savored the joy of reading, however, the emperor seemed intent on keeping close watch on what would be made publicly available to the masses. Good literature, like rare vintage wine, was not meant for common folk, he seemed to think. As the man at the helm, he wanted to be the top judge of what was fit for public consumption and what was not. To that end, the rumor went, he secretly received, for his personal review, a copy of every major work of literature pending publication, while the official censor, Blatta Wolde-Giorgis, held on to his copy and waited for the emperor's verdict.

Tsegaye had been told of Haile-Selassie's secret role and acumen as a literary maven, but had thought little of it until Blatta Wolde-Giorgis mistakenly returned to him a copy of his play, *Petros at the Hour*, which Tsegaye was convinced the emperor had reviewed. Because of Blatta's oversight, he stole a rare glimpse into Janhoy's private thoughts. He read his remarks, scribbled in the margins, in his unmistakable penmanship. Tsegaye saw what the emperor liked and what he disagreed with so vehemently that he had to cross it out with angry strokes of his pen. He read the keen insights and astute commentaries; the questions and exclamations strewn across the pages of the play, and he knew that rumor had it right: Haile-Selassie was an ardent lover of literature and an eagle-eyed reader indeed.

Chapter 24

A WRITER IS HAPPY when his work stirs up in the reader feelings that had surged in him while writing. He exults when his pen has managed to capture in words ideas floating in the ethereal world of his imagination. For a writer like Tsegaye, who had chosen to put his literary calling at the service of his people, the joy ran even deeper. It was a validation of his purpose; a heartening affirmation that he had taken the worthy path.

More than Tsegaye's other plays thus far, *Yekermo Sew* evoked the strongest reaction and caused the most displeasure among the upholders of the status quo. Despite the disparaging reviews from government-owned media and the chilly acknowledgment of his superiors, however, the play had sparked heated debate among intellectuals and brought him the praise of like-minded citizens. By most accounts, *Yekermo Sew* had indeed churned notable waves in the country's hitherto placid literary waters.

Tsegaye would write grander plays that would turn him into a living legend. He would treat his fans and detractors alike to sold-out performances of the milestone works he would write in the 1970s and 1980s. His phenomenal adaptation of Shakespeare's *Othello* had proven, as would his subsequent renditions of *Macbeth*, *Hamlet*, and *King Lear*, that it was indeed possible to make the Anglophone bard speak Amharic. He would experiment with new matrixes and expand linguistic parameters in *Esat Woy Abeba*—*Blaze or Bloom*—a collection of his poems that would be published in 1973. But it was in the aftermath of *Yekermo Sew* that he first came to know the full extent of the writer's delight in a gift well received. The joy was akin to what a parent would feel at beholding signs of his parental gifts blossoming in his children. It was as deeply pleasing as the joy he would feel when, for instance, he learned of his daughter's act of love—a reckless stunt she had pulled off at the risk of her life. He was lying in a hospital bed then, having just awakened from a week-long coma that followed a long spell of what he thought was a virulent cold. The doctors had diagnosed a case of untreated diabetes, but he had come round, thank goodness, and his prognosis was encouraging.

The Black Lion Hospital in Addis Ababa was one of the best in the country in the 1980s. It was well equipped and the doctors were not yet plagued with frustration and discontent. Patients could expect supplies in stock and readily available medicine. Before the disintegration of the health system in following decades, the gravely ill were admitted to clean rooms and received proper treatment. Someone as prominent as Tsegaye would lack for none of the skilled care that money could buy. Yes, the hospital offered quality care in those days, but it remained notoriously inaccessible to visitors. Those were days of military dictatorship when the leaders' paranoia and their mania for control had run amok. Every government institution, be it a bank, a store, or a hospital, was guarded by armed men toting Kalashnikovs. The gatekeepers were given the license to defend their charge by any means, and some among them made ready use of their power by insulting and abusing harmless folk; by roughing them up, threatening to shoot and even shooting to wound or kill. They were called "guardians of the revolution," and they were not held to account even for flagrant abuse of power.

A person needing to enter into a guarded building would have to get permission from someone higher up, or grease the watchman's palm generously. Otherwise it would be entirely up to the guard's whim to let him in or to turn him away. Lakech had chosen to bribe the sentinel. She had paid him to let her slink in with her daughter, Mahlet, who had left school early that day to see her dad. By Lakech's estimate, what she had paid was more than enough to admit two, but the man had his own reckoning.

"I told you, only you can go in. I won't let the girl in," he yelled at her and glowered.

"Please let her come with me. She hasn't seen her father since he was admitted to the hospital. She's been waiting for this day…"

"Don't you understand, lady?" he cut her off. "I can't break the rules for everyone who wants to go in. My job is to do as I am told, and that's that," he said and hustled Mahlet out through the gate. The message was clear: he wanted more money for the girl.

"That's not fair," said Lakech.

"What's fair then, if you don't mind my asking? To leave the gate wide open and let you all walk in and out whenever you feel like it? What do you think this is? A cattle market?"

"You have no pity."

"They don't pay me to feel pity."

"They don't pay you to be so mean either."

"Watch your tongue, woman! You can't insult me for doing my job, okay? Don't push me!" snarled the foul-tempered watchman and tightened his grip on his Kalashnikov.

Tsegaye with his children and other young family members (Addis Ababa, 1970). Back row (l) to (r): Ma'aza Aweke (niece), Estifanos and Hailu Mitiku (step-sons), Tsegaye, Ayenew Mitiku (step-son), and Genet Aweke (niece). Front row (l) to (r): Mahlet and Yodit (daughters), and Abonesh Mekonnen (relative of wife, Lakech).

Lakech opened her purse, pulled out more money, and handed it not to the villain now with specks of eager hope in his eyes, but to her daughter.

"Take a taxi and go home. I'll be there very soon," she said snappily.

Minutes later, in Tsegaye's hospital room, Lakech was busy tending to her husband when the door opened and a grinning Mahlet walked in.

Her mom and dad stared, dumbstruck.

How on earth did she do it? Did she manage to elude the gunman? Or did she stealthily slip in through some backdoor somewhere? Did she slither in through a crack in the wall like a snake, or did she give that scoundrel at the gate the money her mother had given her for taxi fare? Questions, unspoken, streamed out of her parent's eyes and stopped Mahlet in her tracks. "What?" she asked worriedly, attempting to palliate the offense with a smile.

"How did you get in?" Lakech asked.

Mahlet didn't answer right away. She quietly ran to her convalescing father and threw her arms around his neck. He hugged and kissed her back, but he too was anxious to know. Mahlet could no longer keep them guessing.

"I climbed over the wall," she said, and a shocked silence followed. Mahlet's act was deadly and the breach warranted the sternest rebuke. As soon as Lakech got over the shock, she opened her mouth to admonish her daughter, but Tsegaye signaled her to wait. Quietly, he pulled Mahlet and held her close to him. He held her tight and lay still, no less terrified than his wife at what had happened. There was no doubt in their minds what the watchman would have done if he had seen her scaling a wall. He would have fired without a second thought. He would have shot and killed her. He had nothing to fear. His job was to prevent illegal entry—no matter what the method he used, or the age and identity of the trespasser. They would say it was unfortunate, and that the man was only carrying out his duties. The risk Mahlet had taken was immense; she had to be told firmly never to try anything like this ever again. She had to be taught to be afraid of such people.

The thought of his daughter's actions that day would continue to haunt Tsegaye long afterwards and a shiver would run down his back every time he contemplated what could have happened. But for now, he chose to savor the fact that Mahlet had defied the gunman's bullets and scaled a barbed wall to see him.

Chapter 25

HE HAILE-SELASSIE I Prize Trust Award was the Ethiopian equivalent of the Nobel Prize. Established by the emperor for the purpose of encouraging modern learning and rewarding excellence, it was given to those who shone the brightest in the arts and sciences. The prize, a gold medal, was the acme of honors, and came with a hefty sum of money: seven thousand birr. But like most coveted prizes, the award sometimes brought the recipient misery along with its glory.

To be considered for the prize, a writer had to first become a member of the illustrious Ethiopian Writers Association with the blessing of such distinguished veterans as Blatta Wolde-Giorgis Wolde-Yohannes and *Dejazmach* Girmachew Tekle-Hawariyat. Interestingly, not all the important members of the Association were writers. The emperor presided as the patron of the Association and there were a few notables, such as General Diressie Dubale, the security chief, and Abba Habte-Mariam, a highly annointed figure in the Ethiopian Orthodox Church and a loyalist of the monarchy, who wielded as much influence as any legitimate member of the association.

The first ever prize for literature went to Ato Kebede Mikael, a prolific author beloved by the public and adored by the emperor. A year later, another prominent literary figure, *Balambaras* Mahteme-Selassie Wolde-Meskel, was selected. Then in 1966, at the age of 29, Tsegaye became the youngest winner of the prize.

That year, the award ceremony was held in the brightly lit conference hall of the Economic Commission for Africa (ECA) and it was attended by the most glamorous of Ethiopian society. Select artists, writers, and scientists mingled with the power elite, all dressed in formal attire, to honor the winners. It was a grand event that lacked for none of the pomp and glitz befitting a gala attended by the emperor. The band played festive pieces, cameras flashed, and reporters scurried about while guests stood chatting as they waited for the ceremony to begin. There were no surprises; the award committee had not been too discreet it seemed, and word about that year's candidates had already spread. Many knew that Tsegaye had been nominated for the literary award. Behind the forced smiles plastered on the faces of some members of the writer's club, there was simmering umbrage, for there had

Tsegaye is awarded the Haile Sellassie I Prize Trust Award for Amharic Literature (1966).

been a few hopefuls, each older than Tsegaye and no less popular than him, who had hoped to be selected. They were seasoned writers whose works were well known; men with famous pedigrees and lofty connections. And here was a recent arrival on the scene, a no-name from Ambo, about to be crowned as the best in the craft. How unjust! The envy of some of Tsegaye's rivals was so intense that they would bear him ill-will long afterwards and continue to regard him as a usurper who had stolen a title that should have rightly been theirs. On occasion, they would even treat him with open hostility and disdain.

Janhoy handed out the prize and hung gold medals on a parade of jubilant winners as onlookers applauded. The chosen bowed very low to the emperor, and almost as low to the Prime Minister, Aklilu Habte-Wold, who stood next to the sovereign and whispered congratulatory remarks into the ear of each beaming victor. "Congratulations!" he said to Tsegaye. Then getting a bit closer, he added: "Your debt is to the emperor. He made this possible for you. You wouldn't have come this far otherwise. Never forget that," he whispered. Tsegaye smiled and nodded.

Tsegaye converses with Emperor Haile Sellassie while author and minister Kebede Mikael (to Tsegaye's right) looks on. Abdurahman Sherrif, (standing to Tsegaye's left) is painter and former Director of Addis Ababa Fine Arts School (1975-1992). He was Tsegaye's schoolmate at the Commercial School.

At the end of the ceremony, journalists mobbed Tsegaye to ask him a flurry of questions and to take his picture for the papers.

"You are the youngest person to receive the award, Tsegaye. How does that make you feel?"

"Did you expect it?"

"What's your message for young Ethiopians who aspire to become an accomplished writer like you?"

Then a zealous journalist elbowed his way through the noisy throng and asked him: "Is there someone you wish to thank Tsegaye? Someone who has inspired you or played an important role in your literary pursuit?"

Without a second's thought, Tsegaye answered: "Yes, my fifth grade Amharic teacher. Aleqa Me'amir."

Chapter 26

I N 1964, Tsegaye brought his translation of Shakespeare's *Othello* to the stage. The play was an instant success; critics praised it lavishly and theatre lovers came to see it in droves. Tsegaye's masterly rendition of the play and its production with a select cast of actors who reincarnated the British poet's imagination as an Ethiopian reality turned out to be a spellbinding phenomenon so much so that some members of the audience lost their hold on reality and started blurting out fragments of their thoughts and shouting curses at Iago. Outraged men glared at him with clenched teeth and fists while furious women hurled their shoes at him. But there was one member of the audience in particular, a stranger to the make-believe world of theatre, whose outburst rang the loudest. His name was Gabre-Medhin.

Being an important guest of the playwright—his father—Gabre-Medhin was seated just a couple of rows behind even more important guests—Janhoy and his entourage. Haile-Selassie loved *Othello* so much that he had come to see it a second time. As Iago, embodied by the powerful Tesfaye Sahlu, spun his deadly web of malice, lies and deceit, Gabre-Medhin could no longer contain himself. The monster Iago, this hateful villain with an evil heart, was dragging the good man Othello to his destruction. How could any God-fearing person witness such an appalling travesty and remain silent?

Unpreturbed, Iago poured his vicious lie into Othello's ear accusing Desdemona of having slept with Cassio. "Lie with her, on her; what you will," whispered the serpent to gullible Othello. Gabre-Medhin could no longer take it. "When did he say that to you, you viper? Go bring your witness!" he roared, choking with fury. Heads turned and startled eyes stared, but Gabre-Medhin was oblivious to all except the miscreant on the stage, who had now lost his thread of vile thoughts and was looking at Tsegaye with bewildered eyes, mutely begging him to intervene. The actor knew who the raving old man was.

"Don't let this cursed wretch ruin your life. He is lying to you!" bellowed Gabre-Medhin, and Tsegaye quickly rose from his seat to calm his father down. The performance had come to a halt and the audience waited with bated breath as Tsegaye grabbed the old man by the arm and shook him out of his trance. "This is not real, father. It's just a play," he told him in a firm undertone. "Please be quiet and sit down. We'll discuss it later." Gabre-Medhin came to himself and sat down, still furious but subdued. Tsegaye returned to his seat, disbursing apologetic smiles to the audience. The play resumed, but many would later remember that Gabre-Medhin's thunderous eruption had taken the shine out of Tesfaye Sahlu's performance for the remainder of the show that day.

❖ ❖ ❖

After duly savoring *Othello*'s success, Tsegaye began translating yet another of Shakespeare's plays, *Macbeth*, but his plan to stage the work in Amharic was met with stern disapproval. The tale of a king whose dubious ascent to the throne ends in bloody outcome was somewhat suggestive, and attempts were made to persuade him to abandon his idea, first through the medium of his close friend, Richard Pankhurst. A British-born scholar of Ethiopian history, Professor Pankhurst gave Tsegaye the disheartening news that Kebede Mikael had finished translating *Macbeth* into Amharic. Tsegaye had a reputation for stubbornness, but the hope was that once he learned that the emperor's favored author was engaged in the same pursuit, he would be discouraged. But he wasn't. To Pankhurst's remark that a second *Macbeth* in Amharic would be quite superfluous, he replied: "That's even better. We'll have two versions of the play. Better than one." A second emissary was sent to press him to desist, but he refused to yield, and completed the translation. The exasperation he had caused by failing to comply, however, would condemn the script to languish indefinitely at the censorship bureau. Tsegaye's version of *Macbeth* would not be staged for another two years.

It was in those bitter days of disappointment that followed the completion of *Macbeth* and its long confinement that Tsegaye's pen ventured into a new realm of a pan-African content. He wrote a "legend of black peoples" that he called *Oda Oak Oracle*, first in Amharic, and later translated it into English.

Chapter 27

WRITTEN IN VERSE in the style of ancient Grecian plays and published in 1965 by Oxford University Press, *Oda Oak Oracle* tells the story of Goaa, a man "inhabited by the strangers' ways." After being captured by slave-mongers in a small coastal town of east Africa, Goaa and his fellow villagers are chained together and taken aboard "the floating huts" across the sea. In the middle of the voyage, the slave ship is struck by a storm and it sinks, taking down with it all except Goaa, the sole survivor who returns to his village bearing the wisdom of his captors.

The first person that Goaa infects with his foreign wisdom is Shanka, the strongest son of the tribe, for whom the Oracle of the Oda Oak had chosen a bride—Ukutee. Shanka disappoints the Oracle by refusing to consummate the marriage for fear of losing his firstborn, for the Oracle has decreed that Shanka and Ukutee's first child must be sacrificed to appease the ancestral spirits. Emboldened by Goaa's outlandish tales, Shanka disobeys the Oracle. After learning of the secret of the Word from the lips of his friend, he has second thoughts about fulfilling his duty as husband at the price of losing his child. In light of what Goaa has taught him, answering to such a call appears senselessly cruel.

Goaa, Shanka's friend and Ukutee's secret admirer, volunteers to go to the great Oda Oak tree where the Oracle, "the wise interpreter of the voices of the dead" abides, to persuade him with "the weight of his strange wisdom" to absolve Shanka and Ukutee from the obligation of having to kill their firstborn. He tries and fails.

> *"In the sharp stare of the Oracle*
> *I am an object of doubt.*
> *In the eyes of the wise elders.*
> *I am a peril."*

Goaa laments his fate, but he still advises Shanka to overcome his dread of ancestral wrath, which to him is nothing but a nightmare arising from the world of the dead. The truer hell to fear, he counsels his friend, is the bitterness of a neglected woman. He urges Shanka to take Ukutee into his arms, but the thought of what would then follow deters Shanka from embracing the warm body of his bride.

Ukutee too confides in Goaa of her thirst for her husband's affections, and of the pain inflicted on her daily by sharp-tongued women who think she is infertile.

She confides in Goaa:

> *Neither of us sleeps peacefully,*
> *We creep away*
> *From one another*
> *Into the cold wings of darkness.*

Goaa gazes at Ukutee covetously as his words paint the grimness of her fate:

> *Loneliness is*
> *When the ripe fruit fails*
> *To make the bird*
> *Aware of its existence.*

Ukutee is certain that Shanka would never quench her desire as long as the Oracle stands. If she is ever to know the joy of motherhood, she has to lure Goaa, in whose eyes she glimpses a blazing flame of lust. She seizes the moment and tempts him to turn the tempest loose.

> *Would you dare then,*
> *To steal me, even*
> *Against the will of our dead,*
> *Goaa of the strangers' wisdom?*

To which Goaa answers:

> *O the wrath*
> *That must follow!*
> *But I would, woman*
> *I would.*

Nine months later, Ukutee is about to give birth, but Goaa is stricken with remorse. He carries Ukutee to the sacred Oda Oak to ask the Oda-Man to intercede with the ancestors and to beg for mercy. Before the might of the Oracle, Goaa's courage wanes and he blames Ukutee for seducing him into committing a grave sin. He calls:

Awake Old Wise,
Interpreter of heavy winds
Open the trunk
Your holy abode
And smell out the guilty!

In response, the Oda-Man asks the "bygone fathers who see the flutter in the heart of rocks" to speak their will in their language of winds, and he is given the revelation that the man standing before him, Goaa, is possessed by a strange spirit called the Beginning Word. The Oda-Man conveys the message to Goaa:

When the evil ghosts
On the great waves were provoked
And the water rose
Higher than the mountains
And the medicine man
Of the strange ones
Called upon his Beginning Word
You were possessed, Goaa.

Goaa recalls the catastrophe that followed the fateful moment of his possession:

The many, many ceased moaning
The many, many ceased wailing
And the medicine man
Of the strange one ceased calling.

For the guilt of polluting the village with ghosts of strangers, for stealing the bride that was chosen for the strongest son of the tribe, and implanting in her his tainted soul, Goaa's spirit is cursed to live without peace, the Oda-Man interprets. As to the unborn child Ukutee carries, it is "unworthy of life" the Oracle declares.

The ancestors are angry; Shanka has defied their wish and failed to perform his manly deed with Ukutee. Their displeasure has shrouded the sun behind an ominous veil of darkness. Their gnashing teeth thunder over the valley and pesti-

Selamu Bekele as Tewodros, Sophia Yilma as Empress Tewabech, and J. A. Mwanki as Attendant.

lence lurks in the land. The plants are withering in the fields; the cattle are dying, all because of Shanka's guilt. He is responsible for bringing the curse upon his people, and he must pay.

Shanka is taken out of his home by three elders of the village and brought to the Oda Oak to meet his fate. The verdict of the ancestors, according to the Oda-Man, is for the guilty two, Goaa the polluter and Shanka the gullible, to wrestle to the death.

The fight begins; the two fling themselves at each other "like reptiles at midday" while Ukutee's labor pain intensifies, and she moans and shrieks. The deadly combat proceeds as the three elders and the Oda-Man watch. Then Shanka, the strongest son of the tribe, wins the battle by slaying Goaa. He triumphs, but Ukutee has lost her battle. She has given birth to a baby girl but hasn't survived the ordeal.

Being the victor doesn't save Shanka from the fate of an outcast, nor does the blood of Goaa suffice to convince the ancestors to spare the infant. They demand its sacrifice, but Shanka refuses to comply. The play ends as Shanka cradles the wailing orphan in his arms and heads to meet the angry mass of tribesmen creeping ever closer "like a moving forest."

The Oda Oak Oracle was performed in several countries in Africa and Europe. Tsegaye's other plays in English also garnered praise. The English production of *Tewodros* was staged in

A production of *Tewodros* (in English) was directed by Jatinder Verma and staged for the 4th Black Theatre Season at Arts Theatre, London (28 October-21 November, 1987).

The staging of Tsegaye's *Tewodros* (in English) at the University-College of Addis Ababa's newly formed Creative Arts Center in 1963 was deemed a great success. Back row (l) to (r): Dr. Philip Caplan (founder and Director, Creative Arts Center, 1962-64); Tsegaye Debalke (pianist and composer); Halim El-Dabh (ethnomusicologist and founder of Orchestra Ethiopia); and Frances Caplan. Front row: Varkes Nalbandian (son of musician and composer Nerses Nalbandian); Tesfaye Gessese poses as Theodros (he played the role of Messenger): Tsegaye Gabre-Medhin, and Afework Tekle (painter).

May 1963 at the newly opened Creative Arts Center at the University-College of Addis Ababa, founded by Dr. Philip Caplan. An American Fulbright scholar charged with the msision of interesting young students in theatre, Dr. Caplan directed *Tewodros* and drew a team of notable Ethiopian and international musicians and artists to assist in its acclaimed production. *Tewodros* was staged again at the London Arts Theatre in 1987 with a black British cast directed by Jatinder Verma.

Tewodros and *Azmari* were published in the *Ethiopia Observer* in 1967, as was Tsegaye's *Collision of Altars* in London in 1977. This play also drew inspiration from history, exploring the fall of the Axumite Empire of King Kaleb in the sixth century AD. Tsegaye depicts the four main faiths in the powerful Axumite empire whose expansive territory stretched across the Red Sea. As the play unfolds, Christianity, Judaism, Islam and the old religion, the Noble Serpent, are pitted against each other in an epic bid for political and religious dominance.

Chapter 28

N 1961, TANZANIA, the East African country formerly known as Tanganyika, achieved its independence and Julius Nyerere became its president. The occasion, the freedom of an African country from colonial yoke, called for celebration. A date was set for the holiday and several African nations sent representatives to partake in the festivities and deliver congratulatory messages.

The Ethiopian group sent to attend the event in 1964 included Ato Ketema Yifru, the Foreign Minister and the emperor's special envoy, and a cultural group headed by Tsegaye Gabre-Medhin. During an interview in Tanzania, Tsegaye divulged to a journalist that he was a playwright and poet, and that he had begun translating Shakespeare's *Othello*. The interview, published in the country's paper, caught President Nyerere's attention, and he invited the young Ethiopian writer to his home, a sprawling mansion that was formerly the colonial British governor's palace.

President Nyerere's urgent invitation had to do with the fact that he too was a writer, and he had embarked on the daunting task of rendering Shakespeare's *Julius Caesar* into KiSwahili. In time, his efforts would bear fruit and *Julius Kaisari* would appear in print in 1968. But for now, the challenge seemed insurmountable and he sought encouragement and words of advice from a fellow writer wrestling with the same giant.

Those were days of hope for a glorious African future. After plundering the continent's resources and brutalizing its people for decades, colonizing Europeans were finally leaving. The freedom sun was on the rise, and with it came the promise of prosperous days ahead. The ecstasy of liberation intoxicated young and old alike. Orators spoke of a magnificent African renaissance to starry-eyed crowds, and crooners sang of a borderless brotherhood overcoming all ills of Africa. Dancers whirled and leaped in elation to the pulsing rhythm of freedom's drumbeat and poets wrote paeans to the unsung greatness of a bright continent. At the height of idealism before epidemics of corruption, coup d'états, and military dictatorships neutered optimism, it seemed that Africa was on a path to certain glory. Blessed with vastness of land and resources, endowed with an asset of diverse peoples and cultures, braced by the hope and vitality of liberation, guided by the wisdom of

Tsegaye speaks to Sidney Poitier during his visit to Addis Ababa (late 1960s). Also pictured (r-l) are Eshete Hileteworq (Ministry of Information), and Azeb Mebratu, Misrak Tefera, and Wubale Zewde—fans of Poitier.

visionary leaders, the continent, it appeared, was destined to unparalleled greatness.

Léopold Sédar Senghor, president of Senegal, was one such visionary among independent African leaders. A statesman beloved by his people and a prominent cultural theorist, he was also a poet whose superior command of French had earned him a place as the first-ever African member of the Académie Française, the rarefied circle of preeminent authorities of the language. Most significantly, he owed his worldwide renown to his authorship of an ideology that emerged in the 1930s. Together with his intellectual brethren, Aimé Césaire of Martinique and Léon Damas of Guiana, Senghor was founder of a literary and ideological movement known as *negritude*. At a time when colonial powers were expanding their hegemony and trying to assert Western cultural and moral superiority, Senghor and his partners conceived a counter-ideology that called for solidarity among Africans under the banner of a shared black identity. The only way for Africans to resist the insidious attacks of colonial racism, they believed, was to uphold what was theirs. Embracing African values and ways of life was the best defense against the powerful forces of the West. Negritude asserted that the glorified culture of colonizers traced its origin to another civilization that once flourished in Egypt, and later traveled through Greece to Rome before it spread throughout Europe. Africa was thus the cradle of civilization, and Africans should take due credit and pride in the fact.

Tsegaye knew of President Senghor's upright leadership and Africanist voice long before he traveled to Senegal. He had been enthralled by Senghor's vision of African unity and his championship of pan-Africanism in the face of French colonial efforts to undermine African identity. So when Senghor and like-minded leaders planned the First World Festival of Black Arts, a grand festival to celebrate the cultures of Africa to be held in 1966 in Dakar, Tsegaye was excited. Unfortunately though, not all countries were eager to take part in a continental jamboree.

Tsegaye speaks with Nigerian author Chinua Achebe (Addis Ababa, date unknown).

There were a few politicians for whom national identity meant more than what they had in common with the rest of Africa. So, they failed to answer the call. His own Ethiopia, he was mortified to learn, was one of them.

Two years after receiving the invitation, however, the Ethiopian government relented and decided to join the celebration. The change of heart did not come from a belated sense of remorse but from the embarrassing publicity of Ethiopia's disgraceful refusal to participate in the festival. Philip Caplan had quietly posted the unanswered letter on the Arat Kilo campus bulletin board. He was appalled that the invitation had been ignored for so long, and knew that the revelation was sure to cause dismay. As expected, the news sparked outrage. Led by student activists, Berhane-Meskel Redda and Tilahun Gizaw, other students protested until authorities were shamed into reversing course. A committee was quickly created to select the best of the country's cultural heritage, its arts and literature, to present at the festival. While preparations were underway, Tsegaye and Stanislaw Chojnacki, chief librarian and curator of the University-College Museum, were asked to go to Dakar to express Ethiopia's desire to join.

Festival organizers in Dakar had their own pride to preserve. They were not kindly disposed towards a country that needed two long years to make up its mind about celebrating a worthy event. To the two-man delegation from Ethiopia, the organizing committee delivered the bad news: after waiting for a response for two years, it had concluded that Ethiopia was not interested. The official who met

Tsegaye and Chojnacki on behalf of the president told them that it was too late to change plans. "But you are still our honored guests," he added courteously. "Enjoy what Dakar has to offer. We have arranged sightseeing tours for you." If Chojnacki was disappointed, he didn't show it. But Tsegaye was heartbroken. The shame of his government's arrogance and its consequence, exclusion of Ethiopia from an important pan-African celebration, saddened him deeply.

Later that day, while visiting Gorėe Island and the so-called Door of No Return through which captive Africans were shipped to a life of slavery across the Atlantic, Tsegaye wrote a poem entitled *Senegal* and showed it to the official who accompanied them on the tour. The man was moved enough by the poem that he had it translated into French and sent to the editor of Dakar's daily newspaper, *Le Soleil*. The poem was published and quickly came to President Senghor's attention. Then the two messengers from Ethiopia were invited to Senghor's official residence, much to Tsegaye's delight. The chance to meet Senghor, the man he revered, was a rare privilege. And depending on how the meeting went, he might even summon the courage to successfully appeal the committee's decision to the President.

"Vouz-ête bien, Monsieur le Poéte?" the president greeted him when they met the following day. He spoke French, a language with which Tsegaye had a nodding acquaintance, but surprisingly, Mr. Senghor had no trouble understanding him. They conversed cheerfully, the eloquence of their thoughts surmounting the yawning chasm between their mastery of language. Tsegaye brought up a subject dear to Senghor's heart, negritude, and avidly absorbed its philosophy, the tenets and directions of the movement, from the lips of the architect himself. They spoke at length about African cultures and black literature, before turning their attention to their common passion, poetry. At the end of their meeting

Tsegaye and Léopold Sédar Senghor, ca. 1966.

Tsegaye presented Senghor with a copy of his English play, *Oda Oak Oracle*, and just before they parted, raised the topic that had been weighing on his mind all along. He said it was unfortunate that they would have to return empty-handed, and pleaded with the president to intervene.

"I have no authority over the committee's decision," replied Senghor. "I was told that Ethiopia had not responded for a long time. I wish there was something I could do to help, but that is the committee's jurisdiction. It is beyond my power."

Chojnacki cleared his throat dryly to signal to Tsegaye that it was time take their leave. Tsegaye pretended not to notice. "Could you please put us in touch with members of the committee, Your Excellency?" he asked. Senghor quietly pondered the request, "I know the chairman of the committee; he is a good friend," he said. "Unfortunately though, he is in France now. But if you are willing to go to France to talk to him, I can have someone take care of your flight there." Of course Tsegaye would go to France. He would travel to the end of the world if it meant his country's participation would be reconsidered. Without a second's hesitation, he accepted the offer and thanked Senghor.

"That's very kind of you, Mr. President. I am very grateful," he said, grinning joyously.

On their ride back in a chauffeur-driven sedan, Tsegaye was jubilant. He beamed triumphantly, while Chojnacki sat glumly staring through the window. It was clear that something was amiss, but Tsegaye would have to wait until the two were alone to ask.

"I'm not going to France. You'll have to go alone," the professor came out with it as soon as they disembarked.

"Why not?" Tsegaye asked in disbelief.

"Because that's beyond our mandate. We have done what we were asked to do. And I see no need to pursue the matter any further."

"But you realize, don't you, that President Senghor is doing us a great favor. If we don't take the chance, Ethiopia will not participate in the festival. Is that better than making this final effort by going to France? Do you think anyone will care where we go and who we talk to as long as we return home with the good news? We are not even paying for the trip."

Professor Chojnacki was unmoved. "I'm not going; you will have to go by yourself," he said with a determined look on his face.

"Well, I don't care if you are not going, but I'll be damned if I miss the chance," snapped Tsegaye and walked away.

Two days later, Tsegaye flew to Paris and met the director of the festival committee. The man appeared unwilling to bargain, but Tsegaye calmly reasoned with him. He fabricated non-existent remorse on behalf of his government. "The failure to respond was a result of bureaucratic oversight which our government regrets deeply. A case of a inadvertent lapse and nothing else. How could anyone think that Ethiopia would hesitate to take part in an African festival?" The chairman yielded slowly, but he still had to consult with fellow committee members.

In the end, he told Tsegaye that the matter was settled. Ethiopia would be allowed to participate. To make the decision official, he gave him a letter stamped with the seal of the committee. Tsegaye expressed his heartfelt gratitude and left. He was ecstatic! With persistence, he had averted what would have been a shameful exclusion of his country from an African carnival. No one would dare to question his single-handed decision to come all the way to France as long as he had the acceptance letter to show for it. What mattered was that Ethiopia was back on the list! If he had resignedly accepted the first response, he would have had to go back to Addis empty handed. But he had refused to do so, and his protest had earned him a trip to Paris and the chance to convince the decision makers to relent. As a result, he would now return bearing happy tidings. Those who chose him for the mission would receive him with admiration. He would be given a hero's welcome! "Good job, Tsegaye! Thank you for a job well done! Thank you for restoring our pride," they would applaud his efforts.

Chapter 29

THE CONFERENCE HALL at the Ministry of Education was full when Tsegaye entered to submit the letter of admission. The national committee, in charge of selecting and organizing events for the festival, was in session. All the notables were there: artists and writers of renown, as well as top-ranking representatives of cultural institutions. Everyone knew of Tsegaye's trip to France. The committee members were aware of the great lengths he had gone to in order to secure Ethiopia's inclusion, and that didn't sit well with some. How dare the folks in Senegal turn away an Ethiopian delegation? How could they dream of holding a cultural event without Ethiopia, the cultural gem of the continent? Now that Ethiopia had decided to join, shouldn't the organizers have jumped at the chance? And who did Tsegaye think he was flying half way around the world to grovel?

"Hey, Tsegaye! How did the meeting go with President Senghor?" someone jeered.

"Was he impressed with the gift? Your *Oda Oak Oracle*?"

"*Oda Oak Oracle*! A juju story for juju men, hee hee!" sneered a well-known artist.

Some members of the national committee were truly incensed at the fact that the festival organizing nations, recently freed from colonial stranglehold, would have the temerity to give the Ethiopian delegation the cold shoulder despite the much belated response to the invitation. How dare they turn down a request from the brightest star of the show, the flagship of freedom in Africa, the only country in the whole continent to have never been truly colonized?

But there were those others as well, Tsegaye's loudest revilers, who had taken umbrage over another matter. The committee had chosen Tsegaye's *Oda Oak Oracle* to represent Ethiopia's literary heritage at the festival, a fact that had made some of his rivals furious. They had been bemoaning the travesty, fuming what a crying shame it was that this heathenish, outlandish, un-Ethiopian tale of barbaric rituals of blood and sacrifice would be deemed a fitting representative of national literature. His unauthorized trip to Paris presented them with the chance to attack him.

Tsegaye was unaware of the depth of resentment his dual offense had caused. He was stunned by the venom of what he heard and stood rooted to a spot. His eyes mutely searched the somber faces before him for a clue to help make sense of what was taking place, but there was none.

"This is the land of Queen Sheba, lest you have forgotten. We are no bloody savages like the characters in your *Oda Oak Oracle*," went on the eminent artist, the bitterest and most vociferous of his attackers. *Woizero* Mary Tadesse, Vice Minister of Education, knew that a fistfight was imminent. She could feel Tsegaye's bewilderment turning to rage. She could see something wild creeping into his eyes. He was on the brink of exploding unless she got up and pulled him away. She quickly left her seat and seized him by the arm. "Don't do anything stupid, Tsegaye," she told him. "Don't pay attention to this nonsense for God's sake. They are the ones making a fool of themselves," she said and dragged him away. Had it ended then, Tsegaye would have left a wounded man. But one man saw it as his duty to salvage Tsegaye's shattered faith. Gebre-Kristos Desta, a young painter and poet, indignantly rose to his feet.

"What is all this trash talk?" he roared in a voice full of disgust. "Is this a gathering of the country's best minds or a racket in a bar? Can't we be a little more dignified? You were there when we chose Tsegaye's work for the festival. You had your chance to object, but you said nothing. And now this? What a bunch of double-tongued chameleons!"

"Who are you calling a double-tongued chameleon?" shrieked the man who had been making the most disparaging remarks about Tsegaye's play. "Watch yourself, man, or else ..."

"Or else what?"

"I'll bash in your nose!" he shot back. The affront sent Gebre-Kristos lunging at the man, but several people quickly intervened and moved the two apart.

The meeting was adjourned before Tsegaye presented his report, not because of the ugly scene that unfolded but because the person scheduled to preside was unable to attend.

The spite of jealousy was nothing new to Tsegaye. Since becoming a famed poet and playwright, he had garnered as much ill-will and animosity from his rivals as adulation and respect from his fans. Even the extra bitterness that had seeped into the bile after he had won the top prize in literature hadn't escaped his notice. But none of that had prepared him for the brazen attack directed at him at the meeting. How could he have expected such a reward for fulfilling a national errand?

The salve in Gebre-Kristos's words was soothing, but the pain in Tsegaye's guts hadn't subsided as he staggered down the hallway, carrying the bag in which his report lay unread. He shuffled along absently, deaf to the cautious attempts of some sympathetic souls to mollify, until he saw a spectacle that jolted him out of the trance. The same man who minutes earlier had accused Tsegaye of authoring "a juju story for juju men" stood greeting the Senegalese ambassador effusively. "Bienvenue Monsieur l'ambassadeur. C'est un plaîsir de vous voir!" the artist exclaimed as he wrapped up the ambassador in a hug. "What a nice surprise," he said, holding both hands of the "juju man" and grinning with terrifying insincerity. Tsegaye stood still and watched in disbelief. Then he turned, feeling sick to his stomach and headed to the deputy minister's office. The man wanted to see him urgently, he had been told. This was the wrong time to let his fury get the better of him. He had to have his wits about him. But before he could slip away, there came a parting shot from yet another of his attackers, a rival poet and playwright.

"Enough of this juju business, Tsegaye. Stick to writing about our true heritage."

That was it. Tsegaye had reached the limit of his endurance, and there was no one to hold him back this time. No one to reason with him to turn a deaf ear and walk away. He turned around, calmly marched up to the loudmouth who believed that the 1966 Haile-Selassie I Prize Trust Award for literature would have been his had there been no Tsegaye, and slapped him across the face. The man was stunned. Paralyzed by disbelief, he was unable to hit back. It took him a few seconds to realize what had just happened –that Tsegaye, this cheeky upstart, this author of subversive plays and slave stories, this nobody from the backwoods, had the audacity to actually slap *him*, a man of noble birth and connections! And when he finally shook himself out of the stupor and scrambled to salvage his honor, it was too late. Someone stronger than both of them stood in between—Mammo Tessema. "Are you insane, man?" he chided Tsegaye in Oromifa, a mother tongue to both, and took him away. "Don't you know that they are doing this on purpose? They are trying to drag you into the abyss and you are letting them. What's wrong with you?"

Mammo had came to the meeting representing museums for the festival.

The deputy Minister of Education, Dr. Mengesha Gebre-Hiwot, had news for Tsegaye: he had been invited by the cultural minister of Israel for a two-month visit in Tel-Aviv. He broke the news to him with as much air of curt authority as he could muster, but that didn't lessen Tsegaye's bewilderment.

"What is going on in the name of God?" he asked in despair. "I've just been subjected to the most despicable of insults by fellow committee members, and now you are telling me I must go to Israel. What have I done to deserve this?"

Dr. Mengesha would have preferred not to have to explain things. He would have been relieved if Tsegaye had meekly received the order and walked out of the office with bowed head. But Tsegaye wouldn't leave without knowing why. "Could you please tell me what this is all about?" he asked. The deputy hesitated for a moment, then glancing at the closed door and lowering his voice, he said gravely, "I will tell you why, but this must remain between you and me. The emperor is displeased with the subject matter of your play, *Oda Oak Oracle*. He didn't approve of what you did in Senegal, making a present of it to President Senghor. That's what's wrong. And my advice to you is to quietly accept the invitation and go, and let's say no more about it. Good luck, Tsegaye," he said.

So that was it! Someone had gone to the palace and poured poison into the emperor's ear. Someone had told Janhoy that Tsegaye's *Oda Oak Oracle* was grotesquely un-Ethiopian, and that he shouldn't be allowed to sully the country's image with it. They knew this was no joking matter to the emperor. How the world perceived Ethiopia was a matter of paramount importance to him. He was the Conquering Lion of the Tribe of Judah after all, and his reign over an ancient oasis of Christianity surrounded by non-Christians was an abiding source of pride. For Tsegaye to overlook that, to be blinded by his recent love affair with his blackness and to hold his African identity above his Ethiopian heritage was simply inexcusable. His foray into the forbidden subjects of slave-mongering and child sacrifice was a problem that needed address.

If Janhoy had been irked by some of Tsegaye's earlier works, he was now furious. Those other plays that barely concealed his irreverence for the status quo might have been bothersome, but this was a different matter. Tsegaye had now desecrated hallowed ground; he had committed a guilt that warranted penance. The penance to pay would have to be one that would at least open his eyes to the version of Ethiopian history that Haile-Selassie held dearly.

The place of Tsegaye's atonement was chosen with care. Israel was the land of Sheba's pilgrimage where she met King Solomon who fell for her as he did for scores of other women before her, and sired her son Menilek, who would later become the first emperor of Ethiopia, or so went the legend. What better place than that for Tsegaye, to whom it seemed an oak tree was just as worthy an object of worship as a heavenly deity, to learn about his true heritage. He should go to the land of God's chosen people to see the difference. Let his glamorous life of a successful writer be placed on hold while he discovered a more glorious lineage than Shanka and Ukutee. Let him immerse himself in the seemlier history of his ancestors and learn to be proud of it. That was the plan.

Once calm and clearheaded, Tsegaye was grateful to Haile-Selassie for not meting out a worse fate to him. Confinement in Tel-Aviv was not what his accusers had hoped for, he was sure. Considering the gravity of his transgression, the punishment, if one could call it that, was a mere slap on the wrist. It was in fact an act of mercy on the emperor's part.

There was nothing much for Tsegaye to do in Israel. Situated at the Dan Tel-Aviv Hotel, he spent his days visiting numerous cultural centers in the city and counting his blessings. This forced retreat had given him the respite he needed to reflect on his life, to mull over his past, and to ponder his future while translating *Hamlet* in his hotel room at night.

Chapter 30

SEGAYE WAS A 23 year-old student in London when he was made acutely aware of being an African. Not that he didn't know what continent he hailed from till then, but his Ethiopian identity meant much more to him, and he swelled with pride whenever he declared it. Like his compatriots in London, he believed that there were things that set his country apart, such as its ancient history of civilization chronicled in Ethiopic alphabet in centuries old parchment books. Evidence of its art and technology that still stood in Aksum's obelisks and Lalibela's rock-hewn churches. The fascinating diversity of its people and the fantastic profusion of their tongues. The vast expanse of land that was once Abyssinian territory. And most of all, the unity of Ethiopians in times of foreign aggression and their bravery that enabled them to repel formidable armies of invaders. Even in the 1960s, while fellow Africans, future ministers and presidents, held rallies in London demanding the freedom of their countries from colonial occupation, Ethiopia was free. The Italians had repeatedly attempted to occupy the land, but the spirit of their outgunned foes was too indomitable to break. They had failed and left, abandoning all hope of ever reigning over the people of Ethiopia as colonial lords. As a result, Ethiopia remained the only country in Africa to have successfully eluded Europe's colonial design. Yes, that was Ethiopia, the land Tsegaye called home, the source of his pride and swagger. He was an Ethiopian, and wanted to be recognized as such. But as far as the English were concerned, he was an African—just another black man from the dark continent. "Are you African?" they asked him. "Yes, I am Ethiopian," he answered, with emphasis on "Ethiopian," but the distinction meant little to them.

It was somewhat ironic then that Tsegaye, for whom Ethiopianness carried such deep meaning while he was in Europe, would later firmly embrace Africanism and become an enduring voice for African unity.

Tsegaye emerged as a pan-Africanist writer with the publication of *Oda Oak Oracle* in 1965. By creating a literary work that some critics labeled un-Ethiopian, he displeased those who had worked hard to preserve the country's image as a uniquely Judeo-Christian nation situated in a seemingly indistinguishable sea of traditional African religions. The play also became a milestone that signaled the

Tsegaye at Villa Falconieri, which now houses the Centro Europeo dell'Educazione (Frascati, Italy, 1969).

author's coming of age as a transcendent thinker drawn to shared African realities. In light of this transformation as a playwright, his appointment as a member of Ethiopia's delegation for the First World Festival of Black Arts in 1966 was auspicious because it would pave the way for his acquaintance with the founder of the negritude movement, President Senghor of Senegal, and with Cheikh Anta Diop, a towering African intellectual. His friendship with them would add fuel to his Africanist passion, frowned upon back home, and firmly set him on a lifelong quest to prove to the world that Africa was the undisputed genesis of mankind, its arts, and its languages.

At the end of his tenure as Artistic Director of Haile-Selassie I Theatre, Tsegaye began work at Oxford University Press. In 1971 he procured a research grant to study ancient African cultures. His research, anthropological and historical in nature, delved into myths and origins of African peoples, and led him to the conclusion that all Africans were descendants of four original branches: Kama or Ham, Bantu, Chad, and Berber. Of the four, Kama is composed of mixed Kushitic and Semitic ancestry. Kama is also the grandest in that it is the progenitor of the numerous peoples that inhabited northern and eastern Africa, such as the Ethiopians and the black Egyptians of Pharaonic times, the Nubians, the Somalis, the north eastern Kenyans, the Malagasy, and the black Sabeans of south western Arabian Peninsula before it was invaded by Arabs. He explored the notion that the mixed heritage of descendants of Kam or Ham is evident in their skin tone—they are neither as dark-skinned as pure Kushites nor as lighter-skinned as Semites. Among Tsegaye's published research, Art in the life of Ethiopian People and Karmit of Black Egyptian Theatre were presented at Pan-African events in the 1960s.

Tsegaye believed that Ethiopia was the cradle of mankind and its civilization. He saw the unearthing of the oldest known human and hominid fossils in Ethiopia—the 3.5 million-year-old Lucy found in the Afar Region and the 200,000 year-old human skulls discovered in the Omo River—as clear evidence of the fact. He asserted that mankind had spread forth from Ethiopia to the four corners of the earth, a claim that garnered a ringing endorsement through breakthrough findings of DNA studies that appeared in prominent journals of *Science* and *Nature* published in 2008. On February 22 of that year, a Los Angeles Times article entitled "DNA Studies Link Human Migration to Ethiopia" affirmed that "... the pattern of genetic mutations offers evidence that an ancient band of explorers left what is now Ethiopia and went to colonize the rest of the world ... North Africa, the Middle East, Europe, Southern and Central Asia, Australia and its surrounding islands, the Americas and East Asia."

Tsegaye's long poetic essay titled *Footprint of Time*, published in 1984, was an affirmation of his conviction that Ethiopia was the birthplace of humanity. Alberto Tessore's photography accompanies Tsegaye's essay which traces Ethiopian history from prehistoric times of early humanoids and portrays its prominent place in world culture and history.

Like the historian and anthropologist Cheikh Anta Diop, Tsegaye believed that despite superficial differences in physical features such as skin color, facial structure, height, and hair texture, all Africans were descendants of the same family, and he devoted years to exploring this kinship through linguistic clues and shared cultural practices. Like Diop, Tsegaye had no doubt that the inhabitants of ancient Egypt and the authors of its marvelous civilization were black Africans. More forcefully than Diop and almost as vehemently as Martin Bernal in his critically acclaimed book *Black Athena*, Tsegaye argued that the centerpiece of classical Greek culture—theatre—and its paramount subject matter, the mythology of the various gods and the roles they played in shaping human destiny, originated in Africa. He argued that ancient Egypt, a black African civilization, was the source of a Greek literary culture that flourished later.

Tsegaye pointed to the pristine African cultural elements that had survived for millennia despite the recent arrival of non-African gods and ways of life, and noted the striking similarities between them and ancient Grecian culture. The worship of various gods each in its realms of authority—be it rain, sun, harvest or fertility—as well as the roles of rituals and sacrifices as portrayed in Greek tragedies, he maintained, revealed such astonishing resemblance to African realities that the similarity couldn't have been mere coincidence. Even the lyrical rhythm of the Homeric plays, he averred, was evocative of the way the revered village elders of Africa spoke. The discovery of hieroglyphics in the Nile valley depicting the earliest dramatic writings based on the ritual worship of Isis—the black goddess for whom temples were once built in Greece and Rome—was proof to Tsegaye that performances of such plays had taken place on the banks of the Nile since 3,200 B.C. These facts and hypotheses led Tsegaye to the conclusion that the ritualistic worship of black African gods and goddesses and the dramatic representation of the role they played in determining human destiny was an African cultural legacy that predated ancient Greek theatre.

Chapter 31

MORE THAN A decade after General Mengistu Neway tried and failed to depose the king, and paid for the audacity with his life, Haile-Selassie's regime was overthrown in 1974. The ouster was bloodless because this time those who held the guns were at the helm of the coup. Unlike the first attempt when the army took the emperor's side and abandoned the General to his fate, now it was the military that spearheaded the movement to topple the regime.

Mengistu Neway's bold attempt was botched and bloody, but it surely had blazed a dangerous trail to something new. By daring to try to remove the monarch and his autocratic state apparatus, the General had broken a spell; he had taken the taboo out of the notion that forced regime change was possible in Ethiopia. Yes, that treasonous act of 1960 had sown the seeds of doubt in many hearts about the infallibility of Haile-Selassie, and stirred up questions about the fairness of his rule. Students decried the rampant corruption of government officials and the feudalistic land ownership system that had condemned millions of indigent peasants to continue to toil on land that they didn't own. The wretchedness of the landless peasants became their rallying cry; *"Meret larashu!"* they shouted at their protest marches– "Land to the Tiller!" The Ethiopian peasant, the pillar of the country's agriculture-based economy, deserved a better lot, they said. They denounced the status quo for serving the powerful few and allowing them to amass fabulous wealth while commoners languished in poverty. They called for economic and political reforms, and for fairer distribution of resources.

Then came the calamitous drought of 1972/73. Millions went hungry and a quarter million perished. Months of cloudless skies over Wello and Tigray ravaged the badly depleted, rocky farmlands and turned them desolate. The seeds farmers had sown in the fissured fields failed to sprout for lack of water. Starving masses of people abandoned their homes and flocked to nearby towns. Proud country men, with wives and children in tow, wandered in city streets begging for food. In the absence of organized food aid, there was nowhere for them to go. There were no relief sites to hand out food packages and bags of grain. No food dispensaries or soup kitchens to dole out life-saving meals. There was no one to save them from death's ravenous maw; no one to keep the dogged stalker at bay except the generosity of individuals. The severely malnourished who had no strength to beg lay on the sidewalks hugging their knees and waited for the inevitable. For many, death was slow in coming, but it did come in the end. Scores were found dead every morning and townsfolk got used to the sight of truckloads of bodies being carted away to be dumped in mass graves. Even the atrocious spectacle of emaciated infants tugging at the empty bags of their dead mother's breasts ceased to horrify.

How could human misery of such catastrophic proportions occur without the government stepping in to help? How could the world allow such a calamity to take place? Did the affluent nations of the West turn a blind eye when they could have averted the disaster with crumbs from their table? Did they know of the savage famine that was eating men women and children alive in northern Ethiopia?

They didn't.

News of the catastrophe was not allowed to become public, for in the eyes of those who were in charge in the drought-stricken provinces, the colossal misery, the hunger and death of so many, was an ugly blemish, a stain on national pride. It was a shameful stigma better kept out of view at any cost. By some accounts, not even Haile-Selassie himself knew of the devastation that was taking place, and blame was directed at some corrupt officials of Wello and Tigray for keeping it hidden from him. They didn't want to dampen Janhoy's spirits with bad news, it seemed, at a time when preparations had begun for a most lavish party to be held at the palace to mark the emperor's eightieth birthday. Why mar such a joyous event by turning the spotlight to a distressing sideshow of human suffering? There would be time enough for that once the party was over.

The celebration took place as planned, and what a grand affair it was! A banquet to dwarf all the sumptuous banquets the palace had known till then. But the tightly guarded news of the dreadful famine and its ravages leaked out of the country and became headline news around the world. British journalist, Jonathan Dimbleby, smuggled photographs of emaciated corpses and footage of starving children on the brink of death, and the BBC produced a heart-wrenching documentary entitled "The Unknown Famine", which was broadcast by television stations in Europe and North America. People saw the haunting images of little boys and girls, skeletons draped in skin, their eyes staring out of hollow sockets, too weak to move, cry, or even blink. Images of stark hunger that would forever become synonymous with the name of the country itself. The horrifying human misery ignited outrage and spurred the world into action.

By the time Haile-Selassie's government finally turned its attention to the disaster, it was too late. The emperor's seeming indifference and complete ignorance of the tragedy had given powerful impetus to the movement for change. It had emboldened the students, the loudest of the protesters, to call for his ouster. Carrying their accusatory banners and shouting their angry slogans, they paraded through city streets and gave voice to the simmering discontent. Grievances of low pay sprang from various quarters and taxi drivers held a strike over rising fuel prices. But not until the military joined the revolt did things take an ominous turn. Using the excuse of inadequate salaries which the government tried unsuccessfully to resolve by approving a 33 percent raise, the army mutinied and held many commanders hostage, and it became clear to many that a serious insurgency was underway. The unstoppable juggernaut of a revolution was on the move, but there was no one leader guiding it forward. No power had yet assumed the responsibility of charting a new course. The students condemned the system and the underpaid workforce lamented its poverty, but no one knew how the power vacuum would be filled if and when Haile-Selassie's regime was toppled. In the absence of an organized body to assume leadership, the military saw its chance and quickly formed a junta which it christened *Derg*, and chose ten of its boldest members to dethrone the emperor.

On September 12, 1974, a day that ironically ushered in the beginning of a new Ethiopian year, tanks and machinegun-mounted jeeps surrounded the palace as the front men of the Derg, armed with automatic rifles and carrying a piece of paper bearing a decree of the regime's annulment, went to visit Haile-Selassie. The task of informing the emperor of the end of his monarchy had fallen on Major Debela Dinsa, who seemed fearless at the start, but whose knees began to quake when he later found himself confronted by the formidable aura of the eighty-year-old monarch. With a faltering voice, he rattled off the contents of the paper that he held in his trembling hands. The decree charged Janhoy with the crimes of abuse of power and embezzlement of public resources and declared him unfit to be the ruler of the country. To make his humiliation complete, the armed men escorted him out and had him driven away to the place of his confinement not in one of the Rolls-Royce or Mercedes Benz limousines that he was accustomed to, but in an old Volkswagen Beetle that they had arranged for the occasion. Thus came to an inglorious end the glorious reign of His Imperial Majesty Haile-Selassie I, and a seventeen-year reign of terror under the Derg's military dictatorship began.

Chapter 32

TSEGAYE HAD LEFT his position as Artistic Director of Haile-Selassie I Theatre by the time the revolution had begun. Exasperated by a certain individual appointed to oversee activities at the Theatre, he had quit and taken employment at the new Oxford University Press in Addis Ababa.

The man who had made Tsegaye's life at the Theatre miserable was a spy masquerading as manager. As things began to unravel in the waning days of Haile-Selassie's rule, as hostility towards the monarchy proliferated and instances of brazen insubordination became commonplace, the authorities decided to fight back by deploying an army of devoted spies to observe and listen for happenings in the city on their behalf. Especially such places viewed as hotspots of trouble as Haile-Selassie I Theatre were deeply infiltrated and vigilantly watched. The government was well aware of the potential damage that playwrights like Tsegaye could cause if they chose to. Such artists were a self-willed lot; they could easily let themselves be carried away by the swelling tide of unrest and turn their art into incendiary fodder to feed the mutinous frenzy of the herd. Tsegaye was cause for worry; some of his earlier plays had exposed his non-conformist streak.

The so-called manager had little to qualify him for the position. He was assigned to the job by the mere virtue of his unwavering loyalty to his masters and his commitment to being a reliable watchdog. He did what was expected of him, throwing himself wholeheartedly into his duty of prowling after suspicious characters and following the elusive scent trail of treason. He arrived at his office early and spent his days watching, eavesdropping, and asking questions. The trouble was that everyone knew who he was and why he was there. They treated him with barely veiled contempt and left him with no doubt that he was not welcome. But Tsegaye had little patience with the man's meddling and decided to leave. He asked the Information Minister, Ato Getachew Mekasha, for his release, and his request was granted.

In the aftermath of the emperor's deposition, employees of Haile-Selassie I Theatre –renamed the Ethiopian National Theatre—launched their own little coup and ejected the spy. They too had had enough of his incompetent authority and intrusive ubiquity, and they had been biding their time. Their time came when the emperor was dethroned and the man was left stranded in hostile territory. With new hands at the helm, the lion had lost its fearsome tooth overnight, they realized. He had become powerless. They could tell him to leave, and they did. They gathered in protest at the entrance of the Theatre and denied him entry into his office. Performers and administrators joined hands in barring his path, and told him he was no longer welcome in their midst. He acquiesced, wisely.

Emboldened by their success, the employees then decided to rally for yet another prize. After successfully removing the pesky interloper, they wanted Tsegaye to return. The Theatre had lost its way in his absence. So they carried the Ethiopian flag, the green-red-yellow piece of cloth that graced their vociferous rally with a patriotic air, and gathered outside the Ministry of Culture making their demand: "We want Tsegaye back!" they shouted. At other times, whether the minister would choose to give the rowdy men and women an audience or not would depend on his whim. But these were volatile times; a cataclysmic topsy-turvy had put power in the hands of the riffraff. To ignore their request would be ill-advised—even reckless. The minister had to hear their grievances and fulfill their wish. "Tsegaye will return to the Theatre," he informed the crowd and the protestors dispersed triumphantly.

Tsegaye was happy to return to the work he loved and cheerfully went to the Prime Minster's office to accept the official reappointment letter. The former cabinet Minster, Aklilu Habte-Wold, had been removed from office, and Lij Endalkachew Mekonnen had been assigned to the post. Before receiving the letter though, Tsegaye had to fulfill a certain ceremonial procedure—a ludicrously anachronistic ritual—at the new Prime Minister's office where he was met by Abba Habte-Mariam, a close counsel of Emperor Haile-Selassie's and a man held in almost as high regard as the Patriarch of the Orthodox Church. Sitting in the office of the secretary for the Prime Minister, Abba Habte-Mariam greeted Tsegaye, and did what any important member of the clergy would upon meeting a lay person: he took a silver cross out of his pocket and offered it to Tsegaye to kiss.

"Congratulations Tsegaye! The Prime Minster is pleased that you have accepted his request to return to your former position," he said smiling warmly. Then after a brief pause, he quickly recomposed his features, donning the mask of austere dignity to suit the solemnity of the moment. "It will be handed to you once you have sworn the oath of allegiance to the emperor," he said.

"I beg your pardon?" Tsegaye asked wondering if he had heard him right.

"You need to swear allegiance to the emperor before you receive the letter," said Abba Habte-Mariam.

"With all due respect, Father, I can't do that," Tsegaye objected. "I came here because the artists wanted me to return. Besides, Haile-Selassie's government is no longer in charge. How can I swear allegiance to a fading power? I mean no disrespect to you, but you must excuse me, Father," he said and left without the letter.

The following day, the Prime Minister's Trustee, Ato Abeselom, phoned Tsegaye to apologize for the gaffe.

"There was absolutely no need for a pledge of allegiance, Tsegaye. It was a mistake. A blunder. I have the letter of appointment right here with me. I could bring it over to your house if you want," said Abeselom.

"Thank you, but you don't need to do that," answered Tsegaye. "I'll come and pick it up myself."

❖ ❖ ❖

Soon after the popular uprising of 1974, Haile-Selassie's government was confronted by a serious threat to its survival and agreed to revise the constitution. But the revised version of the 1955 constitution didn't go far enough to abate the swelling unrest. That was to be expected since the committee appointed to revise the document included no representatives of the groups that were demanding change. Even the new cabinet was still made up of members of the privileged class; it seemed that the regime had introduced no substantial reforms. And as the government went through the motions of remaking itself, the force at the forefront of the movement for change, the military, created a council that would supposedly work with the government in implementing reform. To the detriment of the weakening monarchy, the Derg had the country's military might under its control; it was now in possession of true power, which it soon began to wield by arresting members of the aristocracy and powerful officials closely associated with the emperor. In trepidation, members of the emperor's inner circle persuaded the age-fuddled ruler to make further concessions. He complied and agreed to release all political prisoners, in addition to allowing the return of political exiles and guaranteeing their safety. But the Derg's demands were endless as they were brazen. The end of Haile-Selassie's forty-year-old-reign was nearing, and all except him saw it looming. The bloodless coup continued to gather speed and the unceremonious end came when Janhoy was quietly taken out of his palace and placed under house arrest.

In the months prior to the demise of the monarchy while the armed force watched impatiently waiting for the slightest misstep by the authorities, the post of prime minster was taken away from Ato Aklilu Habte-Wold and given to a younger successor, Lij Endalkachew Mekonnen. His predecessor, too staunch an ally of Haile-Selassie and firmly set in the old ways of doing governmental business, was seen by the revolutionaries as unfit to hold the high office. Let the youthful Endalkachew take his place and try to placate the belligerent Derg, the thinking went.

Prime Minister Endalkachew Mekonnen came to office determined to set things right by introducing far reaching changes. "I'll do my best to satisfy the people's demands. But I need time. I can't change an old system overnight. I need at least six months to implement meaningful reforms. Give me six months," he earnestly appealed to the masses. His plea for time to make amends for all the things that had gone wrong through decades of autocratic rule, was heard across the country. Knowing that his bid was futile, people felt sorry for Endalkachew. He was cornered prey and it was only a matter of time until the rampaging beast went after his blood. To Tsegaye though, Endalkachew's much publicized and ridiculed request for a spell of six months to perform a miracle became an inspiration for a play based on the unbelievable events leading up to the historic revolution.

Chapter 33

NONE OF THE more than twenty plays that Tsegaye had written prior to 1974 equaled the phenomenal success and daily sold-out performances that graced *Ha Hu Besidist Wor (ABC in Six Months)*. Written in a burst of creative energy in a mere 13 days after Tsegaye's return to the Ethiopian National Theatre, the play was produced by the visionary director, Abate Mekuria, with a stellar cast of actors and actresses, including Wogayehu Nigatu, Tesfaye Sahlu, Awlachew Dejene, Getachew Debalke, Telela Kebede, and Jembere Belay.

Ha Hu Besidist Wor, the first in a series of four plays with *Abugida* (1976), *Melikte Wozader* (1979), and *Mekdim* (1980), to follow in its wake, was a theatrical chronicle of Ethipian history in the late 60s and 70s, a vivid portrayal of the chaotic days of a revolution that was forging ahead to an uncertain destination. It examined the true causes of public discontent that led to the dismantling of the monarchy: the effete incompetence of the ruling class, its inability to adapt to a changing world and its failure to deal with the worsening social ills of the country, the poverty and hunger, the staggering rate of illiteracy, and the gross social injustice. Haile-Selassie's regime was on the wane because it had become hopelessly out of touch. It was on the brink of collapse, but what force would take the reins of government once the monarchy was abolished remained uncertain. Of the various groups angling for power, some appeared to be honest seekers of justice who dreamt of a truly democratic utopia where the people would have a say in the government of their country. There were those as well who sought power for its own sake, the self-aggrandizing wolves who coveted rank and authority for the might and glory that came with it. *Ha Hu Besidist Wor* shed light on them all, and it gave voice to the hope and despair of the people. The pessimists who saw the demise of the emperor's rule as the harbinger of doom and the optimists who welcomed it as the dawn of brighter days had their say in the play. A compelling marriage of Tsegaye's creativity at its best and Abate Mekuria's command of the stage and production, the play was a captivating portrayal of Ethiopia at the crossroads.

Fortunately for Tsegaye, the besieged government was too preoccupied with matters of its own survival to wield the axe of censorship. Unlike his former plays, *Ha Hu Besidist Wor* was left untouched by the emperor's literary police. As for the

Tsegaye with Abate Mekuria in front of a poster advertizing *Melikte Wozader* (translated as "Message of the Proletarian" by Tsegaye). Music by pianist Tefera Abunewold (Addis Ababa City Hall Theatre, ca. 1979).

leaders of the uprising, they were not in complete control yet. They had bigger problems preoccupying them than meddling with artistic freedom. Ironically, they would, in time, prove themselves to be a more virulent enemy of freedom of expression than the imperial government.

The sweet but short-lived freedom that blossomed as the creeping coup gathered speed led many to excess. Shocking speeches were heard on the radio and at mass rallies, and insolent articles were liberally printed in newspapers. For Tsegaye, this absolute freedom brought with it the temptation of indecision regarding the form and content of his play, *Ha Hu Besidist Wor*, which he was unable to resist. With unfettered liberty to write whatever struck his fancy, he kept altering the script—adding and excising, or rewriting portions of it after the actors had completed several sessions of rehearsal. The cast resented this daily evolution of the play, especially the lead actors who had already committed pages of the script to memory through days of hard work. They were disgruntled and bitter, but had to do as they were told because not only was Tsegaye author of the play and manager of the theatre, but he was also the paymaster. The chaotic dismantling of the old bureaucracy had left the National Theatre without an operational budget, and Tsegaye had to depend on box office earnings to pay salaries.

After *Ha Hu Besidist Wor* had become a theatrical phenomenon, Tsegaye collaborated with prominent dramatic artists Wogayehu Nigatu, Haimanot Alemu, and director Abate Mekuria to produce *Atsim Beyegetsu* (*Skeleton on Every Page*). The play, based on Gebre-Kristos Desta's poem *Atsim,* was a vignette of short acts that evoked a damning past jarringly encountering the present.

Following the production of *Ha Hu bebeSidist Wor* and *Atsim Beyegetsu,* a group of pioneer African directors, including Abate, received a grant from UNESCO to produce and direct an African play of their choice. The UNESCO Director General at the time had come across Abate's works while visiting Ethiopia and readily accepted his choice of Tsegaye's *Oda Oak Oracle.* Abate was offered the facilities of Ireland's Abbey Theatre in Dublin, and with a select cast of the theatre's resident professional actors, he began work on the production of the play. Six months later, *Oda Oak Oracle* debuted in Dublin to wide acclaim. The audience enjoyed it immensely and the major newspapers of the city gave it favorable reviews.

Not long after the production of *Oda Oak Oracle,* Abate was offered another opportunity to study at Yale University's School of Drama in 1975, and he returned to Ethiopia in order to take a formal leave of absence from work. Now that he had gained international recognition, the chance to advance his skills at a prestigious university was irresistible. But first he had to get Tsegaye's blessing and formal approval.

Tsegaye was not thrilled by the news. After glancing at the letter of acceptance from Yale and reading Abate's handwritten request to resign from his position, he looked up and said: "You're not going."

"Why not?" asked Abate.

"Because you have work to do. You are the Director of the National Theatre. There's no one to take over your responsibilities."

"But I won't be away for more than a couple of years," replied Abate. "I'll come back as soon as I complete my studies. Besides, the training benefits the theatre just as much as it advances my career."

"I told you; you're not leaving. I'm not going to have my plays mangled by amateurs," said Tsegaye, and to emphasize his point, he tore Abate's letter of resignation and threw the pieces into a dustbin. So that was it; Tsegaye's only worry was that he wouldn't be able to find a person as competent as Abate to direct his plays. The man's dreams and aspirations were of no concern to him. Abate was devastated. The reason Tsegaye gave him for rejecting his request was no less painful than the heartbreak of his dashed hope.

He stormed out of Tsegaye's office angrily and went to see Dr. Aklilu Habte, the Minister of Culture, but Tsegaye, having divined his intent, had called the minister as soon as Abate had left his office, and urged him to decline the request. Dr. Aklilu was gracious enough to hear out Abate's tearful plea, but he refused to give him the release he needed to study abroad. And when Abate became insistent, the minister put an end to the awkward encounter by resorting to the threat of imprisonment for insubordination

Dejected as he was by the outcome, Abate was soon assigned to direct a parallel production of *Ha Hu Besidist Wor* at the City Hall Theatre. The veteran performers at the National Theatre had mastered their parts by then, and Abate was needed to train a younger cast that would tour the country to bring this popular play to the provinces.

❖ ❖ ❖

In 1982, Tsegaye turned his attention to a grand production of Shakespeare's *Hamlet* that he had translated earlier. *Hamlet* had already been staged in 1968, but this later production of the play was going to be magnificent.

Haile-Selassie's government had been done away with by then, and it was widely believed that the emperor had been personally murdered by Mengistu

Haile-Mariam, now occupying the imperial palace as the leader of post-monarchic Ethiopia. With their triumphant ascent to the pinnacle of power, the new rulers had already been possessed by that all too familiar malady of tyrants, relentless paranoia and manic urge for absolute control. Censorship had reared its head once again, more brutal and intolerant than ever before. Tsegaye was aware of the dismal state of personal freedom in the aftermath of the revolution, but he saw no harm in bringing to the people a well-known play written by an English poet of centuries past. It had little bearing on what went on under the totalitarian regime of his country, he thought, and launched a lavish production at the Addis Ababa City Hall Theatre. The play was meant to be a grand

Tsegaye directs the Gravediggers, Jembere Belay (l) and Alemu Gebreab (r) in a production of *Hamlet* (Ethiopian National Theatre, ca. 1982).

dramatic spectacle; preparations had taken a whole year. Tsegaye and Abate had carefully selected the actors; the stage was meticulously designed and rehearsals had been polished to perfection.

Before *Hamlet* was open to the general audience, however, government officials had to approve it and permission had to be granted. The debut performance, attended by invited guests including representatives of authority—the eyes and ears of the Supreme Leader—as well as artists and journalists, was brilliant. The audience watched *Hamlet* spellbound, marveling at Tsegaye's impeccable adaptation of the play and mesmerized by the riveting performance of the actors. They said it was fantastic and expressed their delight with deafening applause. Then came the verdict a few days later: *Hamlet* was not fit for public viewing. No further explanation was given, and it would be reckless of Tsegaye to ask for one. But the reason was obvious to many. In the tale of a scheming power seeker who kills his brother to wear his crown and marry his widow, Mengistu must have suspected a sinister allusion to his own dark deeds on his way to the top. Just as Haile-Selassie was convinced that the character in Tsegaye's *Ugly Girl*—a cruel uncle who enslaves his niece after his brother's death—was meant to portray him, Mengistu Haile-Mariam must have seen his image in Claudius, and that of Halie-Selassie in the dead king of Denmark. Gertrude, of course, was Ethiopia. With memories of the aged emperor he had supposedly asphyxiated to death still fresh on his conscience, the play must have conjured up a likeness too close for comfort. In the imagination of Mengistu, a paranoid dictator, the ghost of a dead emperor exhorting the son to avenge his heinous death may have felt like a disquieting message to loyalists of the fallen regime to rise up and take revenge.

Tsegaye's reckless response to the banning of *Hamlet* was to write an angry comedy, *Ziqegnaw Joro*, a play entirely based on a bantering exchange between two characters: an entertainer at Hager Fikir Theatre and a janitor who cleans the theatre hall after shows. In the play, the entertainer ridicules the janitor as a simpleton who cannot comprehend the high art of theatrical performance. The message wasn't lost on the audience; Tsegaye was baldly insulting as ignoramus those who stood in the way of his play *Hamlet*. "You are unsophisticated. *Hamlet* is beyond your depth," the character tells the janitor. The play, performed only once on the occasion of a convention for professional associations, raised many eyebrows. Within a few days, Tsegaye and Alemtsehai Wodajo, the actress who was instrumental in acquiring permits for the performance of the play during the convention, were both summoned to be censured by irate officials. They were harshly reprimanded. "We are letting you off this once," they told Tsegaye, "but you'd better be careful."

Tsegaye and Abate Mekuria in front of poster advertising *Tewodros*. The cast included Fekadu Tekl-emariam in the lead role, Seyoum Tefera, Abebe Balcha, Kebede Degefu, Getahun Hailu, and others (Addis Ababa City Hall Theatre, ca. 1983-84).

That was the end of *Ziqegnaw Joro*. Tsegaye feigned genuine remorse, but he was secretly happy to have had the chance to vent his fury even just once.

The curse of censorship had bedeviled Tsegaye for much of his life as a poet and playwright. He had resigned himself to the pain of watching his work being dismantled by authorities who never failed to imagine subversive messages lurking inside even the most innocuous of his plays. The emperor's watchdogs, of their own volition or under their master's orders, mutilated most of his plays while banning some of them outright. But even the relentless prying of former days was more lenient in comparison to the military regime's complete stranglehold on artistic freedom. The harshest avatar of censorship under the military regime tolerated nothing that marched out of step or deviated slightly from the official line about the country's state of affairs. And the official line was that thanks to the wisdom and courage of the leader, Mengistu Haile-Mariam, Ethiopia had become an earthly paradise for the working masses. Woe betide the writer, painter, singer, academic, or any imprudent citizen who failed to trumpet the fiction, or worse, dared to tell a different story! Imprisonment, torture, and death were the price to pay.

In a parade of Tsegaye's plays that the new rulers had banned, however, there was one that won favor in the eye of the dictator: *Tewodros.* Mengistu liked it for reasons one could only guess.

Tewodros is the story of Kassa Hailu, later crowned emperor of Ethiopia. Kassa was a shifta—an outlaw—in the early years of his ascent to power. But he was no ordinary shifta; nothing like most outlaws of his time who were feared and hated because they made the lives of ordinary folk miserable by plundering their homes and slaughtering their livestock to feed it to their gangs. Kassa was kind to the inhabitants in regions that he controlled. He ordered his soldiers to treat his

Tsegaye with cast members from *Tewodros:* Daniel Seyoum as the young Alemayehu and Fikirte Desalegn as his mother, Empress Tirunesh.

subjects fairly and even distributed among poor peasants the money and grain he had taken from enemies. People liked him for his benevolence; his humane deeds won him widespread affection and increased his popularity. His following grew rapidly and with a sizeable force under his charge, he was able to easily defeat his rivals and consolidate his power.

Upon his crowning in February 1855, Kassa assumed the throne name Tewodros II. The name was not randomly selected; a prophecy had foretold the coming of an emperor called Tewodros who would rule over a great Ethiopian empire for forty years. Kassa was determined to be that emperor, but alas, in the thirteen years of his reign, Emperor Tewodros would ceaselessly fight a losing battle to realize his vision of unifying and modernizing his country. Vindictive warlords and embittered princelings whom he had defeated and subdued in former years wouldn't leave him in peace. As his army confronted one foe after another in an attempt to quash endless insurgencies, Tewodros became increasingly irritable. Deeply affected as he was by the death of his beloved wife, Empress Tewabech, he had no patience for those who tried to undermine his rule. He lashed out at them mercilessly. As the years went on, the man who had once been liked for his excep-

Saxophonist Getachew Mekuria was part of the *Tewodros* cast at Addis Ababa City Hall Theatre.

tional kindness degenerated into a brutal dictator who resorted to violent ways of punishing his enemies or even those who had crossed him.

In a losing struggle to hold the empire together while fretting over a possible invasion by neighboring Muslim powers, Tewodros realized that he needed assistance if he was to prevail. To that end, he wrote a letter to Britain's Queen Victoria. He was a fellow Christian monarch in dire need of support; she wouldn't deny him his request for expert craftsmen from her land to teach his people the skills of making firearms, he thought. Unfortunately, the letter didn't reach the queen in time. Sent through Captain Charles Cameron, the British Consul in Ethiopia, it was kept hidden. After waiting for two years for a reply that never came, a deeply insulted Tewodros imprisoned Captain Cameron and fellow British citizens living in Ethiopia. In response to the emperor's violation of diplomatic immunity, the British government launched the 1868 Expedition to Abyssinia under the command of Robert Napier. The battle was swift. Tewodros, no longer the popular hero of former days, had more enemies than friends, enemies that were eager to offer their services to the British.

On 10 April 1868, Napier's force defeated the Ethiopian army. When Tewodros understood the predicament he was in, he freed all imprisoned British citizens and committed suicide.

Tsegaye's tale of a farsighted monarch whose noble intentions are thwarted by the perpetual harassment of petty-minded enemies resonated with Colonel Mengistu. And the theatre-loving public that flocked to see *Tewodros* was delighted by the play's sheer lyrical power, its vibrant historicity, and the stellar performance of its cast.

Chapter 34

WHILE TSEGAYE WAS Vice Minister of Culture, he went to the former Soviet Union on an official visit in 1975. Russia, a veteran in the struggle against hostile forces of Western imperialism, had become a dear friend and ally to Ethiopia, an impoverished country on its way to transforming itself into a Marxist-Leninist state upholding the supremacy of the working people. A novice like Ethiopia had much to learn from its experience. Besides, Russia was a military colossus, a mighty big brother in whose protection its puny friend in sub-Saharan Africa felt emboldened enough to revile the U.S. as a blood-sucking monster. Rallying masses shouted anti-American slogans: "Down with Yankee imperialism!" "America is a paper tiger!" they screamed till their voices grew hoarse, and the Kremlin was pleased. It approved of the people's vociferous declaration of their friends and foes. And soon, Ethiopia's determination to forge ahead on the path charted by countries of the Eastern bloc earned it a reward. Tokens of the Soviet Union's solidarity with the people of Ethiopia began arriving: armament to help them fight their enemies—internal and external—came by the shiploads. Ideological ammunition in the form of communist literature translated into the local language inundated the land. Many young Ethiopians went to the Soviet Union on scholarships to be educated at prestigious institutions. High-ranking officials made visits to Moscow to strengthen the bond.

After conducting his official business in Moscow, Tsegaye wanted to meet his fellow countrymen living there. Among the names mentioned to him was that of a young man, Ayalneh Mulatu, held in high regard by the Russians. Ayalneh, he was told, was a brilliant poet and playwright, whose poems regularly appeared in various publications for young readers in the Soviet Union. He even had his own radio show of poetry and literature that aired twice a week.

"He is a bright star, a magnificent poet. We call him Pushkin," Tsegaye's Russian hosts told him, and he asked to be introduced.

Ayalneh and several other Ethiopians were then invited to meet Tsegaye at a lavish dinner reception that the Ethiopian Embassy in Moscow had prepared in his honor. After dinner, guests lounged in comfortable chairs sipping drinks and chatting with the guest of honor. Having been away from his country for six years,

Ayalneh was eager for reliable news from home in the aftermath of the revolution. He listened to Tsegaye's account of the situation, and later when the talk turned to the subject of poetry and literature, he mentioned a play he had recently completed.

"What is it called?" Tsegaye asked him.

"*Esat Sined,*" Ayalneh answered.

The title, which meant Fire Ablaze, didn't tell Tsegaye much about its content.

"I'd like to ask you for big favor, *Gash* Tsegaye," went on Ayalneh. "I'd be very grateful if you would have my play produced at the Ethiopian National Theatre."

The request took Tsegaye by surprise. The young man's audacity riled him. Who did Ayalneh think he was—a nobody as far as Tsegaye was concerned despite the plaudits that the Russians might have piled on him—asking him to stage his mediocre play at the great National Theatre?

"*Hataraw!*" Tsegaye swore, his favorite curse in Oromiffa. The oath sucked the breath out of Ayalneh's lungs. "Where did you get the notion that the National Theatre is a dump yard for plays written by amateurs like you? Do they allow no-name dabblers anywhere near the Bolshoi Theatre here in Moscow?"

Tsegaye's response, callously indignant, humiliated Ayalneh before his Ethiopian and Russian admirers. The Ethiopians spoke Amharic and grasped the full extent of Tsegaye's invective. The Russians could gather from the tone of Tsegaye's voice and Ayalneh's shocked recoil, that he had just been rudely disgraced.

Ayalneh was humiliated. He was furious. He wouldn't let this public insult go unanswered. As spectators watched the showdown in tense silence, he mustered his courage to try to salvage his dignity. He got up from his seat, seething in rage, and stood facing Tsegaye with glaring eyes. "You think you are the reigning king of the Ethiopian National Theatre now. Just give me time. I'll dethrone you one of these days. Mark my words! You'll be ousted. Not one, but ten, twenty of my plays will be performed there!" he vowed, angrily.

An unforeseen crisis was in the making, the observers realized. Tsegaye and Ayalneh could soon be at each other's throats unless someone intervened. But then, to the utter disbelief of all, Tsegaye did something so unexpected that it seemed the two men were acting out a farce, some burlesque in poor taste. He rose from his seat, went over to Ayalneh who stood with clenched fists expecting a fight, gave him a tight bear hug, and kissed him on the cheek.

"Bravo!" he said. You are plucky! You do have a backbone. I respect that. You just told me that your pen is going to outshine mine. And I say: No, it won't! And in our contest for excellence, great works of art will be created. I accept the challenge!"

Ayalneh, a fuming bundle of mounting fury just moments ago, stood motionless with his arms limply hanging down. What was he to make of this sudden about-face?

"Give me the script," Tsegaye said to the dumbfounded Ayalneh.

He took the script as he had promised and had it produced by director Abate Mekuria. *Esat Sined* debuted at the new City Hall Theatre; it became the first play to be staged there, and it was well received by the public.

Before their encounter in Moscow, Ayalneh had met Tsegaye once, long ago. Tsegaye hadn't remembered, but Ayalneh was a student at Addis Ababa University then, working hard to avoid being among those who were sent home for poor performance at the end of every semester. And whenever he had respite from his studies, he sang and played on his harmonica. His friends liked his singing. "You sound just like Tilahun Gessesse," they said to him. Tilahun was the unrivaled king of Ethiopian pop music, and to be compared to him was no small a compliment. After sheepishly savoring the praise, Ayalneh began nursing thoughts of abandoning college education in favor of a singing career. Sweet fantasies of himself crooning to idolizing fans and swooning beauties kept him awake at night. Dreams of fame and glory, and visions of the glamorous life of a pop star, incomparably better than the life that awaited a college graduate, frequented his thoughts, until one day he decided to try his luck by going to the Ethiopian National Theatre for an audition.

Tseagye was writing something in his office when Ayalneh knocked on the door and walked in. As was his wont whenever he was lost in creative reverie, Tsegaye was gesticulating and conversing with himself. With unseeing eyes, he gazed at Ayalneh and came to with a start when Ayalneh cleared his throat.

"I'm here for an audition," said the visitor timidly. "My friends tell me that I have a voice like Tilahun Gessesse's."

"What's your name?" Tsegaye barked at him, visibly annoyed at the intrusion.

"Ayalneh Mulatu."

"Liar! You look like Eskindir Desta."

Eskindir Desta was a prince, a youthful member of the royal family.

Ayalneh stood quietly.

"Are you related to him?"

"No, I'm not."

"Are you sure?"

"I'm sure, sir."

"What do you do?"

"I am a sophomore at Addis Ababa University."

"What else can you do besides singing?"

"I wrote plays when I lived in Gojam."

"What plays? What are they called?"

"One is called *My Wife's Got a Job and She Wants a Divorce*, and the other one is called *Donkey's Meat*."

"So you want to quit writing plays and become a singer?"

"Yes. I'm a good singer. People always tell me so."

"I want to see the plays you have written," Tsegaye said. "Show me your plays."

The following day, Ayalneh brought his handwritten scripts. Tsegaye glanced at them perfunctorily. Then, "Go finish your studies first," he curtly dismissed Ayalneh.

Following the success of *Ha Hu Besidist Wor* (*ABC in Six Months*), Tsegaye then the acting minister of the Ministry of Culture, created what he called the Department of Theatrical Arts within the Ministry. He wanted Ayalneh to head the department and persuaded him to quit his prestigious occupation in Moscow and come to Ethiopia for that purpose.

Upon his return, Ayalneh was dismayed to discover that social and political conditions had degenerated into perilous volatility under the leadership of the new regime. The Derg was officially in charge now, but there was still bloody infighting among its members, which at times resulted in one group accusing another of sabotaging the revolution and calling for its extermination. In the vicious scramble for ultimate power, a handful of parties had sprung up, each claiming to be better suited than the rest to take the helm and lead the country to a communist utopia. There was ebb and flow in the fortunes of each political party; there were times when one of them rose to prominence and it seemed prudent to be in its good graces by joining in or by ingratiating oneself with its members. But soon, another would come to the fore and start a campaign of vilifying its rivals and accusing them of espousing dubious political ideologies. The rivalry was intense. In the minds of the power-hungry legion fighting for supremacy, there was only room for one party. And in time, the party that Mengistu Haile-Mariam belonged to would become the sole ruler.

In these chaotic, bloody days of multi-party strife in the late 1970s before one party stamped out every one of its challengers; imprisoned, tortured, and killed its detractors, and declared itself the only legitimate party with a new name—the Ethiopian Worker's Party—Tsegaye and Ayalneh found themselves caught in the crossfire. As prominent public figures, they had to pledge their political allegiance to a party of their choice. Tsegaye, who had consistently shied away from the trappings of power in the interest of keeping his art unfettered, the man who had repeatedly rebuffed Emperor Haile-Selassie's attempts to rein him in with offers of rank and riches in exchange for his subservience, was in a dire quandary. He had to choose between preserving his independence by refusing to belong to any party and risk being labeled a *mehal-sefari*, an uncommitted individualist straddling the fence—itself a dangerous label that could cost a person his life—or betting on the fortunes of one party by becoming a member.

Having been forced, at the peril of his life, to do something he despised in his heart, Tsegaye had never spoken of his membership to any political party. But some close to him were certain that he had succumbed to the pressure and joined one that had briefly dominated the political

Tsegaye, then Vice Minister of Culture, addresses a crowd assembled to commemmorate Ethiopian victory at the Battle of Adwa (Churchill Road, Addis Ababa, 1975).

scene before being crushed. The victor targeted opposition party members with a vengeance. Tsegaye's life was spared, but he was removed from work.

As it were, throwing in his lot with an ill-fated party, a grievous transgression in its own right, was not Tsegaye's only guilt that condemned him to unemployment and a complete loss of his livelihood. About a year before he was expelled, he had a disagreement with the artists of the National Theatre. The actors and actresses, poorly paid and at the complete mercy of their employers for decades, had decided to take advantage of a promising turn of events. They had demanded permission to form a professional union that would guarantee better wages and give them a say in matters pertaining to the operations of the theatre. Tsegaye, however, was unsympathetic to their cause. He rejected their request, perhaps because he saw the prospect of organized and empowered artists as a threat to his ability to manage the theatre and make decisions with complete independence. When they persisted and threat-ened to cause trouble, Tsegaye took the matter to a higher authority. As a result, eleven performance artists were imprisoned for five months for insubordination.

The jailed artists didn't forget. The wound that Tsegaye had inflicted on them due to his bad judgment clouded by paranoia, was quietly festering. So when the party he was rumored to have joined lost its standing and became a target, the embittered men and women saw their chance for a payback. To make matters even worse for Tsegaye, some of the artists had become members of the party that was on the rise. His fate was sealed, it seemed. The same actors and actresses who had once before publicly rallied for his return to the theatre now marched against him calling him an enemy and demanding that he be hanged. Tsegaye was not hanged, but while he considered himself lucky that he hadn't been taken from his home at night and shot like so many others, a plot was being hatched to lock him up.

In June 1977, Tsegaye and Ayalneh Mulatu were arrested and placed in a prison in Jan Meda. Tsegaye's purported offense was that he had been overheard by a certain employee of the National Theatre slinging his well known expletive, 'hataraw,' at an exalted member of the Derg who had been assigned to manage the Theatre after Tsegaye had left. That was the official charge, but he knew what the true reason was, as did those who authorized his arrest. Ayalneh, on the other hand, had offended members of the Derg with the content of his recent play, *Shatir Beye-ferju*. In it, he had written of a truly democratic Ethiopia that will emerge after the demise of Derg. Naively, he had taken the military regime at its word and believed that the Derg was indeed a transitional power that would in time pass on the reins of government to a publicly elected body, and that its members, all military personnel, would return to their duties in the various sections of the army. He had failed to divine the Derg's true intent of holding onto power for as long as it could. For his audacity in imagining the new Ethiopia without the Derg at the helm, and for the crime of attempting to disseminate so subversive a view through the medium of his play, he was sentenced to languish in a horrible prison.

The prison was tightly packed to the bursting point with members of the Ethiopian People's Revolutionary Party (EPRP), the Derg's mortal foe. Young bright men and women, children of common folk whose parents had paid immense sacrifices to educate, had lately become the brunt of Derg's fury. They had been branded an enemy of the working masses, hunted out of their hideouts throughout the country, and herded into jails where some were subjected to the most gruesome torture before they were shot.

When it became obvious that the leaders of the coup, members of the armed forces, had hijacked the popular revolution and grabbed power with no intention of handing it over to an elected government, the EPRP declared war on them. There was no hope of a peaceful dialogue with Colonel Mengistu and his ilk. They had amply proven their brutality by summarily executing members of the aristocracy. They had exhibited their intolerance to dissent by murdering their own comrades for the guilt of incomplete subservience. The only option left for EPRP to try to wrest power out of the clutches of the Derg was through armed struggle. But thousands of young men and women, brimful of zeal and faith in the righteousness of their cause but scantily armed with a random assortment of woefully outdated weapons were no match for the formidable might of ruthless butchers with the country's military hardware at their disposal. Despite their determination to pay the ultimate sacrifice, despite their breathtaking courage and valiant struggle, the brave men and women, the last of their kind, were crushed beneath the bloody steamroller of the Derg's Red Terror campaign.

On the day Tsegaye and Ayalneh arrived in the prison, the battered men in the crowded prison house, the captured "enemies of socialist Ethiopia" awaiting verdict, were entertaining themselves with a theatrical performance. A large crowd in a dimly lit stuffy room sat raptly watching a play—Tsegaye's *Petros Yachin Se'at* (*Petros at that Hour*)—being performed by a cast of inmates on a cleared patch of floor at one end. The sheer coincidence astonished Tsegaye, and the men's strength of spirit in this godforsaken place in spite of the inevitable nightly knocks on the door and their departure to the torture chamber or the place of their execution, brought tears to his eyes. The prisoners, both actors and spectators, were no less taken aback at the sudden appearance of the playwright before them. Silence reigned for a moment, and was soon followed by thunderous applause and cheers. A welcoming throng mobbed the new arrivals, Tsegaye and Ayalneh.

Over the following three weeks of their confinement at the prison, Ayalneh spent most of his waking hours writing poems on odd bits and pieces of paper and cardboard. Tsegaye, who until then couldn't get through a single day without composing verses or working on a play, avoided pen and paper and whiled away the hours brooding or conversing with fellow inmates. He was heartened to see that even in this den of terror and death, most of the captured foot soldiers of the EPRP remained unbroken. The certainty of their doom hadn't crushed their morale; neither had it rendered them depraved. They were kind to him, the popular poet and playwright in their midst. Their jailers had crammed scores of them into a space meant for a fraction of their number, and they were forced to take turns sleeping. But they gave Tsegaye enough space to sleep whenever he wanted. They even made an exception for him in their rule of arbitrary food distribution. According to the rule, random lots were cast on the parcels of food that family members sent daily, erasing the inequality that prevailed beyond the prison walls. So an inmate whose family had packed a savory meal of buttered lamb stew with injera might end up taking an unappetizing box with barely nourishing content from a destitute kitchen. They allowed Tsegaye to keep whatever came from his home.

The days were relatively uneventful inside the prison, but the nights were filled with terror. While half the prisoners lay down to get a few hours of troubled sleep, their bodies crawling with lice and their heads filled with nightmares of bullets shattering their skulls, the other half would crowd into a corner and await their turn. Then as the night grew old, a loud scrape of a key turning into the keyhole of the large metal door would rouse the sleeping and send chills down the backs of those waiting to lie down. A handful of security officers armed with Uzis and Kalashnikovs would throw open the door and with fingers on triggers, stand barring the path. From a list on a piece of paper, they would call out names. A murderously gloating officer would yell out the names of two, three, four or five inmates whose hour of torment or death had arrived. While those whose names had not been called held their breath and waited, the condemned would get up to follow the miscreants. They would be led to a dungeon where they would be gagged and bound, and the soles of their feet would be beaten with rubber hoses till they split open, or to a street corner where they would be told to lie face down to be shot in the head. Some of those whose names were called quietly followed the predators in resignation, but there were some brave souls—full of defiance to the end—who vilified the brutes and spat in their faces.

Half way through their prison term, Tsegaye and Ayalneh were surprised to see a very young boy of about twelve or thirteen, in battered canvas shoes and faded khaki pants, being brought into the prison. All eyes stared at him in disbelief. He couldn't have been involved in anything that might have threatened the Derg. Desperate as it might have been for recruits in the days of its heavy losses, the EPRP wouldn't be so cruel and reckless as to enlist a child. What could this confused and terrified young boy have done?

The boy, carrying a plastic bag with a few buns of bread in it, found an empty spot on the floor next to Ayalneh and sat. Then turning to Ayalneh, "What have I done? Why did they bring me here?" he asked tearfully.

"What have you done?" Ayalneh asked him back.

"My mother sent me to buy bread. I bought the bread and then on my way home, I saw people causing trouble at the parade. As I stood watching, armed soldiers came. They jumped out of their trucks and began arresting people. I tried to run, but they caught me. Then they brought me here," he said. "What are they going to do with me? My mother doesn't even know where I am."

"They won't do anything to you. You are too young. Tell them what you just told me when they ask you. They'll let you go," said Ayalneh patting his head to calm him down.

When the nightly specters opened the door later that night to haul off their prey, the boy's name was on their list.

"They're going to let me go," he said excitedly, nimbly rising to his feet. He picked up the bag of bread to take it with him, then changed his mind. Overjoyed at the prospect of his ordeal coming to an end, he handed the bag to Ayalneh . "You can have the bread. I'll tell my mom what happened," he said. "She won't mind. She won't be mad at me."

He left following the men and was never heard of again.

Both Tsegaye and Ayalneh were freed three weeks after their arrest. They were told that they had been pardoned, and that they ought to carefully ponder the consequences of their thoughts and actions in the future.

Chapter 35

T SEGAYE REVISED HIS translation of Shakespeare's *Macbeth* and signed a contract in 1998 for the play to be staged at Ras Theatre in Merkato, Addis Ababa. His health had gravely deteriorated by then, but consumed as he was by the relentless pace of his creative work, he was unaware of how ominous his condition had become. Attempts had been made to convince him to go to the U.S., where his daughters lived, to get medical treatment. But he had refused to oblige with the excuse that he was busy with the new production. "I can't walk away from my commitment. I have already signed a contract," he said. Tsegaye was stubborn, even more so in matters of his health. The doctors who examined him had prescribed medication and essential life-style changes, most of which he simply brushed aside. They told him what to eat and what to avoid. They cautioned him to slow down and to get regular check-ups.

As if the fact of his failing health were a minor setback that would remain just that if he paid it no heed, Tsegaye went on refusing to change his ways. He was grateful not to be homebound. He was free to go where he pleased and to frequent his favorite haunts in the city. Writing was his raison d'être. Reading, thinking, imagining and creating. His vision was intact, as were those vital faculties he relied on to give life to the whispers of his muse. Why should he let the malfunction of the less vital organs cow him into submission to the impossible demands of overbearing physicians, and by so doing risk disturbing his placid poet's life? He wouldn't. At least not until the revised *Macbeth* had been brought to the stage and until he had completed writing the new play that he had started. Not until he had put on paper the various poems he had conceived. So as his wife fretted and his daughters desperately tried to convince him to share their concern, he heedlessly carried on with his life until one day someone "tricked" him into surrendering for a thorough medical checkup. The diagnosis was bleak; his condition was dire.

Her name was Tizita Gebru, the woman who persuaded him to follow her into the doctor's office. He first met her in Sweden while attending an event organized by the Ethiopian community in Stockholm. He had been invited to speak and his reading of a series of poems titled "Ethiopianness" had stirred up the audience's patriotic fervor. Tizita, a devoted Ethiopian who had been trying to get Tsegaye's work international recognition, was one of the organizers of the event

Tizita was in Addis Ababa and had met him for coffee. After telling Tsegaye about the progress she had made in directing the attention of some European literary award establishments to his achievements she said she wanted to go to a clinic and he offered to drive her there. When they arrived, she asked him to go in with her. "I'd really like you to get a quick medical exam. Just a routine checkup. I promise it won't take long," she said. Caught unaware, he let himself be cajoled out of the car and into the examining room of a Danish physician with whom Tizita had made prior arrangements for a complete checkup without Tsegaye's knowledge. He was quickly ushered in. The visit was not brief, but the results came soon enough and they were quite alarming. His heart had badly weakened and his kidneys were in severe distress, the doctor said. Nothing short of immediate treatment would save his life. And the kind of treatment Tsegaye needed, added the Danish physician, was not available in Ethiopia. He would have to go to Europe or the United States.

On another front, Tsegaye's wife Lakech, after conferring with her daughters, Yodit, Mahlet and Adey, and her physician cousin, Dr. Negash, had decided that Tsegaye should be seen by the renowned endocrinologist, Dr. Ahmed Reja of Bete Zata Clinic. What he had heard at the Swedish Clinic had finally softened Tsegaye's resolve not to be intimidated by the gloomy pronouncements of those despots in white coats. Without actually saying it, the Scandinavian doctor had made it clear that his days were numbered unless he got immediate treatment. Half believing the verdict and yet hoping for a gentler, more clement outcome that would leave him alone with little or no changes, Tsegaye submitted to the prodding fingers and prying eyes of Dr. Reja. But to his consternation, the second diagnosis was no less disquieting than the first. Tsegaye's health was in grave jeopardy. The doctor was prudent; he divulged the grim news to Lakech but not to Tsegaye. Being a keen reader of faces, Tsegaye had seen the truth in Dr. Reja's eyes. His wife confirmed his suspicion.

"What did he tell you?" he asked her on their way home.

"He said he couldn't believe that you're still on your feet," she answered. She would have said it more discreetly; tactfully, but her husband needed to be jolted out of his defiance and realize the deadly seriousness of his illness.

Tsegaye and Lakech arrived in New York City on a muggy day in July 1998. Their daughters lived in the neighborhood of Washington Heights in Uptown Manhattan. After the grueling fourteen-hour flight, Tsegaye did look sickly and tired, but to his daughters' relief, he didn't seem to be on the brink of death as the doctors in Addis had intimated. He hugged and kissed each of them and told them

Tsegaye shortly before leaving Addis Ababa for medical treatment (October, 1997)
Photo by Wendy Belcher.

he was fine. He warmly greeted those who came to visit him; he even had the energy
to chat and laugh with them. There was no need to rush him to a hospital right away,
it appeared. Let him rest for a few days first, his daughters thought. But the illness
that was quietly lurking thus far reared its head on the fifth day of his arrival. Tsegaye
woke up one night gasping for air, unable to breathe or to call for help. His wife
found him in the throes of a mute struggle, his eyes bulging and his body drenched
in sweat. In panic, she woke her daughters and they rushed him to St. Barnabas
Hospital in the Bronx.

When he regained consciousness, Tsegaye was pleased to see an Ethiopian
among the team of emergency care staff that treated him. Dr. Abdurahman Ahmed,
a nephrologist at St. Barnabas Hospital, was there to reassure him that he was being
well taken care of. There was no imminent danger, he told him, and as gently as he
could, disclosed the truth about his condition. Both his kidneys had failed, and he
would have to undergo dialysis three times a week for the remainder of his life.

Chapter 36

THE DIALYSIS MACHINE is an ingenious medical device intended to save a life when the kidneys are no longer functional. When the twin blood-cleansing organs, each smaller than a fist, abandon their post and give free passage to what the body discards, the unfiltered dross enters the bloodstream and poisons the body. Wondrous as it is for mere bits of flesh to sift through almost 200 liters of blood, separating the wheat from the chaff, day after day, year after year, that alone is not all that the kidneys are good for. They manufacture three types of hormones as well, medical science tells us; hormones that produce red blood cells, regulate blood pressure, and maintain a healthy balance of chemicals in the body. They are miraculous, the kidneys, and their task is herculean. But the invention meant to come to the rescue when they quit their service, the dialysis machine, is good only for purifying blood. The machine is a life-saving medical wonder, complete with various tubes, control devices, signal-light panels and sophisticated filtering, gauging and regulating contraptions. It is a hefty apparatus too, as big as a refrigerator, but alas, it is no match for those small lumps of flesh mostly taken for granted until they fail to function.

Tsegaye acclimatized himself to his treatment with relative ease. With an effort of will that he had mustered when faced with an only choice that brooked no protest, he submitted to the torment of dialysis three times a week; the procedure became an inviolable routine. He got used to heading to St. Barnabas's dialysis center where a Philippina nurse would weigh him, take his blood pressure, and connect him up to the machine. In time, he got accustomed to lying in a cold, whitewashed room and turning his face away from the gruesome sight of needles puncturing the skin and flesh of his arm and tubes draining his blood and pumping it back in. He smiled and nodded at the frivolous chatter of the nurse, small talk meant to take his mind off the ordeal he had to endure for three to four hours. On days that the nurse was less garrulous, Tsegaye watched the overhead television, got something out of his back-pack to read, took a nap or simply immersed himself in thought, interrupted every now and then by the hum and gurgle of the machine and its occasional beeping, signaling to the nurse that there was something amiss. Without betraying the pain of his illness and the anguish of dislocation, he surrendered to his drastically altered

Tsegaye presents his gift of poem during a young family friend's wedding (Long Island City, Spring 2003).

life in New York City and learned to live with the heart-wrenching possibility that he may never go back to the country that he loved above everything else.

To one like Tsegaye, a towering embodiment of all that is preciously Ethiopian, life outside his country would have been out of the question had it not been the only option. Living in a foreign land to combat a merciless illness and submitting to a cruel regimen of medical procedures were devastating concessions that he had to make. Without the comfort of having his family with him and the constant stream of visitors who came from near and far to see him, Tsegaye's twilight years in New York City would have been unbearable. They came to sit and chat with him, to join him for a walk, for a movie, for coffee or dinner. Those who were unable to come and see him called or wrote letters. Even in his moments of solitude, he kept himself occupied by reading, writing, or simply drifting into his private thoughts and meditations, losing himself in an entrancing world of contemplation so intense and engrossing as to lead one to believe that what he had in his head was more real and engaging than what lay before his eyes.

That is not to say he was aloof or withdrawn. Tsegaye wasn't an introvert who would rather be left alone with his quiet musings than communing with those around him. On the contrary, he reveled in company and enjoyed conversing with all types of people. He was a spellbound listener as he was a hypnotizing speaker, and with his gifts of easily connecting with those he had just met, his childlike curiosity, and unflagging attention, he had no trouble charming even the most stolid into sharing their stories with him. But he was as attached to his inner world as he was to the world outside, and being a perennial thinker and a prolific writer, he had moments of inwardness when the sheer intensity of his daydreaming and reverie would leave him oblivious to what went on around him. In a piece titled "Our Father's Daughters" that Yodit and Mahlet wrote for the once popular online magazine Seleda, Mahlet described her dad as having the makings of an "absent minded professor." Recalling memories of Tsegaye in her childhood while he was writing plays or composing verses, she writes "… he reads, hums, and sometimes sings his material aloud." Those who were strangers to his habit, such as a newly hired housemaid, found his soliloquy worrisomely bizarre. People didn't talk to themselves where she came from, and spilling out one's thoughts to no one in particular was a symptom of incipient madness.

When ideas brewed in his thoughts demanded to be captured on paper, Tsegaye would frantically grab at anything to write on. "His writing takes place everywhere and anytime," wrote Yodit. There were days when, driving his children home from school, he would "… reach for any piece of paper at hand to jot down his inspiration of the moment… receipts, the back of business cards, the margins of whatever newspaper or magazine he happens to be reading. The light would turn green, but the car would remain motionless."

Tsegaye's writing didn't abate even while he was fighting a losing battle against the disease away from home. The ravages of diabetes and the toll that dialysis had taken were apparent in his emaciated limbs, his uncertain gait and halting stride, the weariness etched in his brows and the fatigue that compelled him to take long naps. But his will to continue his work remained unbroken. As it became clear to him that his health was in unstoppable decline, he felt he had little time to write, and he wrote incessantly from dawn to dusk. The more aggressive and advanced his illness became, the more doggedly he held on to his most precious possession—his mind—and bravely battled to protect it from the scourge. The flesh has already fallen prey to the enemy, he knew. It had let him down by quickly succumbing to the disease. That to him was an act of betrayal he wouldn't pardon, and so he loosened his hold on his body and became somewhat estranged to it. He still felt its aches and pains, its torment and distress, but he refused to coddle it by wallowing in self-pity or by bemoaning its torment. Tsegaye rarely talked about his illness or indulged in sharing details about his pain. Like a heartbroken parent who would no longer have anything to do with a disowned child, he avoided discussing the havoc diabetes was wreaking on his body. Coming from a culture where it was customary for the sick to dole out detailed accounts of their pain to anyone willing to lend an ear, Tsegaye's

An afternoon in the park - Tsegaye with wife Lakech Bitew, grandson Menelik Bordier, and author Fasil Yitbarek (New York, Fort Tyron Park, 2002).

refusal to complain, even to members of his own family who needed to know, was quite uncommon.

Dr. Adey, Tsegaye's youngest daughter and coincidentally enough a pulmonologist at St. Barnabas Hospital where her father was a patient, recalled occasions when the dialysis nurse inadvertently put excessive blood-thinner to prevent clotting in the graft connecting the vein to the artery in Tsegaye's arm. He would come home with his shirtsleeve soaked in blood, but he would tell no one at home about this. After discovering copious blood stains on his shirt and even on his *gabi*, a cotton blanket that Tsegaye took with him to the clinic for warmth, Lakech began checking his clothes thoroughly whenever he returned from dialysis. "It was as if his body were no longer his," recalls Adey. Let blood flow as though it were water. Let them cut and mangle his flesh; he wouldn't protest, as long as they left his mind alone. And his eyes. But to his grief, his eyes were not immune to the onslaught. As his illness worsened, his eyesight deteriorated at an alarming speed and he despaired. The looming threat to his vision became the only harm to his body that terrified him. "I can't live without my vision," he said, and meant it. He asked his daughters to seek specialists and urged the doctors to save him from blindness. Mercifully though, his eyesight didn't desert him completely. It was impaired, especially during his final years, but it served him to the end.

❖ ❖ ❖

Christmas Eve, 1998. In the cafeteria hall of the dialysis clinic at St. Barnabas Hospital, a holiday celebration is underway. The hospital's staff and dialysis patients are milling around tables laden with food and drink.

Tsegaye has been on dialysis for a few months already. The dialysis center has become a familiar place, and Tsegaye's endearing qualities, his calm dignity, his wit and humor, and even his cheerfulness in an otherwise gloomy setting, has won him the affection of his doctors, his nurses, and fellow patients.

St. Barnabas is in South Bronx, an ethnic and racial potpourri like most other parts of the city. The diversity is evident in the skin tones all around Tsegaye at the holiday party, from lily-white to pitch-dark and every shade in between, and in the Babel of tongues spoken: English, Spanish, Ebonics, Tagalog, Hindi, French, Creole.

Christmas is a day of giving in the U.S., Tsegaye knows, and he has come with a gift for those who care for him at the clinic, and for his comrades-in-suffering, the victims of kidney disease. But his gift is unusual; not something bought in a store, put in a box, wrapped in colorful paper and tied with a ribbon. What he has brought for the folks at the holiday gathering is a gift of words, verses he has sat composing in the wee hours the night before—a poem titled 'Dialysis'.

There are close to a hundred revelers in the hall, as many in wheelchairs as those standing on their feet. Most of the patients, being severely ill, are downcast on most days, but the holiday atmosphere has lightened their spirits today. Their faces are brighter and there are twinkles in their eyes.

As Tsegaye rises to read his poem, the clamor in the hall abates briefly, and gives way to the subdued buzz and murmur, the clinking of glasses and silverware, and the creaks and groans of wheelchairs.

"Happy Holidays Ivan, Cecil, Sandra, Annette, Luz, Celi, Anna, Selza, Judy, Alena, Elena, Joseph, Gladys, Al, Malcolm, Stephen, Christina," reads Tsegaye from the paper in his hands, names of the hospital staff he has come to know over the past months. A warm smile breaks on the face of each person whose name he calls. "The doctors, the nurses, the dieticians, the social workers, the guards, the receptionists, the ambulance chauffeurs, and all my fellow patients. Happy Holidays to you all!"

"Happy holidays to you, too!" various voices chime in.

"I come from the land of the beginning of all mankind in Africa. In fact, in some sense, we are all extensions of Mother Africa," he says. Some smile faintly, and others nod in agreement. "The name Africa was first coined by our mutual ancestors about eight thousand years ago from *Afa*, meaning Earth and all that dwells on Earth. *Ra*, meaning the Sun King, for kings were the children of the Sun. And *Ka*, which means God. Afa-Ra-Ka, therefore, means Land of the Sun King and God.

Then the Europeans came recently and distorted the name Afaraka into Africa, since they are in the habit of mispronouncing names which they find hard to leave alone." Tsegaye looks up briefly and glances at the faces before him, some blank and others smiling politely, while in the farther end of the hall, the commotion around the food table has resumed.

"I don't write in English. I think in Ethiopian and write in Ethiopian. But sometimes I try to translate into English a poem or a play I thought out in Ethiopian. This is what I tried to do with this poem: Dialysis."

He begins.

"In the wasted eyes of an old black alien poet like me
It is only through the infinite mercy of God
That one would emerge from the ancient depths of Africa
Floating like a toy ship lost in endless space
To land on the glowing wings of Saint Barnabas's emergency
To rediscover the healing touch of miracle
And to marvel in the dead of night that was not dead at all!
Here, where the lights inside were suddenly more brilliant than those outside,
Where the shining coats stretch out their tenderest hands,
Where the "nightingales" on their endless wings,
With unflagging patience, gifted fingers, and inner insights
Mend our open wounds, recycle our bloods, restore our lives
That even I who came to die may also live again..."

Tsegaye goes on reading his poem calmly, raising his voice above the swelling din. The fleeting interest that had hushed his audience at the start begins to dissipate as hurried doctors and nurses briskly walk in and out of the hall to attend to their duties. Noise and clatter return as some are lured back to the irresistible glut of free food and drinks. They like the idea; it is beautiful. It is touching: an elderly African patient—a poet—presenting a gift he has brought for all, a poem about dialysis. But to most people in the hall, many of whom are terribly sick, Tsegaye's words, lovely as they sound despite his accent that at times makes it hard for them to make out what he is saying, neither spark a poetic flame in their souls nor soothe the ache of their flesh. Partaking in the holiday feast on a Christmas Eve that could very well be their last is what they are here for. They would rather eat, drink, chatter, laugh, and try their best to be merry.

Chapter 37

TSEGAYE WAS A playwright, a director, an anthropologist, etymologist and an Africanist. But he was a poet more than anything else. He lived poetry and saw the world around him through poetic lenses. He saw poetic moments even in the most mundane of occasions and found inspiration in the most ordinary of events. He composed verses mentally or on paper whenever he got the chance. In poetry, he expressed his deepest feelings and private thoughts.

When Tsegaye published a collection of his poems that he called *Isat Woy Abeba—Blaze or Bloom*—in 1973, those who read it had no doubt that Amharic poetry had risen to new heights. Poetry has always been an integral part of self-expression in Ethiopia. The literary landscape was not barren, but it was littered with mediocrity. Shallow verses, cute couplets and silly doggerels abounded. But the breadth and depth of Tsegaye's poems in *Isat Woy Abeba* illuminated new possibilities. His poems pioneered a new form and caliber and astonishingly, Amharic was not even the poet's native tongue.

Rhymes had always been a deeply cherished means of expression to Ethiopians. The folklore was awash with them; the moralistic allegories, the devotional hymns, the popular ballads and love songs, the battlefield rallying cries and the elegies to war heroes, all testified to the fact. Despite this age-old tradition of verses and rhymes, however, Amharic poetry's pace of development had remained glacial. That is not to say there had not been occasional flashes of brilliance, but they were few and far between until Tsegaye, at age 37, burst onto the scene with a collection of fifty two poems.

What made *Isat Woy Abeba* an outstanding achievement? What qualities set it apart from other poems that had come before it? Well, for one thing, the wide variety of subject matter the poems delved into was something new. At a time when conventional poetry seldom ventured beyond clichéd themes, Tsegaye's foray into untrodden paths of poetic thought and imagination was thrilling as it was refreshing.

The first poem titled 'To a Brother Whom I've Never Encountered' is a seven-page tour-de-force of soul-searching and self-reproach. It deplores the abysmal gulf that separates elite city-dwellers from their impoverished, unlettered brethren in rural Ethiopia, members of the various ethnicities in the country commonly regarded as inferior. It is a lamentation of the alienation that has rendered the urbanite callously indifferent to his underprivileged countrymen. It is a poignant exposé of the estrangement that has sown mistrust and resentment in the hearts of the impoverished farmer, the nomad, and the herdsman. Despite the noisy lip service paid to glorifying the beauty of ethnic diversity; despite the colorful images depicting the exotic looks and attires of indigenous folks adorning magazine pages and postcards, the wall of segregation dividing ethnic minorities from their exalted compatriots remained intact. The poem, written in first person, is self-accusatory, but blame is obviously shared by all members of Tsegaye's social class.

In 'Merkato', a poem about the open-air market in Addis Ababa, Tsegaye shares his fascination with the perpetual hustle and bustle, the daily chaotic trading and polyglottic haggling, the lies, hoodwinking, pickpocketing, the row and scuffle and all the hurly-burly that takes place there. Tsegaye's keen imagination and his gift for words join forces to paint such vivid images of the popular market that one almost feels the shoving and jostling of Merkato's restless crowd; one almost hears the clamor and smells the mélange of odors that pervade the market.

The pain and remorse of unconfessed love are the subject of another poem: 'Love's Regret'. A mature, sober man ruefully recalls the narcissistic pride and vanity of his youth that had held him back from revealing his true feelings to his beloved. Years later, with the smoldering ember of unrequited love weakly glowing in his heart, thoughts of his foolish conceit come to haunt him. He assesses the price he has paid for spurning the love of a woman he secretly adored.

Tsegaye was just nearing middle age when he wrote *Isat Woy Abeba*, yet his poem, 'Enough', is a stirring meditation on the profound weariness, the debilitating exhaustion that comes with old age. A tired old man worn by the daily grind of life is now at the end of his tether and passes the baton on to a younger runner and retires to calmly await the end.

There are also historical poems in *Isat Woy Abeba*, such as 'Metemma in Dreams', 'Maichew', 'Lamentations of Petros', and 'Adwa' where Tsegaye pays homage to heroic Ethiopians who fought invaders, the Italians and the British, and paid with their life and blood to preserve their country's sovereignty.

Like in most of his plays, the subjects of some of Tsegaye's poems emanate from his hypersensitivity to the ugly realities of his society and from his precocious awareness of them since his early youth. For instance, in his poem titled 'Who is What?', he poses a clear-eyed question about who really ought to be called a prostitute: the wretched pauper of a woman compelled to sell her body out of desperation, or the dirty lecher of a husband who leaves his wife behind and slinks into a brothel to sully the sanctity of marriage? At the time that Tsegaye came of age as a mature poet and playwright in the late sixties, philandering with prostitutes was commonplace among the elite. Nightly visits to Wube Berha, a warren of brothels between Piazza and Arat Kilo, had become fashionable. Prominent gentlemen flocked there to swill high-priced alcohol and to dance to western music, and as the night grew old, to take their pick of women and to escort them to bed for a fee. And yet, in the broad daylight of sham decency and sanctimony, it was not the man, the unrepentant profligate, who had to bear the brunt of societal resentment and denunciation, but the woman he had paid to scratch his carnal itch. They called her a prostitute, a whore, a loose, fallen woman who should be chased out of town for luring respectable men into her den of depravity and for ruining happy marriages. Tsegaye's 'Who is What?', a poem written in the voice of the prostitute, is a rebuke reminiscent of Christ's challenge to a mob clamoring to stone an adulteress to death: *Let he who is without sin cast the first stone.*

Tsegaye's poetic material is diverse. In *Isat Woy Abeba*, there are recollections of memorable places in Ethiopia that the poet had visited, places that had left lasting impressions on him. Poems such as 'Harar', 'Dire Dawa', and 'Asmara', named after the burgeoning cities that had once captured his imagination, recreate the unique dynamics and defining features of these cities. His poem 'Abbay' is a paean to the prominent place the that Nile River has always had in the civilizations of north-eastern Africa, and of ancient Egypt and Ethiopia in particular. It is a tribute to the Nile's constant bounty and life-nourishing indispensability. In 'Ankober', Tsegaye marvels at the giddying altitude of the old town and its perpetual shroud of fog. He recalls its bygone glory as the seat of government power before losing the status to Addis Ababa. In his poem, 'Goal', he conjures up the mad passion that a soccer game inside a stadium turns loose. He depicts the electric tension and impending melee, the cursing, shouting, howling, and fist fight, the racket and stampede that are a hallmark of the game. In 'Let Death too Perish', Tsegaye imagines mourners turning a funeral procession into a carnival. He pictures the bereaved denying death its due by withholding tears and sorrow, and lifting their voices in song. They ululate in jubilation instead as they bury death itself along with the deceased. Pallbearers dance on death's grave to stop it from rearing its head again.

The heartbreak of watching his beloved aunt, Adde Argaatu, growing ever fuddled and decrepit is the subject of 'Adde Adaye', while in another poem, 'Let's Commune in Silence', he pictures a blissful escape away from the hectic rush of everyday life to a quiet place where he and his beloved, accompanied by the serenely eloquent beauty of nature, will have no need for words. In his poem, 'Back to the Summit at Nightfall', Tsegaye ponders the insatiability of red-hot infatuation. A besotted lover, lusting for the body of his beloved, climbs to the top of a hill at night to meet her. He quenches his desire and returns home only to realize that the hunger has returned the following night, more intense and unbearable. He has become an addict to the wild joy, the intoxicating ecstasy that sweeps through him when he holds her in his arms. His days are spent in eager anticipation of the nightly tryst with his lover who dwells on top of a hill. Yet a closer reading of the poem suggests a different kind of rendezvous, one of the poet's daily pilgrimage to the goddess of his muse. It hints at his flight on the wings of imagination to the summit of his artistic abilities where he basks in the rapture of creation. It evokes the joy that surges inside him when he manages to capture in words the fleeting flashes of inspiration and renders them tangible. Tsegaye was at the peak of his creative years then, and like the smitten lover who couldn't get enough of his mistress's body, each conceived and realized poetic challenge seemed to intensify his hunger for more of the thrill.

More than the variety of themes in *Isat Woy Abeba*, it was the unfettered eloquence of Tsegaye's language, the sheer brilliance in choice of words and the masterful way that he wove them together that enthralled readers. *Isat Woy Abeba* had none of the blemishes –unfinished thoughts and lackluster diction, cramped vision and constipated delivery—that marred most poems of its time. Tsegaye searched far and wide to capture just the right word, just the apt phrasing and seamless rhyming, and proved to skeptics that like other "more developed" languages elsewhere, Amharic too was rich enough, versatile enough, beautiful and elegant enough to allow one to create poetry that transfixed.

Tsegaye wrote poems in English as well, over eighty of them throughout his productive life, but unlike his Amharic poems, those he wrote in English were somewhat less visceral. They lacked the striking originality and impeccable beauty of his Amharic poetry. "I think in Amharic and write in Amharic," he said. In fact, some of his English poems were translations of Amharic versions. Amharic was the language he was marvelously versed in. Thinking in Amharic, he rose higher, probed deeper, and created beautiful verses. Yet, he had penned some English poems that had received wide acclaim, such as his 'OAU Anthem' chosen to be the Anthem of the Organization of African Union, and 'Esop', which was selected by the United Poet Laureates International during its 15th Congress of World Poets. Tsegaye was invited to take part in the event which took place between July 21 and 25, 1997 at Buckinghamshire, England, but he was unable to travel. In his absence, he was awarded the 1997 Honorable Poets Laureate Golden Laurel Award given by the Congress of World Poets and United Poets Laureate International. In its communiqué documenting the invitation and regretting Tsegaye's inability to attend, the Congress wrote:

Tsegaye addresses the United Nations in New York (June, 1991).

"Although Poet Laureate Tsegaye's doctors didn't as yet encourage him to make a long journey due to a recent fracture in his leg, President Ronald Shafer of the Congress has assured him that his poem, "Esop" (an epic on the life of the black Greek poet—philosopher of Ethiopian origin) and his paper entitled "Poetry Conquered Darkness and the World was Saved" shall be presented at the Congress. The President has also assured Tsegaye that, as it had earlier done during the 12th session, the Congress shall also this time very kindly observe a silent prayer for the peace of Ethiopia at the opening of its session."

Tsegaye continued to write poetry until his last days, and most written in his final year in New York dwelt on a matter uppermost in his thoughts: the fate of his country under the leadership of EPRDF, the regime that has been in power since ousting the military dictatorship in 1991.

Chapter 38

THE FORCE THAT overthrew the military government of Ethiopia, the Tigrean People's Liberation Front (TPLF), started out as a small group of guerilla fighters. Its members were of Tigrean ethnicity, and its name implied that the movement's apparent object seemed to be liberating the people of Tigray, one of the fourteen provinces of pre-1991 Ethiopia, from the atrocious rule of the military government under Mengistu Haile-Mariam. In the early years of Colonel Mengistu's rule, the TPLF's armed struggle against Ethiopia's formidable war machine—the second largest army in sub-Saharan Africa—seemed hopelessly ambitious. But as the ponderously bloated, ill-managed Ethiopian army was thrust into one bloody war after another, troop morale dwindled and opposing TPLF and EPLF (Eritrean People's Liberation Front) forces grew into formidable enemies to contend with. To make matters worse, some of those entrusted with engineering the strike against the rebels proved to be inept as well as corrupt, weaknesses the insurgents were quick to exploit. As losses mounted, the army resorted to brutal measures of bombing villages and indiscriminately killing civilians. The government even went as far as denying international food aid to the drought-stricken parts of Tigray, home of the rebels. But none of these attempts could stop the tide from rising. Quixotic as it had seemed for a small group of TPLF insurgents to try to wrest power from a military colossus, the uprising, initially viewed as a minor annoyance, eventually became a potent force that overthrew Mengistu's regime in 1991.

In the aftermath of the TPLF's triumphant march to the capital, other opposition forces joined its ranks. Now that the military dictatorship was ousted, its foes had gathered to take their share of the prize. The TPLF, by far the strongest force of all, christened this coalition the Ethiopian People's Revolutionary Democratic Front (EPRDF). Soon after seizing control of power in May 1991, the TPLF-dominated EPRDF organized a national conference to establish a transitional government and invited representatives of various ethnic groups to attend. The leader of the TPLF, Meles Zenawi, was declared president of the coalition. At the conference, a charter was produced marking a new division of political power, and later, the country's provinces were redrawn along ethnic lines.

Tsegaye meets with Prof. Taye Woldesemayat (former Chairman, Ethiopian Teachers Association) and Kefyalew Mamo, (former President, Ethiopian Free Journalists Association), 1996.

TPLF's political tendencies alarmed Tsegaye as it did many like-minded Ethiopians. Its conferring of the right of secession to any ethnic group that sought it, Tsegaye saw as a perilous move that could cause serious problems in the future. Its endorsement of Eritrea's independence from Ethiopia, he took for reckless sundering of one people and a consignment of Ethiopia into landlocked poverty.

In 1990, Tsegaye wrote *Ha Hu Woyim Pe Pu* (*ABC or XYZ*), a sequel to his popular post-revolution plays *Ha Hu Besidist Wor, Abugida Qeyiso, Melikte Wozader,* and *Mekdim*. *Ha Hu Woyim Pe Pu* recounts the story of two brothers born in the early years of the Derg period. One of them, representing the force that triumphed over Mengistu's regime, comes to the capital as a conqueror from the north. The other, a city-bred political broker, owns a tourist-entertainment business in Addis Ababa with a nightly show featuring three folk dancers reminiscent of the three witches in Shakespeare's *Macbeth*. Trained by him to mock and ridicule the political conflicts that have caused a rift between him and his brother, the dancers lament the end of peace and harmonious existence. Their songs are ritual tragic songs foreshadowing discord and mutual destruction. The play embodied timely issues that preoccupied many Ethiopians: Where was the country headed? What was in store for Ethiopia with the new leadership at the helm? What did this change of government usher in? Was it the dawn of a brighter future, the ABC of democracy and fair

Tesfaye Sima and Wuhibe-Sellassie Girma in *HaHu Woyim PePu*, (Ethiopian National Theatre, 1993). Backdrop by Gebre Kristos Desta, created for *HaHu Besidist Wor* ca. 1973.

governance, or the end—the XYZ—of hope, the end of tolerance and peaceful coexistence?

Ha Hu Woyim Pe Pu opened at the Ethiopian National Theatre in 1991 and became an instant success. In the few days of its thrice-a-week run, the theatre hall was packed to capacity, and crowds were turned away from sold-out performances. This mushrooming interest alarmed the government. Already displeased by the play's subject matter, the authorities became increasingly uneasy and withdrew their consent for its performance in Addis Ababa. But because the play had not been banned altogether, the cast was free to go on a nation-wide tour, which it set out to do, starting with three towns in southern Ethiopia: Ziway, Dilla and Hawassa.

Audiences flocked to performances in Ziway and Dilla and, on opening day tickets in Hawassa were sold out. Judging by the hushed attention of the audience in the first few minutes, the play had everyone riveted. Things were going fine, it seemed, until half an hour later when shots were fired from inside the theatre.

In the commotion that ensued, stick-brandishing men leapt onto the stage and viciously attacked performers while a few others hurled chairs that noisily shattered the glass windows of the theatre hall. The sound of gunfire and the violence that followed unleashed chaos in the still-dark hall. Men and women

Tsegaye with the cast of *HaHu Woyim PePu*. Front row (l) to (r): Rahel Assefa, Amelework Tesfaye, Azeb Worku. Middle: Tsegaye. Back row (l) to (r): Tesfaye Sima, Ayenew Mitiku (Tsegaye's step-son, not member of cast); Alemu Gebreab; Getachew Sileshi (sound technichian), and Wuhibe-Sellassie Girma.

were injured while trying to flee. Those trampled underfoot in the melee lay screaming as terrified cast members ran out of the hall and fled away with their attackers following close behind. Their pursuers were dogged; they seemed intent on chasing them to the ends of the earth. But fortunately, some courageous souls came to the rescue.

That was the end of *ABC or XYZ*; the play was never again staged in Ethiopia. Tsegaye wanted to revive the production, but the traumatized cast was too frightened to oblige.

Chapter 39

TSEGAYE'S FEAR WHEN leaving his country was that his voice of protest against what he perceived to be an undemocratic government would be muted by distance. He feared that exile would render him an observer-from-afar, a critic-in-absentia whose pen would certainly become less potent from across the ocean.

In New York, Tsegaye found the care he needed to survive the ravages of a long-neglected illness, but no peace of mind about the fate of the country he had left behind. Unhappy tidings from his homeland kept coming, and his concern about EPRDF's handling of the country's political affairs mounted. The war that the government had declared against Eritrea in May 1998 over a disputed piece of land named Badme went on claiming lives and sapping the country's resources. Thousands of young recruits were killed in the fighting. The war ended in 2002, and a UN-appointed arbitrating commission later ruled that Badme belonged to Eritrea.

In 2005, good news reached Tsegaye and kindled hope in his heart. Elections were to be held in May of that year and the competing party, the Coalition for Unity and Democracy, seemed a worthy contender. He was sorely disappointed, however, as the EPRDF was later declared the winner amid accusations of irregularities at the polls and repression of marches in which dozens of protesters reportedly lost their lives.

Tsegaye increasingly felt that his beloved Ethiopia was not faring well. His absence distressed him; his inability to live among his people and to wield the power of his art in a quest for justice, as he had done under previous regimes, caused him anguish. But he didn't stop writing and speaking. The series of long poems entitled 'Ethiopianness' that he wrote in the final years of his life were forceful indictments of the folly he perceived in the leaders. They were impassioned exhortations for Ethiopians everywhere to unite.

Tsegaye's strength was already gravely undermined by his worsening illness, but sheer force of will drove his devotion to keeping abreast of political developments in his country and to speaking out through his writing and public appearances. He wrote poems and articles that were published in the U.S. and in Ethiopia. He was often invited to events organized by Ethiopians in various areas of the United

Tsegaye attends the memorial service for Professor Asrat Woldeyes, distinguished surgeon, academic, and national political figure (Washington, D.C., 1999). Photo by Robert Hale

States—gatherings to exchange views and share concern of homeland developments. He attended these events despite sometimes difficult circumstances that even involved the risky business of rescheduling his life-saving dialysis treatment. His message to fellow Ethiopians was always the same. He urged them to put aside their differences and to stand united.

Tsegaye was famously inept with modern gadgets. Even using such simple devices as a microwave oven or a TV remote control flustered him time and again. But he pushed himself to learn to use a computer so that he would access online writings and discussions about Ethiopia. His venture into this modern medium of information wasn't without its frustrations. There were days when things would go wrong with the machine, depriving him of his daily dose of tidings from his homeland, and he had to call his daughters to ask them what to do. Or he would phone Elsabeth Demissie, a friend of his daughters' who had become a very close friend and confidant in New York. "I can't get this thing to work," he would say to her. "Find out what is in the news and let me know." He was despotic over those he loved the most, she knew, and she would obediently scour the web and report back.

Beyond the gifted poet and playwright that everyone else knew Tsegaye to be, Elsabeth saw in him a wise and kind human being whose fatherly thoughts and advice were precious to her. She found in him a dear friend who had no trouble transcending their age difference and relating to her as an equal. She basked in his genuine concern for her well-being and marveled at his keen sensitivity to her feelings. In his profound love for his country, his encyclopedic knowledge of Ethiopian history, and his embodiment of Ethiopian values, Elsabeth found a constant fountain that nourished her identity away from home.

To Tsegaye, she was a doting daughter and a devoted friend whose constancy he counted on. She telephoned often and dropped in regularly to keep him company. She even accompanied him on his travels to various events across the Unites States where he was invited to speak.

Tsegaye loved Elsabeth. He trusted her. He let her into the guarded universe of his thoughts that was off limits to many. He shared with her stories, tales from the days of his boyhood in Ambo and his adult life in Addis. He missed his country terribly, especially towards the end of his life. There were days when Elsabeth found him wrapped in nostalgia. He spoke of nothing else on those days but his memories of sundry Ethiopian realities. The way he recreated minor details and mundane routines of everyday life, with such yearning fervor, seeped into Elsabeth and filled her with intense longing. Being a steadfast Ethiopian and an unwilling immigrant like Tsegaye, she was often a spellbound audience to his conjuring up of the tastes, smells, and sounds of home.

Chapter 40

O<small>N DAYS THAT HE</small> had no dialysis, Tsegaye enjoyed sitting at Starbucks, located just around the corner from his home. He often went there carrying his books and writing pads, along with a cushion to help him bear the long hours that he would sit in the hard chairs of the coffee shop. The regulars saw him and smiled, a frail elderly man intensely engrossed in reading or scribbling something in exotic script that they could not make out. The attendants were used to him. They didn't mind his eccentricities: his coming with his own cushion and a paper cup of coffee from a nearby deli which he preferred because it wasn't as bitter and strong as theirs. Even his audacity in asking them to warm it up for him when it got cold, they found amusing.

Jessie's Place, a restaurant across the street from his home, was Tsegaye's other haunt in the neighborhood. If people came with a private matter to discuss with him or if he wanted to relieve his family of the chore of hosting his numerous visitors, he took his guests to Jessie's Place where he was also a familiar face. There he met and dined with friends or held council with out-of-town guests.

Tsegaye had no dialysis treatment on Fridays. And had this particular Friday in February not been nippy, he might have gone to Starbucks. But it was one of those bitterly cold days that Tsegaye hated the most because the icy wind pierced through layers of his clothing and chilled his bones. So he stayed indoors, wrapped up in his thick gabi that he often donned on top of his pajamas.

At around noon that day, guests came to visit the family, and since the apartment where Lakech and Tsegaye lived was small, Lakech suggested meeting the visitors at their daughters' larger apartment nearby. She headed there first and Tsegaye followed. He bundled himself in winter attire: layers topped with a thick sweater, a scarf and a woolen coat; he covered his head with a knit ski hat, and walked to his daughters' place as quickly as he could.

Lakech and Tsegaye enjoyed that afternoon. They dined with their guests, talked and laughed with them, and then retired to their apartment in the evening.

At 3:30 a.m. on Saturday morning, Lakech was awakened by the sound of Tsegaye coughing. The cough was persistent, as if something was lodged in his windpipe, something sticky that refused to move.

"Are you okay?" she asked him from her bed in the living room.

"I think I'm having an asthma attack. Can you get me one of your asthma medicines?" he asked between coughing fits. He had forgotten that Lakech's asthma was a thing of the past by then.

"You don't have asthma. You can't be asthmatic all of a sudden," she said getting out of her bed and heading to the bathroom where he stood bent over the washbasin trying to cough up whatever had clogged his lungs. Lakech stood next to him and worriedly scanned his face, hoping that the coughing would abate. It didn't.

"Should I call Adey?" she asked him.

"Yes, call her," he gasped.

Lakech quickly dialed the number then went back to the bathroom. Gradually, the coughing subsided, but Tsegaye's breathing was still labored. Lakech held him by the arm and led him to the comfortable recliner in the living room. He sank into it in relief and leaned back. He closed his eyes and sat quietly as Lakech waited for her physician daughter to come.

Mahlet was up nursing Yared, her six-month-old son, when the phone rang. The sound was infernal at such a late hour. It triggered a slew of morbid thoughts that shot through her head at lightning speed.

When Adey arrived, she found her dad quietly resting in the chair, with Lakech sitting on the floor at his feet.

"I think he is better now," said Lakech, glancing at the becalmed face of her husband. "He is not coughing anymore."

Even to the trained eyes of Adey, it appeared that Tsegaye was dozing off in his chair, as she had seen him doing many times before.

"How are you doing now, Dad? Are you feeling better?" she asked him, but there was no response. When she held his arms , she found them to be limp. She tugged and prodded at him to wake him up, in vain. Panicking, she told her mother to call an ambulance and went on trying to rouse her unresponsive father.

The emergency operator asked if Tsegaye was breathing, and when Adey said she was not sure, she told her to lay him flat on his back on the floor. Mahlet had arrived by then, and the three of them together lifted Tsegaye out of the chair and put him on the floor. It was now up to Adey to try to resuscitate him, desperately, hoping and praying that the ambulance would arrive soon. It did, less than ten minutes after the call was made. About eight men, EMS personnel, policemen and firemen filed into the small living room and quickly got to work trying to save Tsegaye. but he kept slipping farther and farther away.

While the men did their best to wake Tsegaye, Adey glanced at the clock. She knew that if deprived of oxygen for six to seven minutes, the human brain started to die. If a person came back after a long resuscitation attempt, it would surely be with much reduced cognitive faculties. Her dad wouldn't want that, Adey was certain, and the foolish thought crossed her mind that if he returned in such a condition, he would never forgive her.

A half-hour went by with the men still working hard to perform a miracle. Yet the monitor that received signals from sensors placed on Tsegaye's chest showed no signs of life. Their attempts to revive him, at times bordering on the violent, was painful for the family to watch, so Adey told them to stop. "I think we have lost him," she said tearfully. The men hadn't admitted defeat yet. They carried him out of the house and into an ambulance, heading to the emergency room of Columbia Presbyterian Hospital in Manhattan.

He was pronounced dead upon arrival.

Chapter 41

A bleak winter day on March 4th 2006. In the large assembly hall of the majestic Riverside Church in Manhattan, hundreds of people have gathered from all over the United States and beyond to pay their last respects to Tsegaye. Men and women, young and old, whose lives he has touched in various ways, have come to bid him farewell before he is taken to his final resting place in the country he loved.

Some among those gathered in the hall remember him as a supremely gifted poet who had penned sublime verses. To them he was a peerless wordsmith whose poems are a spectacular union of brilliant thoughts and mesmerizing language.

He was a phenomenal playwright to others; a pioneer who changed the course of Ethiopian theatre culture by lifting it to a higher purpose and molding it into a socially responsible art form. He was author of unforgettable plays that laid bare the fair and foul realities of his land; a dramatist par excellence whose works had the power to unleash emotional tempest in the audience. He was a maverick who courageously wielded his potent weapon—his pen—against the tyrannical might of those who ruled over the people of Ethiopia.

There were those who saw him as a paragon of Ethiopianness whose all-consuming love for his country had no equal. He was the pride of his people in their eyes, a giant whose steadfast commitment to upholding the best and condemning the worst of his society filled them with awe.

As the farewell ceremony begins, priests from Ethiopian Orthodox churches in New York City conduct a prayer service for the repose of Tsegaye's soul.

Then invited speakers address the congregation in the hall. Tsegaye's friends, former colleagues, artists, members of his family appear in turn to speak of his virtues and to share their cherished memories of him.

Tesfaye Sima, a young artist that Tsegaye mentored, performs a segment from *Tewodros*, one of Tsegaye's most powerful plays about the futile, desperate attempts of Emperor Tewodros to unify his country. The brief act, the emperor's soliloquy before he takes his own life as the enemy draws near, invokes for a fleeting moment the magic that Tsegaye's plays conjured up in theatre halls.

Following the performance, the vice president of the Norwegian Authors' Union, Mr. Terje, takes the stage. He says that the Authors' Union has awarded its 2005 Freedom of Expression Prize to Tsegaye. Arrangements had been made for a prize-awarding ceremony to be held in Norway in April of that year, but with Tsegaye's unexpected passing, the Union has decided to present the prize on this occasion.

"Tsegaye was a worthy person in the contemporary world of literature," Mr. Terje speaks to the people in the hall. "He was a poet, playwright, translator and essayist, considered one of Africa's leading intellectuals. He was a key representative and symbol for the struggle for freedom of expression and tolerance. He was imprisoned because of his work and he suffered censorship throughout the years. The prize has been awarded twelve times, and this is the first time it has been awarded to an author from the African continent."

Tsegaye's wife, Lakech, accepts the prize on his behalf.

The last speaker is Dr. Abdurahman Ahmed, Tsegaye's nephrologist at St. Barnabas Hospital since 1998. He stands at the lectern and shares the poem that Tsegaye had written and read for his fellow kidney patients at the hospital one Christmas Eve seven years ago:

> "In the wasted eyes of an old black alien poet like me
> It is only through the infinite mercy of God
> That one would emerge from the ancient depths of Africa
> Floating like a toy ship lost in endless space
> To land on the glowing wings of Saint Barnabas's emergency...."

The stifled sobs of mourners from various parts of the hall punctuate his reading.

GLOSSARY

abba	form of a title for ordinary priests
aleqa	head of church, a learned priest
atse	emperor
ato	a formal equivalent of 'mister'
basha	derivative of the Turkish 'pasha' for low-level government official
balambaras	low-level administrative title
bitowded	highly favored courtier, imperial counselor
blatta	a title signifying learning, given in the 20th century to government officials of the director-general level or quivalent
blatten geta	'master of the *blatta*,' an exalted version of the title *blatta*, given to government officials of the ministerial level
dajazmach	'commander of the gate,' a politico-military title below *ras*
etege	empress, sometimes also translated as queen
gashe	a less formal term signifying respect, akin to 'sir'
grazmach	'commander of the left,' a politico-military title above *balambaras*
janhoy	honorific address used for emperors
leul	'prince,' title borne by sons of the royal family and upper nobility
lij	'child,' an honorific title usually reserved for sons of the royal family or upper nobility
negus	king
negadras	'head of merchants,' originally leader of a merchant caravan, later chief government official in charge of collecting customs
ras	'head,' the highest traditional title next to *negus*
woizero	a formal equivalent of 'Mrs.'

Select glossary words adapted from Bahru Zewde, *History of Modern Ethiopia 1855-1974*, London: James Currey, first published 1991.

APPENDIX I
Education & Awards

17 August 1936: Born in Ambo (Bodda), Shewa province, Ethiopia

1945 to 1948: Attended Zema and Kine Ethiopian Orthodox Church Schools

1948 to 1952: Student at Ambo Elementary School

1952 to 1956: Student at General Wingate and Commercial Secondary Schools

1956 to 1959: LL.B., Blackstone School of Law, Chicago (Correspondence Program)

1959 to 1960: Studied British Experimental Theatre at the Royal Court Theatre, London and French Experimental Theatre at the Comédie Française, Paris

1959 to 1960: UNESCO Fellowship to study Theatre Arts in Britain, France, and Italy

1961 to 1971: Director of the former Haile Sellassie I Theatre, now the Ethiopian National Theatre

1965: International Theatre Institute Fellowship Award to study Israeli Theatre

1966: Awarded the Haile Selassie I International Prize for Amharic Literature

1968: Fulbright Award, lecture tour of U.S. universities on African theatre; guest of the U.S. Department of State.

1971 to 1972: Editor at Oxford University Press, Addis Ababa

1971: Fulbright Award, lecture tour of U.S. universities on African and Ethiopian arts and literature; conducted research study on African antiquities.

1971: Research Fellow in African cultural antiquities at the University of Dakar, now Cheikh Anta Diop University.

1971: Commander of the National Order of the Republic of Senegal in recognition of outstanding merit in African Literature and Black Egyptian studies.

1972 to 1974:	General Manager, Ethiopian National Theatre
1975:	*Fulbright awardee, Selected as BFS Bi-Continental Scholar, "International Education: Link for Human Understanding".
1975 to 1976:	Vice-Minister, Ministry of Culture and Sports
1977 to 1978:	Assistant Professor, Department of Education, Addis Ababa University Founder/Director, Department of Theatre, Addis Ababa University
1978 to 1979:	Secretary General, Ethiopian Peace, Solidarity, and Friendship House
1982:	Gold Mercury International Ad Persona Award for Ethiopian Literature
1985 to 1992:	Cultural Adviser, Ministry of Culture
1985:	Fulbright, Senior Resident Scholar Fellowship Award Columbia University, New York
1986:	Co-winner of the Organization of African Unity (OAU) Anthem
1987:	Winner, Ethiopian Golden Red Sea Star
1994:	Human Rights Watch, Free Expression Award, NewYork
1997:	Honorable Poet Laureate, Golden Laurel Award, Congress of World Poets and United Poets Laureate International, Buckinghamshire, England, July 25, 1997
2005:	Freedom of Expression Prize, the Norwegian Author's Union and the Royal Norwegian Ministry of Cultural Affairs (awarded posthumously).

*Editor's note: Unable to participate because Tsegaye was imprisoned and later released by appeal of Amnesty International.

APPENDIX II
Chronology of Select Works & Productions

Works in Amharic

2003   'Abren Zim Inibel' Audio recording of poems in Amharic & English. CD launched at the National Museum of African Art, Smithsonian (Washington, DC, United States).

*1996   *Teratiregnoch, (The Theatricalists)*. Unpublished. Banned.

1994   *Petros Yachin Se 'at*. A play about Ethiopian martyr Patriarch, Petros. Produced: Addis Ababa, 1968; the first Pan African Cultural Festival, Algiers, 1969; Ethiopian National Theatre, 1973. (Banned at the Ethiopian National Theatre); Patriots Theatre, Addis Ababa, 1981; and reproduced at the Addis Ababa Commercial College.

           Included in *Tsegaye Gabre-Medhin, Tarikawi Tewnetoch (Historical Plays)*, an anthology of four works, edited by Heran Sereke-Brhan. Addis Ababa University Press, 2011.

*1993   *Ha Hu Weyim Pe Pu, (ABC or XYZ)*. A political play and an appeal for peace. Banned.

           (Editor's note: Part V of a series of thematically connected works)

1991   *Abeba Wey Issat, (Flower or Fire)*. A collection of poems in Amharic, Vol. 2. Unpublished.

*1989   *Menilik*. A historical play on the life of Emperor Menilik. Banned.

           Included in *Tsegaye Gabre-Medhin, Tarikawi Tewnetoch (Historical Plays)*, an anthology of four works, edited by Heran Sereke-Brhan. Addis Ababa University Press, 2011.

1984   *Zikegna Joro*. A tragiccomedy on the life of Abera Joro, a popular Ethiopian comedian. Congress Hall. Banned after one performance.

1983-1984   *Tewodros*. A new version of *Tewodros* produced at City Hall Theatre, Addis Ababa.

Included in *Tsegaye Gabre-Medhin, Tarikawi Tewnetoch* (*Historical Plays*), an anthology of four works, edited by Heran Sereke-Brhan. Addis Ababa University Press, 2011.

(Tsegaye's note: *Tewodros* is a new Amharic version and not a translation into Amharic of my original English play.)

*1982   *Hamlet.* Translation from William Shakespeare. Produced at the Ethiopian National Theatre, Addis Ababa, 1968. Published by Oxford University Press, Addis Ababa, 1972. Reproduced, 1996. Produced at the Ethiopian National Theatre, Addis Ababa. Banned.

1981   *Zeray.* A tragedy on the life of Ethiopian patriot, Zeray Deres. Produced at Asmara Theatre, Eritrea.

Included in *Tsegaye Gabre-Medhin, Tarikawi Tewnetoch* (*Historical Plays*), an anthology of four works, edited by Heran Sereke-Brhan. Addis Ababa University Press, 2011.

1981   *Gamo.* A play on the Ethiopian revolution produced at City Hall Theatre, Addis Ababa. Banned immediately after production.

Tsegaye's note: Gamo means 'Lion's Cub' – it is an Oromo 'word.

1980   *Mekdim,* (Preface). A play about the Ethiopian revolution. Produced at City Hall Theatre, Addis Ababa.

(Editor's note: Part IV of a series of thematically connected works.)

*1979   *Melikte Woz Ader.* A play about the Ethiopian revolution. Produced at the Ethiopian National Theatre and City Hall Theatre, Addis Ababa. Banned.

(Editor's note: Part III of a series of thematically connected works.)

(Tsegaye's note: *Melikte Proletarian* is (an) 'Anglo-Amharic' combined word forming the title of another Amharic play. It means, 'Message of the Proletarian'.)

1976   *Abugida Keyiso.* A play about the Ethiopian revolution. Produced at the Ethiopian National Theatre and City Hall Theatre, Addis Ababa.

Playwright imprisoned as a result of this play.

(Editor's note: Part II of a series of thematically connected works.)

(Tsegaye's note: *Abugida Transform* an 'Anglo-Amharic combined word forming the title of my Amharic play based on the story of the Chinese Revolution. 'Abugida' is the Amharic name of the second-level Ge'ez alphabet reading, as taught in our traditional church school. There is no equivalent word for it in English, I'm afraid.)

*1974   *Inat Alem Tenu*, (*Mother Courage*). Adaptation from Bertolt Brecht. Produced at the Ethiopian National Theatre, Addis Ababa. Banned.

1973-1974   *Atsim Beyegetsu*, (*Skeleton in Pages*). A play about the Ethiopian revolution. Produced at the Ethiopian National Theatre, Addis Ababa.

(Tsegaye's note: Five one-act plays.)

1973   *Ha Hu Besidist Wor*, (*ABC in Six Months*). A play about the Ethiopian revolution. Produced at the Ethiopian National Theatre, Addis Ababa. Banned for reproduction, 1997.

(Editor's note: Part I of a series of thematically connected works).

1973   *Isat Woy Abeba*, (*Fire or Flower*) Vol. 1. A collection of poems in Amharic. Published by Berhanena Selam, Addis Ababa.

1969   *Kirar Siker*, (*Kirar Tight-Tuned*). Produced at the Haile Sellassie I Theatre, Addis Ababa.

1968   *Macbeth*. Adaptation from William Shakespeare. Published by Oxford University Press, Addis Ababa, 1972. Produced in part at the Haile Sellassie I Theatre, Addis Ababa.

*1968   *King Lear*. Adaptation from William Shakespeare. Produced in part at the Haile Sellassie I Theatre, Addis Ababa. Banned.

1966   *Yekermo Sew*, (*The Seasoned*). Produced at the Haile Sellassie I Theatre. Published by Berhanena Selam, Addis Ababa, 1967.

1963   *Othello*. Adaptation from William Shakespeare. Produced at the Haile Sellassie I Theatre, Addis Ababa. Published by Berhanena Selam, 1965. Produced at City Hall Theatre, Addis Ababa, 1980-1982.

1963   *Tartouffe*. Adaptation from Moliére. Produced at the Haile Sellassie I Theatre, Addis Ababa.

1962   *YeFez Doctor*. Adaptation from Moliére's play, *Doctor In Spite of Himself*. Produced at the Haile Sellassie I Theatre, Addis Ababa.

*1961   *YeMama Zetegn Melk*, (*Mother's Nine Faces*). Produced at the Haile Sellassie I Theatre, Addis Ababa. Banned.

1961   *Kosho Cigara*, (*Cheap Cigarettes*). Produced at the Haile Sellassie I Theatre, Addis Ababa.

*1961   *Chulo*, (*Errand Boy*). Produced at the Haile Sellassie I Theatre, Addis Ababa, Banned.

1960   *Ign Biye Metahu*, (*Back With a Grin*). Produced at the Haile Sellassie I Theatre, Addis Ababa.

*1960   *Listro*, (*Shoeshine Boy*). Produced at the Haile Sellassie I Theatre, Addis Ababa. Banned.

*1959   *Joro Degif*, (*Mumps*). Produced at the Haile Sellassie I Theatre, Addis Ababa. Banned.

1959   *Askeyami Lijagered*, (*The Ugly Girl*). Produced at the Haile Sellassie I Theatre, Addis Ababa.

1959   *Yeshoh Aklil*, (*Crown of Thorns*). Produced at the Haile Sellassie I Theatre, Addis Ababa. Published by Berhanena Selam, Addis Ababa.

*1957   *Belg*, (*Autumn*). Produced at the Haile Sellassie I Theatre. Published by Berhanena Selam, 1972. Banned.

1951   *Yedem Azmera*, (*Blood Harvest*). A play about Fascist Italy's occupation of Ethiopia during World War II. Produced at the Addis Ababa Commercial Secondary School, Addis Ababa.

*1951   *Lelaw Adam*, (*The Other Adam*). A play of social criticism and a reflection on the times. Produced at the Addis Ababa Commercial Secondary School. Banned.

---

*Editor's note: A total of thirteen of Tsegaye's plays were banned.

APPENDIX III

Chronology of Select Works & Productions

Works in English

1993-2006	Work that was in progress: *Afraka Kabara: The First Religion of Humankind as Sources of Judaic, Christian, Greco-Roman, and Islamic Cultures.* A book on pre-classical African culture.
1993	*Hand and Voice.* A play on the appeal for peace dedicated to Fantahun, a martyr of the Ethiopian students' peace movement in Sidist Kilo, Addis Ababa. Unpublished.
1993	(Untitled) - Collection of poems in English, Vol. 2. Unpublished.
1986	*FANA.* A musical drama. Unpublished
1986	"Deliver the World." Poem representing Ethiopia in the *International Year of Peace* "Poetry for Peace".
1984	*Footprint of Time.* Ethiopian travel book. Published by Magnus Institute (in Italian, French, and English) for the Ethiopian Tourist Organization.
1981	*Petros, Black Electron.* A play about Ethiopian martyr patriarch, Petros. An earlier short version of the same was published in *Ethiopia Observer*, London & Edinburgh, 1967.
1968	*Collision of Altars.* A play set in 6th century AD, with Ethiopia as the third greatest power in the world. Rex Collins Publishers, Ltd., London, 1977.
1967	*Tewodros.* A play about the tragic death of Emperor Tewodros. Published in *Ethiopia Observer*, London & Edinburgh. Produced at the Haile Sellassie I University-College Creative Arts Center, 1963 and London Arts Theatre, 1987.
1967	*Azmari, (Singer).* Produced at Addis Ababa University Creative Arts Center. Published in *Ethiopia Observer*. London & Edinburgh.

1965   Collection of poems in English, Vol. 1. Published in *Ethiopia Observer*, Vol. IX No. 1, London & Edinburgh. Poems have also been published in other anthologies and reviews.

1964   *Isis Atys*. Musical drama presented for the Inaugural Ceremony of the Organization of African Unity, Addis Ababa.

1964   *Oda Oak Oracle: A Legend of Black Peoples, Told of Gods and God, Of Hope and Love, of Fears and Sacrifices*. Published by Oxford University Press. Produced at Haile Sellassie I University-College Creative Arts Center, 1964. Also produced in Britain, Denmark, Italy, Kenya, Nigeria, Rumania, Tanzania, and United States, 19651971. Presented at the National Arts Center of Canada. Performed at the Stanford Summer Theatre "Africa on Stage" Festival, August 2007, Stanford University and other venues in northern California.

1960   *Suspended Steps*. Drama written for Experimental Theatre Study, Royal Court Theatre, London.

1942   *The Story of King Dionysus and of the Two Brothers*. Produced for His Imperial Majesty Haile Sellassie I, Ambo Elementary School Hall, Ethiopia.

---

* Tsegaye's notes: The editor has added Tsegaye's notes from various sources to these entries.
* Unless otherwise indicated, dates provided are those of performances.
Additional performance dates and publication dates are noted within entries.

APPENDIX IV
Research Papers

1997   "Increasing our Understanding of other Cultures." Paper presented at the Congress of World Poets, Buckinghamshire, England.

1988   "The Last Hours of Tewodros." Paper presented at the Kasa and Kasa Symposium, Addis Ababa University, Institute of Ethiopian Studies, published in 1990.

1982   Isis in Ethiopian Antiquities." Presented at the International Symposium on History and Ethnography in Ethiopian Studies, Addis Ababa University, November 1982.

1980   "The World Dimensions of the Community of Black People." Presented at the First PreColloquium of the Third World of Negro Arts. Organized by The Society of African Cultures and the Government of Senegal, Dakar.

1977   "Ikher Qf Nagada: The First Actor in the First City of Humankind." Presented at the 2nd World Black Arts Festival Colloquium. Organized by the Organization of African Unity (OAU), United Nations Educational Scientific and Cultural Organization (UNESCO), Society of African Cultures, and the Government of Nigeria, Lagos.

1973   "Africa as the Origin of the Early Greek Theatre Culture." Presented at the International Congress of Africanists, Third Session, Organization of African Unity (OAU), Addis Ababa, December 919.

1970   "Literature and the African Public." Presented at the AfroScandinavian Seminar on African Humanism and Scandinavian Culture, Copenhagen.

1968   "Ancient Performing Arts of Ancient Africans." Presented at the AfroEuropean Writers Conference. Organized by the Society of African Cultures and the Vatican Office of Culture, Rome.

1967   "Kamit of Black Egyptian Theatre." First Pan-African Cultural Festival, Colloquium. Organized by the Organization of

African Unity (OAU), the Society of African Cultures, and the Government of Algeria, Algiers.

1966   "Art in the Life of the Ethiopian People." First World Black Arts Festival, Colloquium. Organized by the Society of African Cultures, UNESCO, and the Government of Senegal, Dakar

1958   "What Does World Brotherhood Mean To Me?" Fulbright Fellowship prize-winning essay.

APPENDIX V
Official Travels, Research Residencies & Visits

June 1998 – February 2006: Resident, New York City, U.S.A.

25 March 1994: U.S.A. Guest of UNICEF, 25th Year Celebration of Oral Rehydration Therapy, Washington, D.C.

June, 1993: U.S.A. Invited to the United Poets Laureate International Symposium, Phoenix, Arizona, USA. *Tsegaye's notes: Could not attend because government troops came on stage and beat up the actors in my play, *ABC or XYZ* (*HaHu Woyim PePu*) – an appeal for peace, which was running in Ethiopia at the time.

June 1991: U.S.A. Guest of UNICEF, United Nations and Organization of African Unity (OAU) Declaration of the "Year of the African Child," June 16, New York.

April 1991: U.S.A. Participant in the International Symposium on "Shakespeare in the NonEnglish Speaking World", Globe Theatre North America Inc., Los Angeles.

1989-1990: Zimbabwe and Mali. Chairman of African Artists and Intellectuals for UNICEF Africa, Harare and Bamako.

1987: U.S.A. Guest of The City University of New York, Writer-in-Residence.

October -November, 1987: United Kingdom. Present at the opening of English play Tewodros at the London Arts Theatre by the Black Theatre Forum, London.

July 1986: Congo. First Congress of African Scientists.

May 1986: Senegal. Competition of African Poets and Musicians for the Organization of African Unity (OAU) Anthem.

March 1986: Poland. Represented Ethiopia at the "Congress of Intellectuals for the Peaceful Future of the World," Warsaw.

1985: U.S.A. Senior African Scholar, Fulbright Resident Fellow, Columbia University, New York and guest of the U.S. Department of State, the Library of Congress, Washington, D.C.

1980:	Senegal. Guest of the Government of Senegal and member of the colloquium, First PreColloquies of the Third World Festival of Black Arts, Dakar.
1979:	Bulgaria. Member of the Ethiopian Peace Delegation.
1978:	U.S.A. Fulbright Grant as Resident Writer, Sarah Lawrence College, New York and the Library of Congress, Washington D.C.; Tour of several universities and colleges.
1976:	Nigeria. Research at Lagos, Ife and Kano.
1975:	U.S.S.R. Guest of Soviet Writer's Union, Moscow.
1975:	United Kingdom. Research at the British Museum, London and the University of Liverpool, Department of Oriental Studies.
1974:	Tanzania. Guest lecturer, Department of Theatre Arts, University of Dar Es Salaam.
1973:	Cameroon. Guest of the Government of Cameroon at the African Writer's Conference.
1971–1972:	Senegal. Guest of the Government of Senegal. Research Fellowship at University of Dakar; also conducted research at the Institute Fundamental d'Afrique Noir.
1970:	Congo. Guest of the Government of Congo Government at the Conference of African Writers.
1969–1970:	Egypt and Sudan. Research at the Cairo National Museum, Dandara, Luxor, Abu Symbol, Edfu, Wadi Halfa and the Sudan National Museum.
1969–1970:	Greece. Research at the National Museum of Athens, University of Athens and Crete.
1969–1970:	United Kingdom and France, Research at British Museum, London Library, Louvre and Maîson des science de l'homme.
1969:	Algeria. Head of the Ethiopian Cultural Delegation to the first Pan-African Cultural Festival, Organization of African Unity, Algiers.
1969:	Italy. Guest of the Government of Italy at the Afro-European Writer's Conference, Rome.
1968:	Yugoslavia. Ethiopian Delegate to the International Poets' Night, Struga

1968:   France, Guest of the Government of France and of the International Theatre Institute Committee, Mancy.

1968:   U.S.A. Fulbright and guest of U.S. Department of State, "Leaders and Experts Visit"; visited several universities and theatres, and lectured on African cultures.

1967:   Denmark. Guest of the Government of Denmark at the Afro-Scandinavian Cultural Conference, Copenhagen.

1967:   USSR, Guest of the Afro-Asian Writers' Union, Moscow.

1967:   German Federal Republic, guest of the government. Toured theatres, film centers and city halls

1966:   Israel, International Theatre Institute. Fellowship and Guest of the Government of Israel, Tel Aviv.

1966:   Senegal. Head of the Ethiopian Cultural Delegation to the First World Negro Arts Festival, Dakar.

1964–1968: Kenya, Tanzania, Uganda. Served as External Examiner for the Department of Arts and Literaturein the Universities of Nairobi, Dar es Salaam, and Makarere.

1964:   Tanzania. Head of the Ethiopian Cultural Delegation to the Independence Day of Tanzania, Dar es Salaam.

1963:   Kenya. Head of the Ethiopian Cultural Delegation to the Independence Day of Kenya, Nairobi.

1959–1960: United Kingdom, France, Italy, UNESCO Fellowship. Visited and studied at the Royal Court Theatre, London; Royal Theatre, Windsor; Comédie Française, Paris; Rome Opera, Rome.

APPENDIX VI

Tsegaye held professional membership with the following:

Ethiopian Writers' Association (Executive Committee)

Society of African Cultures

African Writers' Union

African Researchers' Union

AfroAsian Writers' Union

Organization of African Unity (OAU) "ThinkTank" Forum Africa 2000

Black Arts International Festival Committee: Senegal

Congress of World Poets: United Poets Laureate International, Member 1990

UNESCO, National Committee, Member 1988

Member of Advisory Council for UNICEF; African Artists and Intellectuals 1989

Goodwill Ambassador for International Red Cross and Red Crescent, Ethiopia Branch, 1991

He was recognized in:

International Who's Who

Contemporary Dramatists Who's Who

International Who's Who in Poetry

Who's Who in the Middle East

Who's Who in Africa

The Worlds' Who's Who of Authors

INDEX

BOOKS THAT BELONG ON YOUR SHELF

Tsehai's
Sharf-Pankhurst
Series

Edited by: Frederic A. Sharf and Richard Pankhurst

Expedition from Abyssinia to Somaliland (1901)
ISBN: 978-1-59907-045-2

Expedition From The Sudan to Abyssinia (1899 – 1900)
ISBN: 978-1-59907-006-3

Expedition From Uganda to Abyssinia (1898)
ISBN: 1599070073

Ethiopia in Wartime (1941-1942) A Memoir by Brian F. Macdona
ISBN: 0974819824

Letters from Abyssinia: 1916 and 1917 by Major Hugh D. Pearson
ISBN: 0974819808

Abyssinia, 1867 - 1868: Artists on Campaign
ISBN: 0972317244

and MORE...

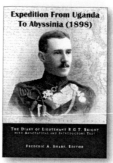

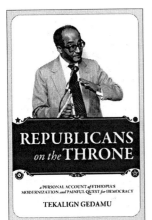

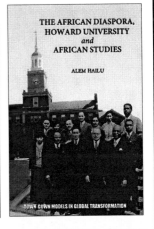
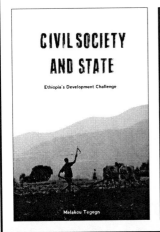

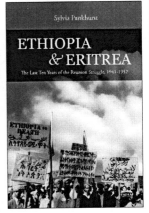

CPSIA information can be obtained at www.ICGtesting.com
Printed in the USA
BVOW021631170613

323528BV00004B/9/P